MOONRISE

"If you have ever wondered why some of us believe that women have the power to change the world or if you have asked yourself why so many women are remarkable and brave leaders (and even in the case that you are skeptical about these claims and want to see some concrete evidence), this is the book for you. Such a rich range of experience is described in these pages, stories of resistance, creativity, and care fueled by a profound sense of connection with the earth, family, neighborhoods, community, and widening circles of common cause. To a war-torn world, beset by poverty, pollution, and global warming, this collection seeds not only hope but also courage by presenting us with so many clear paths to action."

SUSAN GRIFFIN, AUTHOR OF
WOMAN AND NATURE, A CHORUS OF STONES,
AND *WRESTLING WITH THE ANGEL OF DEMOCRACY*

"*Moonrise* is like a warm blanket on a cold night. Its nurturing stories touch the heart. And it is like a dip in the pool on a hot day, enlivening the mind. You'll keep this book by your bed always, ready when you need to read or reread the essays for leadership inspiration and aspiration."

GLORIA FELDT, AUTHOR OF *NO EXCUSES: 9 WAYS WOMEN CAN
CHANGE HOW WE THINK ABOUT POWER*

"*Moonrise* shows us the power of leading with love—a power we must all learn the use of if we are to save our planet and civilization."

JUDY WICKS, FOUNDER OF WHITE DOG CAFÉ AND BUSINESS
ALLIANCE FOR LOCAL LIVING ECONOMIES

MOONRISE

The Power of Women
Leading from the Heart

EDITED BY NINA SIMONS

WITH ANNEKE CAMPBELL

Park Street Press
Rochester, Vermont • Toronto, Canada

Park Street Press
One Park Street
Rochester, Vermont 05767
www.ParkStPress.com

Text paper is SFI certified

Park Street Press is a division of Inner Traditions International

Library of Congress Cataloging-in-Publication Data

[Moonrise : the power of women leading from the heart / edited by Nina Simons
with Anneke Campbell.
  p. cm.
  Summary: "Explores the flourishing, passionate forms of leadership emerging
from women on behalf of the earth and community"—Provided by publisher.
  ISBN 978-1-59477-352-5 (pbk.)
  1. Women social reformers—Case studies. 2. Leadership in women—
Case studies. 3. Women environmentalists—Case studies. 4. Women in
development—Case studies. 5. Social action—Case studies. I. Simons, Nina. II.
Campbell, Anneke.
  HQ1123.M66 2010
  303.48'4082—dc22

                                                                2010019640

Printed and bound in the United States by Lake Book Manufacturing
The text paper is 100% SFI certified. The Sustainable Forestry Initiative® program
promotes sustainable forest management.

10   9   8   7   6   5   4   3   2   1

Text design and layout by Virginia Scott Bowman
This book was typeset in Garamond Premier Pro and Legacy Sansa with Berkeley
Oldstyle and Gill Sans as display typefaces

To send correspondence to the author of this book, mail a first-class letter to the author
c/o Inner Traditions • Bear & Company, One Park Street, Rochester, VT 05767, and
we will forward the communication, or visit the author's website **www.bioneers.org.**

This book is dedicated to everyone who has ever felt powerless, experienced being the dissenting or minority voice, or felt unfairly judged, devalued, or dismissed for being different. It is intended for anyone who has experienced a culture that elevates some while denigrating others. As women in a society that privileges attributes and people who are "masculine," I believe we all have a particular empathic window on injustice.

Injustice raises appropriate anger, and our ire rises up to defend and protect our hearts. Since many women are taught to stifle their anger, and to avoid being called a "bitch," this feeling often remains unexperienced. This reservoir of unexpressed rage at injustice may armor or callous our hearts, impeding our capacity to fully feel the passion that can ignite and strengthen leadership.

Moonrise is meant to speak to and strengthen the "feminine" within us all, regardless of where we may see ourselves situated on a wide spectrum of gender possibilities. The stories within it come from women of many ages, ethnicities, orientations, and perspectives, as well as from a few men. If one story doesn't resonate with your reality, I hope you'll move on to read another. We all reflect the biases of our own condition and unique vantage point, and our perspectives and life experiences are endlessly diverse. It is my intention to offer as many inclusive and invitational entry points as possible, to inspire reflection, learning, and integration.

Contents

PART ONE

Knowing Our Selves, Our Inner Landscape, and Our Sense of Purpose

PART TWO

Leadership Sourced from Inner Authority

PART THREE

Reweaving the Web of Connection

PART FOUR

Renegotiating Power: Generosity, Mentorship, and Respectful Relations

PART FIVE

Restoring the Feminine in Our Strategies, Institutions, and Culture

Acknowledgments

First and foremost, my heartfelt thanks to all of you who've helped co-create the living social system sculpture that is Bioneers. So many of you have contributed in diverse ways over the years with your voices, resources, creativity, caring, and wisdom. Thank you for your generosity, for all of your gifts have been needed to help make Bioneers a fount of hope, connection, and learning that offers so much to so many, on behalf of the sacred web of life on Earth. Thank you.

My enduring gratitude to Anneke Campbell, whose deft editing and wise communication skills artfully contributed to the process of helping me select, refine, and weave these many voices into a coherent and integral offering. *Moonrise* and I have benefited greatly from her insight, passion, and friendship. A deep bow of thanks to my colleague and friend Felice Marohn, whose commitment, clarity, unerring precision, relational sensitivity, and consistent, conscious equilibrium have been a gift to this book and to my life and learning.

To Kenny Ausubel, my partner on my path in life and love: thank you for your clear vision in seeing the need to create Bioneers as a regenerative wellspring so many years ago. Thank you for your mentorship as an author and entrepreneur, and for your perseverance in keeping the sacred fire burning through difficult times. Thank you for suggesting I create this book and for seeing its value to me and to the world long before I saw it myself.

My heartfelt thanks to my mother, Rhea Goodman, whose lust for dancing and juicy, embodied wisdom inspire me to stretch, celebrate, and breathe, daily. To my mother-in-law, Anya Ausubel, whose nimble articulateness, peregrinating ways, and artful celebration of kinship remind me how to love life no matter what. To my near-daughter Ramona Ausubel, your balance of compassion and focus, your eloquence, and the breadth of your creative purpose fill my heart with glee. My brother Tony, we share a passion for how integrity may transform the world. I am thankful for your translating it for business. Our beloved father, Barnett, gave me the heft of his lion heart to stand on as I grew, for which words will never adequately express my gratitude.

I have been gifted to partner with many remarkable women who've advanced my learning and inner liberation. My collaboration with Toby Herzlich is deep, magical, and profound, and I am especially grateful to her for helping me develop some skillfulness as a teacher and facilitator. Akaya Windwood made many contributions to the early design of the Cultivating Women's Leadership training, and her generosity, challenges, and forgiveness have helped me to find, stay connected with, and learn to value myself.

Laura Loescher has taught me of the value of brilliance offered homeopathically, and gifted me with true friendship and consistent love. Micah Bazant created the elegant and original logo design that represents our trainings and also graces this book, for which I am profoundly grateful.

Joanna, Jess, Sarita, and Miquela, my mutual mentoring friends, you have shown me how much power, authenticity, and grace abide in our younger sisters. The many women who have participated in Cultivating Women's Leadership trainings have expanded my understanding and vision, and I am grateful to you all. To my many other remarkable women friends, donor activists, and leaders of all shapes and sizes: your kinship, companionship, belief in me, and love are gifts that buoy me ongoingly, and I am deeply thankful.

Many men have been central to my discoveries, integration, and healing, and your reflections, caring, and support have been medicine beyond measure for me. I offer my heartfelt gratitude especially to J. P. Harpignies, Jan Sultan, Peter Mattair, and Robert Gass for being brothers of my soul and gifting me with your insight, love, and encouragement.

Jeannette Armstrong and Marlowe Sam are cherished friends and teachers who have invested powerfully and generously in my leadership. I thank you both, as your wisdom has provided me with vision in some of my most uncertain times. There are women whom I look to for guidance in the invisible realms, including particularly Alice Walker, Joy Harjo, Terry Tempest Williams, and Paula Gunn Allen. Thank you for being so audacious, lyrical, funny, and utterly yourselves, and for reminding me that combining a hypnotic chant with a belly laugh and a saxophone's forlorn howl, or a peoples' prayer with pulsating poetry, expands what is possible.

My appreciation and gratitude to my colleagues at Inner Traditions: to Ehud Sperling, Jon Graham, Jeanie Levitan, and Anne Dillon. Your belief in this book has helped it to be born in a good way.

My heart swells with thankfulness to all of you who've taken a stand and risked expressing yourselves courageously on behalf of the sacred web of life. Though some of you are included in this book, many more who have inspired, influenced, and shaped me—and so many of us—are not. You have gifted me—and our movement of movements—with your stories, your audacity, your authenticity, your love, your reverence, your creativity, and your bravery. I am thankful beyond measure for the generosity and commitment you keep offering to the community of life on Earth.

I bow in gratitude to the many women and men who have expanded my options by revealing new ways to lead and who have demonstrated how to make a strong, strategic, determined stand with your hearts remaining open. You have stayed connected with all of your intelligences—body, heart, mind, and spirit—remaining faithful to all your human wholeness as you've responded to a call to effect progressive change. You have broken my forgetfulness open by revealing your pain, grief, or sorrow, and awakened me to the value of healthy anger. You have refused to take no for an answer and you have known you were on track when, as my friend

Diane Wilson says, you "smelled your fear and headed straight for it." You have persevered with your work when it was ahead of its time and misunderstood, and you proceeded against the flow, without compensation, your offerings fueled by your love and devotion.

I offer a special and humble bow of thanks, while respecting your privacy, to the following women, whose friendship and ideas have gifted me with insights and learning: Melissa, Dawna, Sue, Barbara, Nancy, Betsy, Ginny, Linda, Kristin, Effie, Kat, Laura, Betsy, Maggie, Amanda, Lorraine, and Barbara.

Finally, I offer my sincere and humble gratitude to you who are reading this book. Your love for the wonder of life, for each other, and for this sacred Earth represents the most hopeful and transformative tsunami I can imagine. May the stories contained herein expand your engaged action and ignite your full creativity and purposefulness. May their power let your fear lose its sway and inspire your leadership to offer all that you are here to give, in reinventing how we live on Earth at this pivotal time.

Most of the stories contained in *Moonrise* began as talks offered at Bioneers conferences and have been adapted for this book. Anneke Campbell and I selected and edited them to help illustrate five essential elements of how we are collectively redefining leadership. Some exemplify several or all of the elements, offering a kind of holographic vision. Many of the contributors have authored books themselves, and all have active websites. I hope their stories encourage and expand your sense of what's possible.

NINA SIMONS

About Bioneers

Bioneers (www.bioneers.org) is a nonprofit educational organization that highlights breakthrough solutions for restoring people and planet. Founded in 1990 in Santa Fe, New Mexico, by social entrepreneurs Kenny Ausubel and Nina Simons, Bioneers has acted as a fertile hub of social and scientific innovators with practical and visionary solutions for the world's most pressing environmental and social challenges.

A celebration of the genius of nature and human ingenuity, Bioneers connects people with solutions and each other. Its acclaimed annual national and local conferences are complemented by extensive media outreach including an award-winning radio series, a book series, and a role in third-party media projects such as Leonardo DiCaprio's film *The 11th Hour.*

The mission of Bioneers is to inspire a shift to live on Earth in ways that honor the web of life, each other, and future generations.

For over twenty years the annual Bioneers conference has served as a dynamic, leading-edge forum of both practical and visionary solutions to real-world challenges. As a network of networks, Bioneers celebrates people and nature—"human ingenuity wedded to the wisdom of the wild." It brings together the most innovative and effective leaders, from the grassroots to the canopy, focused on nature-based solutions and innovative social strategies for restoring Earth's imperiled ecosystems and healing our human communities. The Bioneers framework of interdependence brings together all the parts—and diverse voices—to build connections among many communities and constituencies across boundaries of issues, gender, race, culture, class, and age.

By illuminating the interdependence of the web of life and the unity of human and natural systems, Bioneers fosters a culture of solutions grounded in four billion years of evolutionary intelligence. The solutions in nature consistently surpass our concept of what is possible. Bioneers reflects a larger global movement devoted to creating conditions conducive to life: a world that's healthy, equitable, democratic, and diverse—and beautiful and fun.

Bioneers has received numerous honors and awards. These include awards from the California State Senate, the Marin County Board of Supervisors, the Rainforest Action Network, and Global Green and the New York Festivals and Crystal Communicator radio awards as well as the Buckminster Fuller Challenge Award.

We invite you to learn more about Bioneers and its programs, including the annual national Bioneers conference, local Beaming Bioneers satellite conferences, the Cultivating Women's Leadership program and trainings, the Dreaming New Mexico state-level localization project, radio series, book series, youth program, and food and farming program. By becoming a member, you can connect locally and globally with the dynamic Bioneers network.

Visit www.bioneers.org or call 1-877-BIONEER.

BIONEERS

Revolution from the Heart of Nature

It's all alive—it's all connected—it's all intelligent—it's all relatives.

Milk and Blood

Terry Tempest Williams

Why these two words?

Because milk is what we desired first. Because blood is what drives the human heart.

Because milk comes from our breasts and blood comes from our wombs.

Because what every woman knows is that we are remade each time we make love, each time we give birth; each time we feel the blood making its way through our body into our cupped hands, we remember it is our destiny to make change.

Milk and blood. Why these two words?

Because milk as in cow as in goat as in breast as in semen as in any substance that nurtures and nourishes at once is at the heart of pleasure. Because we drink deeply. Because we drink deeply out of both need and desire.

Because blood as in flow as in menses as in moon as in cycle means I am not pregnant. Because what every woman knows each month when she bleeds is that life begins anew now. Because what every woman understands each time she makes love is that life could be in the making now. Which is why when a woman allows another to enter her, it is not just a physical act, but a spiritual one.

Milk and blood.

Milk and blood. Men and women. Pleasure and pain. Love is to life what inevitability is to death. And so we risk everything to try to touch the ineffable by touching each other. Again and again. Over and over. With little control. We wish we could control. Out of control. We lose our minds and find them as we lose ourselves in fire.

We are Fire. We are Water. We are Earth. We are Air. We are all things elemental.

What a woman never forgets is this: we hold the moon in our bellies and the sun in our hearts. In darkness, we shine. In daylight, we burn. We are milk and blood. We enter a pact with angels that when a child is conceived in us, dear sisters, we will give our lives to love. Always, to love. In love, our bodies are remade. Women are remade. Because until we bleed, we check our wombs every day for the stirrings of life. Because until we bleed, we wonder if our life will be one or two or three. Because until we bleed, we imagine every possibility from pleasure to pain to birth to death and wonder, day and night, how we will do what needs to be done and when we stop bleeding, we enter the pause of wisdom that says, what needs to be done is the work of women. Unreasonable women. Wild women. Smart women. All women. We join hands in the great circling of life and remember what binds us together is milk and blood.

What Nina Simons has brought together in *Moonrise: The Power of Women Leading from the Heart* is a call and a cry for authentic leadership born out of the bodies of women. By coming to understand and embrace her own power, she found not only her voice but her vocation as one of the cofounders of Bioneers with her life-partner, Kenny Ausubel.

She writes: "I came to understand the fabric of the world in a new way. A way that integrates respectful relationship to all of life while remaining deeply connected to the mystery and complexity of creation. . . . A way that listens for *all* the voices, especially those that are rarely heard or valued in our culture. A way that attends to dreams, intuition, the invisible world, and the wisdom of our animal bodies and authentic selves as vital sources of information."

This anthology of intelligence and contemplation, artistry and action inspires us to be our highest and deepest selves. When I look at these contributors, I see my mentors: Lily Yeh, Rachel Naomi Remen, Eve Ensler, Joanna Macy, Alice Walker, Jean Bolen, Janine Benyus, Gloria Flora, and Julia Butterfly Hill.

I see them making mosaics in Rwanda from the rubble of war. I see them healing the sick with the grace of stories. I seem them demanding that we speak the words, say the words, honor the word "vagina." I see them unflinching as they face the waves of grief. I see them creating both disturbance and peace with their pens. I see them educating our souls through psychology, biology, and illuminating the patterns that sustain us as human beings in relationship to the larger communities on the planet. I see them standing in front of bulldozers, confronting policies that compromise our public lands at the risk of being fired. I see them climbing trees and choosing to stay as they embrace a redwood named Luna.

Nina Simons calls for a different way of being in the world through presence and instinct and the courage that comes from falling in love with the earth.

Could it be that the "genius of women" is our capacity to transform the world through creation? Life. This is our gift: what we take in through our bodies and release through birth. This is our art—the art of living. This is our life—the life of giving. We can be fierce and compassionate, at once. It is how we create beauty in a broken world. To lead is to follow our hearts. We do it alone and we do it together in the name of community.

I have watched Nina Simons's vision of an embodied voice evolve over time as she has questioned her own power and leadership. I have seen her reluctance to take her place at the heart of her own creation, which is Bioneers. Now, she stands through the peace of her authority that has been mirrored back to her through the light of all those she has supported. Her emotional intelligence is eloquent and elegiac on behalf of a world in need of being both cradled and challenged. Nina Simons's voice speaks lovingly and fearlessly, calling us toward courageous action, personally and collectively, as we cut the bonds of oppression and liberate ourselves.

To engage in a leadership of the heart is to nurture the creation of a new kind of human being, one who embraces the arts and humanities, science and technology into a rubric of emancipatory expression. This is what I continue to learn from Nina's commitment to evolutionary change on the planet. I have seen her weep with joy and cry out in pain; in both instances, her tears fall as water in the desert. I have watched her doubt the strength of her soul, even as she lifts and carries us through landscapes of despair. It is her power of perception that I have come to count on when I have lost my way. She understands that to collapse under the weight of loss is necessary if we are to kneel together and bless the ground where the seeds of our sacred rage have been sown. Anger can also be an unfolding of love. We are just beginning to understand the language of an ecological literacy, a liturgy born through the empathy of witness. When a painted bunting appears in Maine on the tail of a winter storm, who can doubt the flames of beauty and the transformative power of its inner heat to melt a frozen terrain?

Authentic leadership inspires the work of joy.

We are women joined with men, holding the hands of our children who know how to read and write, speak and play from the vitality of experience—reading the landscape, reading people, reading the situation before us, as we find ourselves standing in the center of complexity and paradox. Nothing makes sense anymore except how we face each other with kindness. Our clarity of hearts inspires a clarity of leadership that is dependent upon love. We listen and we respond as we face a changing world.

The Australian poet and activist Judith Wright saw that "our dream was the wrong dream, our strength was the wrong strength," recognizing that "wounded we cross the desert's emptiness, and must be false to what would make us whole."

For far too long, we have been seduced into walking a path that did not lead us to ourselves. For far too long, we have said yes, when we wanted to say no. And in our confusion, we said no, when we desperately wanted to answer yes. These are our secrets, what we long for and how we have suffered privately. But regrets are making love to the past, and there is no movement there. What I choose to embrace is the woman I am becoming, here, now, growing beyond my own conditioning, breaking set with what was breaking me.

I turn to the wisdom of women. I rely on the words of women. And I am inspired by the lives of women as a reminder of how I can untangle the great challenges before us in the name of family and begin to knit ourselves together.

> *Then all a world I made in me;*
> *all the world you hear and see*
> *hung upon my dreaming blood.*
> *There hung the multitudinous stars,*
> *and coloured birds and fishes moved.*
> *There swam the sliding continents.*
> JUDITH WRIGHT, "WOMAN TO CHILD"

We are Fire. We are Water. We are Earth. We are Air. We are all things elemental.

Milk and blood. We can no longer afford to distance ourselves from what is real and true and life-affirming.

We can no longer deny the destiny that is ours, individually and collectively, as women who wait—waiting to love, waiting to speak, waiting to act. In our withholding of power, we abrogate our power, and that creates war.

Moonrise is a compilation of peace. It is a procession of women's words and wisdom born out of the work of creation. Milk and blood. Our voice is our passion and our passion is our path that leads us to a leadership of the heart.

In this century, if we fail, it is because we are too timid. May we be brave. May we be bold. May we be brave and bold together. May we read these words, may we hold these words, may we embody these stories, as we locate our own and break them as bread for the birds, for our children, as sacrament.

Terry Tempest Williams (www.coyoteclan.com), one of the nation's most celebrated writers, is the author of *Refuge; Leap; Red: Passion and Patience in the Desert;* and, most recently, *The Open Space of Democracy.* Recipient of both a Guggenheim Fellowship and a Lannan Literary Fellowship, she is an active voice on behalf of social and environmental issues. She lives in Castle Valley, Utah, with her husband, Brooke Williams.

Cultivating Connection and Capacity Through Story

Nina Simons

Perhaps you have come to this place, to this moment, to these people, to this challenge, for just such a time as this.

MORDECAI TO ESTHER, IN THE BOOK OF RUTH

Around the globe, women are rising up in creative and unexpected ways to defend what they love—protecting their families, villages, neighborhoods, homelands, and lifeways, while creating community and connection to strengthen resiliency and healing. Responding to urgent calls from the earth, and to social harms that threaten the livability and fabric of our world, women are leading efforts to defend what they love, reinventing and challenging facets of society everywhere. Recognizing the ineffectiveness of conventional approaches, they're midwifing new models and ways of relating to the earth and each other that want to be born. Women are inventing new forms (and reclaiming old ones) in every area of life, ranging from childbirth to education, and spanning peacemaking, healing, economics, and restorative justice. Many are also reimagining business, governance, and education.

These women and many men are leading as pathfinders, whose

vision and passion for a better world motivate others to act to help heal our collective home (the earth) and advance the common good. We may choose to risk reaching for our dreams not only for the benefit of those around us, but because making a stand on behalf of what we most love, of the future we yearn for, is the most fulfilling, joyful, and meaningful way to spend our short and precious lives.

Though people today often lament a lack of leadership, a new form is arising everywhere—largely from women—and is as unstoppable as grass that grows up through the cracks in concrete. Since it does not resemble what we were taught to expect leadership to look like, this emergence is largely unseen.

In the new leadership landscape described in this book, women (and some men) are wielding power in different ways than what we have been taught to expect. Like Sarah Crowell, whose students keep her practice vulnerable and deeply honest, many are experimenting with collaborative, win-win structures, in which each participant is enriched and expanded by her engagement. Some, like Judy Wicks and her vision to improve business, what we eat, and how we treat each other, are sharing their accomplishments openly and freely, to better equip even their competitors in order to help transform a whole community.

Leslie Gray's story offers insight into an alternate use of power that comes from within, reminding us of the profound value of somatic and intuitive cues. Women leaders often opt to lead from behind or alongside their colleagues, and less frequently from out in front. As the stories here so amply illustrate, being a leader does not necessitate asserting dominance, but rather asks that we listen actively and inwardly, reach across the differences that tend to divide us, initiate and choose the hard work of collaboration, stay connected with our passion, and inspire enthusiastic engagement to strengthen and catalyze others into action.

For most of my career, though I had many accomplishments and successes, I did not consider myself a leader. I have worked in the arts, as a social entrepreneur, in the corporate world, and as co-leader of a nonprofit organization. The way my path meandered and changed embarrassed me, until I identified the common thread: I loved helping orchestrate diverse groups of people to work together toward a higher purpose, a common goal. Rather than diminishing my inclusiveness and ability to inspire cooperation as having little value, I have come to appreciate them as leadership skills. The twists and turns my life has taken have become a source of pleasure for me, as they have given me greater flexibility and a wide range of experiences to draw upon.

After college, I pursued a career in theater, as I believed the arts were the most powerful way to reach people's hearts and minds in order to transform culture. Once I realized how difficult it would be to make a living at "transformational theater," I became disillusioned, took a practical turn at managing restaurants, and then continued to work in music and film.

When I met my husband and partner, Kenny Ausubel, he was finishing a feature-length documentary about alternative cancer remedies, *Hoxsey: How Healing Becomes a Crime.* I learned about the corrupt history of medical politics that has obstructed patients' access to natural treatments, and felt the pain of patients recently diagnosed with cancer, without access to adequate information. My idealism was rekindled. I helped him to market and distribute the film; we got it widely reviewed, broadcast internationally, and screened for Congress. We discovered we were a remarkably compatible and complementary team, and we have worked together ever since.

My first sense of feeling called toward leadership took me completely by surprise, shifting my path toward serving the beauty, health, and fertility of the natural world. In 1989, Kenny and I spent a weekend near the tiny town of Gila, New Mexico, visiting with master gardener Gabriel Howearth. Upon our arrival, Gabriel offered us a tour through his biodiversity garden, which was an orgy of colors, smells, tastes, and sounds. Entering, I saw whole societies of tomatoes—of every size, shape, and color—more varieties than I had known existed. The sweet scent of their juices, warmed by the afternoon sun, intoxicated me as it mingled with the smell of the dark, moist soil. Bees, ladybugs, butterflies, and birds circled overhead, attracted by the fertility below. My senses were dancing. Having grown up in New York City, I never grew food. I wondered whether a garden like this might have inspired the myth of the Garden of Eden.

This one was filled with unusual heirloom and traditional varieties, foods I had never heard of before. As Gabriel fondly introduced us to each plant, he explained how it was related to those on either side. He related to these plants as intimately as one might one's own family.

I learned that this diverse abundance of food plants was threatened by the concentration of corporate agribusiness, and that a tremendous effort was needed to conserve and spread them. I understood that diversity is not only evidence of nature's complexity, wisdom, and beauty, but it is also life's best strategy for survival, offering options for adaptation and resilience in response to change. I knew that what I experienced in that garden was sacred.

I felt as if the spirit of the natural world tapped me on the shoulder and said, "You're working for me now."

Though I felt utterly unprepared and knew nothing about farming, biodiversity, or business, the call was undeniable. I never paused to doubt myself. I returned home and quit my job to work for Seeds of Change, the entrepreneurial organic seed start-up that Kenny founded with Gabriel.

I embarked on the steepest learning curve of my life, eventually becoming the company's president. I quickly learned to trust my instincts and innate business sense. I chose to let go of my embarrassment about not having formal training or knowing all the answers, and to instead appreciate my common sense and beginner's mind. We grew the company rapidly over the next five years, developing it through innovative social marketing into a successful national brand.

My husband, Kenny, first came to me with the idea of producing a Bioneers Conference in 1990. His research had unearthed visionary leaders who were effectively responding to many of our most pressing environmental and social challenges with solutions often inspired by nature. We imagined it would be valuable to spread news of their many effective innovations for restoring the relationship among people and planet, and thereby help leverage the pressure for change.

We assumed that these leaders would already know each other. We were surprised to discover that almost all of them were operating separately, many having no knowledge of each other's work. One primary purpose of Bioneers became to cross-pollinate ideas, best practices, and approaches across fields of endeavor. Connecting the people became as important as spreading the ideas and solutions.

As people new to producing conferences, we created a form that we hoped might affect people deeply—not only intellectually, but to reach their hearts and even touch their sense of the sacred. We came to think of Bioneers as a three-day ceremony, one that integrates arts and culture in a tapestry woven to include and integrate many ways of knowing. Without ever consciously intending it, and in a form I would never have dreamed of, I had found a way to do transformational theater after all!

Through Bioneers' diverse combination of people and perspectives, I came to understand the fabric of the world in a new way. A way that integrates respectful relationship to all of life while remaining deeply connected to the mystery and complexity of creation. A way that values the lessons of history and recognizes the subjectivity of its stories. A way that recognizes the wisdom of indigenous peoples as having essential instructions for how to live on Earth in a good way. A way that listens for the voices of ancestors, as well as those of the land, plants, and creatures. A way that listens for *all* the voices, especially those that are rarely heard or valued in our culture. A way that attends to dreams, intuition, the invisible world, and the wisdom of our animal bodies and authentic selves as vital sources of information.

I learned from hearing scores of leaders' stories over many years, stories of what called to them, of their challenges and victories, and stories of what they had to overcome to respond in wholehearted and creative ways. Appreciating gifts in others sometimes helped me to identify similar capacities in myself that I would not otherwise have recognized. Stories can encourage compassion among people who are different. I was changed by so many stories offered with honesty, heart, and courage. The love and sense of serving something sacred that motivated so many of them reshaped my understanding of leadership. As they transformed me, I realized that perhaps they can shift our culture. Few things can create connection and grow our own capacities more meaningfully than immersing ourselves in each other's stories.

Five years after starting Bioneers, a documentary film added a gender lens to my worldview, shifting my sense of purpose and calling. *The Burning Times* tells the story of the 500- to 600-year period in European history when—depending on which historian's estimates you believe—somewhere between fifty thousand and millions of women were tortured and murdered as "witches." Suddenly, the irrational fear I had of speaking my truth publicly had a possible explanation in our collective history. That sustained reign of terror against women seemed to live deep within my unconscious, that lineage residing in the marrow of my bones.

As I considered this information in light of the various environmental, economic, and social challenges we face, I saw a pattern of imbalance of "masculine" over "feminine" qualities everywhere I looked. Rational, linear, goal-oriented, quantitative, short-term, and competitive approaches were consistently front and center. Concerns about future generations, emotional intelligence, subjective experience, process, relationships, aesthetics, and qualitative and cooperative efforts were hard to measure and therefore generally discounted as "soft" or irrelevant.

I began to see an insidious and largely invisible cultural legacy of devaluing or even demonizing those human characteristics relegated to the domain of the "feminine," and elevating and institutionalizing those qualities associated with the "masculine." I realized that it was not only women who have been systematically culturally devalued, but the "feminine" qualities within us all. This legacy of cultural bias has damaged *everyone*.

Fritjof Capra notes that the transition toward becoming an eco-literate society (one that understands how to live in balance with the natural world) requires a shift in emphasis from counting things to focusing on mapping relationships. Seen through my gender lens, this change in our priorities reflects a reintegration of the feminine back into our human wholeness.

As I explored this idea, it was striking to discover that, from a Jungian perspective, the feminine is associated with the inner, and the masculine with the external or outer. I began seeing twin pathways to help restore our cultural health—one of inspiring and equipping women toward greater leadership, and the other of elevating and restoring the qualities of the feminine within us all. I began to program panel discussions at Bioneers to explore a theme I called "Restoring the Feminine."

When I investigated my own relationship to leadership, I noticed a disturbing incongruity. Although others saw me as an accomplished woman leader, having entrepreneurially helped to develop a national company and having cofounded an influential nonprofit, I did not see myself that way. Inwardly, I felt uncertain and deflected compliments so consistently that Kenny teased me for being Teflon. I began the inner work to find a way to align how others saw me and how I saw myself. I started seeing that the ways in which I undervalued my common sense and intuition, my relational intelligence and creative contributions, might have roots in a larger cultural story.

I knew that these innate gifts were essential for my work, but I saw them as lesser contributions than the rigorously fact-based, analytical and intellectual gifts of my husband and other male (as well as some female) colleagues. To grow into my own sense of purpose in the world, or my own potential, I realized I had to stop comparing myself to others. I practiced receiving compliments, really letting myself feel them, and began appreciating my own very different brand of eloquence. I forgave myself for not remembering facts and figures.

Reflecting inwardly, I realized that I had a deeply embedded belief that I was serving Kenny's vision, and saw myself as the "woman behind the man." When I encountered obstacles, I was quick to attribute them to a sexist system, or to inwardly blame his or others' leadership style. Once I recognized the story I was telling myself and saw how self-limiting it was, I knew that I could shed that narrative and adopt a new one—one in which I became the generative actor in my own story. Though a small voice within me worried about being self-centered, my desire to serve the world's healing helped me to shed it. I was elated, and I knew that I had found the keys to my own liberation.

My relationship to Bioneers began to change. With the help of feedback from colleagues and friends I trusted, I reassessed and reclaimed the value of my contribution. For the first time, I began to perceive Bioneers as an authentic cocreation. In reality, it is a collaborative social sculpture that is the product of many hands, hearts, and minds. My own story changed from seeing it as one man's vision to a collaborative cocreation, a place where my leadership is both welcomed and needed.

Through Bioneers, I occupy an unusual catbird seat in knowing so many disparate women leaders. Motivated by the opportunity I saw to find common ground among them, I organized a retreat for diverse women leaders, called UnReasonable Women for the Earth. I invited thirty-two women leaders, most of whom did not know each other, to come together to imagine what a women's movement with Earth at its heart might look like.

Over several joyful and tumultuous days, we explored what we commonly believed was most essential to transforming culture. We agreed that it was our interconnectedness, our interdependence, that was most crucial to invoke and impart—the reality that the suffering of one person or species anywhere affects us all. We saw our illusions of separateness and "safety" as creating compartmentalized thinking, feeling, and being. We recognized that seeing life as interconnected and utterly interdependent is central to most spiritual and sacred traditions, and also to systems thinking. Three of the participants went on to found CODEPINK: Women for Peace, as the United States prepared to invade Iraq.

I began to understand producing and convening as vital elements of social-change work, and they became a potent part of my tool kit as a leader.

As I changed my inner story and developed a more vital sense of myself, I learned from many mentors among Bioneers' networks. Often their stories showed me that it is possible to integrate vulnerability, not-knowing, and compassion with strength. I began sharing my discoveries with other women around me. Each time I did, women nodded their heads in recognition of similar patterns and stories within themselves. It seemed that much of what I was learning had value for others.

Wanting to translate what I was learning into tools and practices for other women and girls, I sought to help strengthen their capacity to lead the transition toward a healthy, peaceful, sustainable, and just world. I invited a friend and colleague, Toby Herzlich, to partner with me to cocreate and cofacilitate a residential training. Toby had been a professional facilitator of groups for many years, was a Rockwood Leadership* trainer, and had worked previously with women in Bosnia and Herzegovina. I knew she had the skills and knowledge we would need to create a transformational experience for women. I also knew it was necessary to gather women of differing backgrounds, ages, and ethnicities to connect across their differences and learn practices to help grow themselves and each other.

Since we began five years ago, over 190 women have participated in Cultivating Women's Leadership trainings. Everyone leaves with a stronger sense of her own purpose, understanding more clearly her unique "assignment" and what lights her up, and with a preliminary toolkit to continue to cultivate her own ongoing, emergent leadership. Most discover how strengthening it can be to be honest and caring while challenging each other to do our best, to authentically support each other's dreams and vision.

When we first began offering the workshop, women called to say, "Sure, I would like to come and learn with a group of passionate, capable, and engaged women, but I'm not so sure about this leadership thing." As we discovered how many of us have conflicting views about leadership, we designed processes to unpack our beliefs and to sort through our fears, conflicts, and dreams.

---

*The Rockwood Leadership Institute is an organization whose mission is to provide individuals, organizations, and networks with powerful and effective training in leadership and collaboration. Founded in 2000, it focuses on equipping individuals with the skills and tools necessary to overcome challenges and inspire the outcomes of social policy reform and grassroots movements.

Since many of our concepts of leadership have been unconsciously informed by the biases of our culture, relatively few women actually aspire to leadership roles. Frequently we found that women assume that leadership is conferred principally through privilege, job stature, or other symbols of authority that some of us simply do not possess. Often women imagine leadership as an innate talent available only to a select few, rather than one that is learnable and may be cultivated intentionally over time.

I came to see that many of us have an inherent distrust and antipathy toward leadership because of our negative experiences of it, and the way it often manifests in the world. Many of us associate it with ways of relating to others that are disrespectful, damaging, and top-down, perhaps seeing power as a zero-sum game in which putting people down is required if one is to stay on top. Many women see leadership as necessarily involving lots of conflict, which many might prefer to avoid. It is often seen as a solitary practice, which isolates those who pursue it. Our inherited models have frequently involved compulsive self-sacrifice, becoming a target, and relinquishing any work-life balance. Since these characteristics and the lifestyle that accompanies them are often profoundly unappealing to many women and girls, many avoid leadership roles altogether. The women we worked with were not signed on for leadership like that.

The generous and caringly motivated forms of leadership I knew from Bioneers were rarely reported in the media or seen in popular culture—rather, they were emerging largely under the radar. Reflecting on the many leaders who have helped inform my life and learning, I wanted to find a way to share their voices and stories with a wider audience.

This, then, is a book to describe this new form of leadership that is arising all over the world. Though this new way of leading embraces the value of our "feminine" characteristics, values relationships as essential to individual and social health, and is being practiced mainly by women, some courageous and innovative men are doing it too. While this book seeks to encourage and equip women to step more fully into leadership, my larger purpose is to inspire anyone interested in bringing her or his fullest capacity to transforming how we live on Earth and with each other. The goal of *Moonrise* is to ignite the power and capacity within us all to create change by leading in ways that are joyful, healthy, and whole.

These leaders' stories express an integration of both their "feminine" and "masculine" natures. Their ways of leading value the discipline, focus, and determination that are often attributed to the "masculine." Their approaches illustrate that by wedding these "masculine" traits to our relational intelligence—our compassion, humility, intuition, somatic wisdom, empathy, and receptivity—we can each express a potent union. Reflecting the ancient wisdom of the Tao, the Yin/Yang symbol, and most indigenous and shamanic traditions, our leadership and institutions will achieve their greatest influence to transform our cultures only when they integrate all aspects of our human potential.

This leadership arises from the heart and the soles of our feet, and it is motivated from within. It stems from a desire to protect, defend, and nurture whatever we most love, whatever in life has the most meaning for each of us. For that reason, this book describes a progression that flows from the inside out. This perspective, in line with the ancient Hermetic axiom "As above, so below," is that authentic leadership in the world emerges from and reflects the personal, inner work we do. As Gandhi famously said, "We must first be the change we wish to see in the world."

These stories arise from a diverse array of voices, reflecting the prism of who we are. The call to leadership that these stories collectively present is an invitation to us all, to people of every hue, age, shape, and history. All our contributions, all our collective creativity and imagination, are needed to remake this world. By reading and reflecting on these richly differing perspectives from people of many backgrounds, ethnicities, and ages, a *whole* picture of how we are reinventing leadership can surface. Only then may the themes and through-lines of a new pattern emerge.

Gandhi also knew that "social change occurs when deeply felt private experiences are given public legitimacy." The stories in this book unfold in an intimate and personal way that is a key element of this new leadership, a style rarely heard today when leaders tell their stories. Since most were originally delivered as talks at Bioneers conferences, they are also more conversational in tone than if they'd been written for the printed page.

Here is an overview of the arc of the stories contained in this book.

In the first section, "Knowing Our Selves, Our Inner Landscape, and Our Sense of Purpose," you will encounter women who have learned that their own self-knowledge and sense of purpose and authenticity are central to how they show up in the world. They conduct themselves impeccably and kindly, holding themselves rigorously accountable to being honest and real with the people they encounter. Their actions are informed by their self-awareness and sense of purpose. Each has paid exquisite attention to what makes her flame grow brighter, to identifying her unique "assignment," and has used that to inform her leadership pathway. These women have listened inwardly and have been informed by all their emotions as well as their body's own somatic intelligence. When we realize that whatever we have to offer the world and what lights us up are both clues to the same assignment, we can reconcile the false dichotomy between self and service. This leadership is inherently both joyful and fulfilling, and through practicing it, we may each become beacons to attract, strengthen, and inspire others along the way.

The stories of "Leadership Sourced from Inner Authority" describe how women have found all the authority and power needed to face adversity by tapping into their hearts, their souls, their bellies, and their convictions. None of these women required or sought the support of any power outside herself, but rather they were ignited to act, strengthened by a knowingness that came from deep within. No job title or institution gave them permission to innovate and inspire others, to be resolute and fearless. When they feel uncertain or need support, they look within to find the strength, courage, and guidance they seek. It is there they find their most valued, or sacred, instructions. Though connection and collaboration offer further resources, their first connection and sustenance arises from within.

In the third section, "Reweaving the Web of Connection," we explore the heart of this leadership: how we form, cultivate, and strengthen relationships to advance a vision. This emphasis on relatedness and connection offers medicine for a world torn apart by individualism and greed. It expands from the deeply personal outward to our relationships with each other and the natural world. This reawakening of the wisdom within us invites awareness and contact with the invisible worlds of energy, intention, and intuition. Some of the stories reveal ancient relations among women and land, plants, and culture. They speak to a mindfulness of our lineage, ancestors, and those yet unborn. In service to our wholeness, they also invite reclaiming our connections to loss, grief, and the "dark" emotions that have been chronically avoided, ignored, or denied, but which are needed for the reinvention of what it means to be fully human.

Section four, "Renegotiating Power: Generosity, Mentorship, and Respectful Relations," offers some novel approaches to help morph the old paradigm that sees power as a limited resource, in which someone has to lose for another to win. Ranging from business to philanthropy and economics to mentorship to the natural world, these stories explore the power of generosity and humility to transform ourselves and others. Describing a social transformation with roots in our indigenous past, these stories look to our hearts' desires, indigenous cultures, and how nature operates to identify, create, and spread strategies of mutual aid and abundance.

In the fifth section, "Restoring the Feminine in Our Strategies, Institutions, and Culture," we visit with leaders responding to ways the systemic devaluing of the feminine—the relational, intuitive, spiritual, and embodied experiential qualities—have created imbalance and caused inequity or harm in our culture. Three bold and innovative men's stories are included here, as each integrates qualities of the feminine central to his approach to healing, innovation, or conservation. They remind us how accessible and inviting this new leadership form may be to us all. The women tackle institutions including science, media, health, and governance to help create systems of balance, wholeness, and health.

Their stories offer solutions that speak to the needs of constituencies ranging from women and children to war veterans, and from inner-city dwellers seeking cooperative employment to the oceans' inhabitants. Their systemic solutions offer relevant ideas for all global citizens. While each relates a vision for addressing an aspect of our culture, so many other facets still call urgently for reinvention. Their examples illuminate pathways for seeing how much positive change is possible through the leadership of one impassioned, intentional, and loving person.

Their stories have ignited, catalyzed, and strengthened me in countless ways. To further articulate the vision contained within them, I have, at the head of each of them, added my own sense of the person who is telling the story. I am grateful, honored, and deeply enthused to share them with you. The Dalai Lama noted recently that "the world will be saved by Western women." If, as His Holiness, Alice Walker, the indigenous Wisdomkeepers, and Sweet Honey in the Rock suggest, we *are* the ones we have been waiting for, then let us reorient our vision, strengthen our hearts, and liberate our capacities, so that we can see, appreciate, and participate fully in the leadership that is emerging. To really *become* the ones we have been waiting for, we need a call to leadership that we can relate to, be inspired by, and embrace wholeheartedly. That is the medicine these stories have to offer.

> *May we convey stories like birds carry seeds in their feathers,*
> *to sow them in purposeful and transformational ways.*
> *May we fully embrace all of our human wholeness—*
> *honoring the depth of our losses and the breadth and power*
> *   of our love.*
> *May we find our way to right relationship with ourselves,*
> *each other, and the whole Earth community that is "all our*
> *   relations."*

May we lead in ways that are joyful, rigorous, kind, and effective,
Serving the beauty and mystery of Mother Earth and all her kin,
Enlivening, inspiring, and encouraging others along the way.
Awomen, Amen, Aho, and Ashé.

Nina Simons, the editor of this book with Anneke Campbell, is a social entrepreneur experienced in both the nonprofit and corporate worlds. In 1990, she cofounded Bioneers (www.bioneers.org) and, as co-CEO, she has helped lead the organization through twenty-one years of identifying, gathering, and disseminating breakthrough solutions for restoring people and planet.

Nina was also the marketing director and later president of the entrepreneurial start-up company Seeds of Change from 1989 to 1994, helping grow it into an emerging national brand in a mere five years. Subsequently, she was the director of strategic marketing at Odwalla, the fresh juice company from 1995 to 1997, a time when it was expanding rapidly across the nation. Both of these professional experiences instilled strong leadership skills in her, which were later refined and strengthened and further developed through her seminal work with Bioneers.

Nina currently focuses largely on writing and teaching about leadership, women, and nature—while cultivating her own leadership—and on leveraging Bioneers' abundant solutions and stories to catalyze and inspire greater social and environmental transformation worldwide.

PART ONE

Knowing Our Selves,
Our Inner Landscape,
and Our Sense of Purpose

1

To Walk in Beauty

Sarah Crowell

Sarah Crowell leads by embodying the transformative and regenerative power of art, love, and truth. She is fiercely committed to being awake, loving, and fully engaged, while igniting healing through the physical training and creative expression of young people. Her honesty, joy, and commitment are potent and effective medicine for the indifference and cynicism that is so prevalent among today's youth. Because she knows herself so well, she can bring her fullest capacity as a leader to liberating the expressive vision and capacities of young people.

NINA SIMONS

I am the artistic director of a nonprofit arts education and violence-prevention organization called Destiny Arts Center, based in Oakland, California. Our mission is to end isolation, prejudice, and violence in the lives of young people. We've been around for twenty-one years; I've been at the center for nineteen. Our instructors stay with us for many years and, in so doing, continue to deepen their connection to the youth and families we serve. I believe it takes this kind of commitment and longevity for young people to trust us as mentors and to make lasting change in their lives and in the lives of their communities.

We're located in a small community center in the middle of a residential neighborhood. Here we intentionally limit the number of youths to 150 individuals so that we can remain true to our commitment to serve them at a deep level in a place that feels like home to them. To serve larger numbers, we send our instructors out into twenty-five public preschools and elementary, middle, and high schools each year. And our performance groups perform for up to 25,000 audience members annually.

In addition to being the artistic director, I am a performing arts instructor. However, in this capacity, I do not "teach" young people; I mentor them by being a role model to them. I do my own work. I come to them as authentic and humble and fierce as I can be, and I create dances and theater pieces with them. I show up and I teach the *plié* and the *tendue* and I ask them questions and I listen to their stories, and then we make beautiful pieces of art together. I come back the next day and teach the *plié* and the *tendue* again and get the class to quiet down and sit in a circle and meditate. I breathe with them and get them excited about sitting still for thirty seconds and the following week for forty-five seconds. In our programs in the public schools, teachers and students meditate before every single class. One of these teachers came to me and said, "My class sat for five whole minutes today, and they were so excited!" These are eight-, nine-, and ten-year-olds who have found the benefit of meditation.

Every single day we, the staff, just show up, with our hearts as open as possible. We teach violence prevention by serving young people aged three to eighteen in after-school, weekend, and summer programs featuring dance, martial arts, theater, self-defense, conflict resolution, and leadership. It takes a whole lot of time, a whole lot of love, a whole lot of spirit and patience for young people to recognize that they have the power to make change.

We as their role models have the responsibility to show them that we understand our *own* power to make change so that they see that it's possible. And we have to come correct with them too. If I walk into a rehearsal with my teenagers, who are creating art about personal and political issues with me, and I have an attitude that says, "I've got a lot to do, we have a piece to finish about global warming, and dammit, everybody's wearing the wrong dance attire, and you are all getting on my nerves!" then the youths look at me like: "You want me to do *what?* You want me to move? You want me to create work about changing the world? You want me to do *anything* with you?"

Sometimes it's hard for me to be in the space of love that is required to *be the change,* but I know that if I face these young people in a space of irritation or fear, that's what I'll get back: the reflection of whatever I'm bringing to them. Then what we will create together is not an authentic expression of what we say we want to create—a peaceful, more loving world.

How will the children know that the earth is theirs to care about? *We,* their elders, have got to know it first, and then *live* in that knowing, *alongside* this generation that would appear—to so many of us—not to care. But how *can* they care when we're selling them doses of self-hatred wrapped in fancy TV/Wal-Mart/Gap/gotta-have-it flashy stuff? Get good grades, get a good man, make the right decisions, go to college stuff. E-mail and cell phone, don't talk to each other face-to-face fear stuff. Ignore the racism, sexism, consumerism, ageism, and homophobia that keeps selling us stuff stuff. Then we turn around and tell them they need to care because the world is falling apart and they are the leaders of tomorrow. We say, "Get it together, y'all. You're the ones who will make the difference." That is some bullshit. We have to work *with* the next generation.

I have to tell you a story. I did a theater exercise where I asked a group of young people to get into a circle to play a game called the emotion game. In this we play with or create emotions with increasing intensity, from one to ten, ten being huge. The first emotion I gave them was fear. I said, "Let's experience fear." I said, "In the middle of the circle, picture something that you're really afraid of." I counted from one to ten, and by the time I got to ten, they were trembling and contorting their bodies in terror. It was palpable. Then we did anger. Again, their bodies were really into it. One, two, three . . . I slowly counted all the way up to ten, and their faces and bodies were gripped and clenched in anger.

You think teenagers would be shy with their bodies in front of you? Ha! They were right there with the fear and the anger. Then I said, "Okay, let's try bliss. Who knows what that is?" Somebody defined it as extreme happiness. I said, "That's good enough. Here we go, imagine something in the center of the circle, and we're going to go big for this bliss thing." I started the counting, one, two, three—and nothing happened. They just stood there giggling, telling me it was stupid. They couldn't do it. I said: "Okay, wait. You mean to tell me that you can feel and express fear and anger but not bliss? What are we here for, then? Do you want to change the world? Start right here. Experience bliss. I dare you."

I admit it; this was a dare to myself. I was praying at the same time. *Lord, they already think I'm crazy. And now I'm taking them to bliss?* Then I prayed, and I centered myself. I recognized that I had recently been in this space of noticing how terrifying it is to want something and then ask and expect to get it. It's subtle, this releasing the fear of scarcity, which is a story so safe it's habitual. My exploration has been to see if I can be in the energy of abundance. Living in the world in front of people—whether in a classroom or at a conference, as I believe is my purpose—my task is to allow the fear to exist but to step past it, and choose something different than fear in each interaction. This has been my personal journey, and I always drag my students along with me on whatever journey I am taking.

I want my students to be removed from the terror of wanting something different, to know that they belong on the planet, that they belong in their bodies, that they're here as precious beings for a purpose: to connect with other beings and to remove the illusion of separation between us all. I'm not talking about having youths deny that institutionalized prejudice and injustice exist in this world, but I want them to know that, inside the context of all the suffering, they can dare to want something different, and they can create that. I want them to know that it requires incredible discipline and perseverance—and imagination—to create real change.

So here I was in a circle of teenagers daring them to experience, just for a few moments, something other than the fear, anger, and disempowerment they feel over and over again in their lives. I was asking them to be bold, to be true revolutionaries. I said to them: "Let us be willing to be in bliss, because if we can't do that, what are we creating? What are we dreaming up for this world? It takes courage to be in this place of joy and bliss together—maybe more so than to be in a place of fear or anger." I could feel the group resonate with what I was saying.

We all held hands and we looked at each other, and I asked: "Are you with me? Can you make the commitment to be in bliss with me right now?" Everybody was nodding. Their expressions were determined. So I counted, "One, two, three, four . . ." Their bodies softened. Their expressions sweetened. Their defenses dropped. By the time I got to ten, every single kid in that circle was weeping with pure joy and amazement. They were weeping because they saw each other's beauty and felt their own. Afterward, we sat and we debriefed. One girl, choking through her tears, asked: "If we could just see each other from this place all the time, who would we be, what would this world be like?"

What happens when we create this space for young people? What happens when we witness and testify to their fear, anger, and hopelessness and then model for them complete recognition that we can also choose bliss, that we have the ability to see beauty in one another? Giving them that opportunity lights up their hidden spaces and lets them make bold strokes on life's paper. Big brush strokes with the words, "I know what I want and I deserve to get it," and big wide strides with the intention, "I know that I belong here. And if I know that I belong here, then I can care about the air, and the earth, and the water, about the person next to me suffering, the person across the street or across the ocean suffering. I can care if the globe is warming up."

It takes a ton of courage to rise above the despair to ecstasy. So I go back to my job every single day and I look into the eyes of the children, and I have to be real with them. That's my discipline, and that's my daily practice. It's a constant remembering that there is no separation. If I am holding the space that I do not have to be in my story of scarcity, something shifts for them too. Some days it's small, but, nevertheless, something shifts. If we make that decision on a collaborative level regularly, slowly but surely things change in momentous ways. So let us be a generation not afraid to look into each other's eyes and proclaim that we see something beautiful there. Because if we don't, the globe is going heat up and the water is going to rise up and we won't even notice. Let's walk the talk together. Let's be afraid and then dare to love each other anyway.

Sarah Crowell is the artistic director at Destiny Arts Center (www.destinyarts.org), an arts education/violence-prevention center for youth based in Oakland, California. Crowell received nine California Arts Council Artist in Residency grants for her work at Destiny and a National Endowment for the Arts grant to author a curriculum guide called *Youth on the Move: A Teacher's Guidebook to Co-Creating Original Movement/Theater Performances with Teens*. Crowell is the recipient of the 2007 KPFA peace award and the 2006 Purple Moon DreamSpeakers award. She has performed both nationally and internationally with modern, jazz, and theater dance companies in Boston and the Bay Area since 1984.

2

Women Reimagining the World

Jean Shinoda Bolen, M.D., Joanna Macy, Nina Simons, Alice Walker, and Akaya Windwood

From her practice as a Jungian analyst, with an intimate and deep focus on the inner world, Jean Shinoda Bolen's sense of her own assignment has prompted her to turn increasingly outward to offer insight to thousands of women globally. Her book Goddesses in Everywoman *unearthed stories, dreams, and archetypes that offer kinship, context, and connection to women as we reclaim the feminine. As her life path and purpose evolve, she speaks about how forming supportive circles of women can help us grow into our potential, and awaken women everywhere to heal our relationship to nature and to the living Earth.*

Joanna Macy is a widely beloved mentor and wise elder who marries traditional indigenous wisdom, living systems thinking, Buddhist cosmology, empathic connection, and engaged action in an unstoppable and piercing combination. She teaches through experience and example that, in order to be whole and fully potent, love's power to transform our world must be inextricably woven with our outrage, grief, and loss. Joanna reminds me that transformative learning must reach our whole selves, including body, heart, mind, and spirit, to be fully integrated. She embodies the values of practice, lifelong learning, ceaseless commitment, and the regenerative power of love.

Alice Walker's curious, adventurous, and expansive soul seems to permeate her writing, conveying a quality of personal invention and self-knowledge that has inspired my own emergence. By acknowledging the presence of the ancestors—and weaving intuition, dreams, and mystery into her story-telling—she affirms all of our desires to reclaim them. In openly exploring her history, spirituality, and relationships, vulnerably and unflinchingly, she offers affirmation and strength. The story she tells here gave me the cour-age to make it a priority, above anything else, to spend time with a dearly beloved dog when he was leaving life.

Akaya Winwood's brand of leadership is demanding, loving, and uncom-promising. Her commitment to liberation—her own and others'—informs the evolution of the Rockwood Leadership Institute's work. She is a mentor for many, and her haikus of insight and irreverent humor have flung open doors for me, helping me become more of who I was born to be. Akaya's insightful questions, fierce commitment, and demand that we each be our best are expanding the lives, power, and capacity of thousands of nonprofit leaders for progressive change.

NINA SIMONS

Nina Simons exemplifies the kind of leadership that this book is all about—balancing heart with head, strength with flexibility, honesty with sensitivity, fierce purposefulness with compassion, relational brilliance with organizational effectiveness. She leads by joyful inspiration, by generous collaboration, by ever-increasing inclusion. Fearlessly plumbing her own depths and constantly expanding the net of her interest and understanding, she translates these learning experiences into tools for serving the emerging leadership of others. Her inner purpose radiates out into the world, encouraging and motivating the rest of us to find what sparks us so that we may join her in the adventure of helping to shift our collective course.

ANNEKE CAMPBELL

Akaya Windwood: Arundati Roy tells us: "Another world is not only possible, she's on her way. On a quiet day, I can hear her breathing." What practical, everyday actions can we take to move us along to this world that we are reimagining?

Jean Shinoda Bolen: Well, I have been doing what I call my assignment, and I've been encouraging others to do their assignment. This assignment is something that feels like it has your name on it. The principles are: is it meaningful to you; will it be fun being with others on this project, on this cause; and is it motivated by love? It could appear to be motivated by outrage, but you're only outraged if something you love is being trashed.

So for anybody who's waiting for an assignment, if you really are open to serve, some assignment will come along with your name on it. You do have a choice as to whether or not you will step up to it and say, That one's mine.

My assignment was to move from my much more introverted work as a Jungian analyst into seeding circles all over the place, circles with a spiritual center. When that metaphoric millionth circle is formed, patriarchy will be over. It doesn't seem that hard. After that, my next assignment was to be a message carrier, through writing *Urgent Message from Mother: Gather the Women, Save the World,* and by taking the message out further through the spoken word. Simple, really.

Alice Walker: I totally agree. At this point, it has to be about service. It's not about career, it's not about hardly anything else but where you can serve the people and all the rest of the animals and where you can serve the planet, and finding the joy of that.

Sometimes it's hard to know where you will serve next, because the place that you're standing is not holding, or you don't see the effectiveness of what you're doing. For instance, all those marches and all those speeches and all that anguish to try to stop the war, the last big war against Iraq, and before that against Afghanistan. It's not that I personally gave up on that—I still march in protest against war—but I also realize that we have to change the consciousness of our children about war. They don't know what war is, and how could they when their parents give them camouflage diapers and buy them war toys? They think war is a game.

If you really love your children, you try to tell them where they are. So it was necessary for me to move on to writing a children's book about war to help shift the consciousness of our children. It seems to me that it may be a very long shot, but it certainly seems worth doing, and in my own life, the now and the distant yonder are held together by hard work.

I find guidance in my dreams. I know that the ability to dream was given to human beings as a guide, and for the most part we've lost it or we ignore it. I protect my dream world as much as possible from television, from a lot of conversations, from things that I really don't need to know. This is very helpful, because as my dream self trusts me to protect it, I am given more guidance in dreaming.

Sometimes, like Durga, I feel like I have eighteen or nineteen arms, and all of them are whirling. Then someone comes along and they want me to use a twentieth arm, and I don't have it. This is how it often is for the people who are holding up the hoop. If everybody showed up, the hoop wouldn't be so heavy.

Jean Shinoda Bolen: You don't do everything at once. There is an internal priority, the sense of what your sacred work is. There's something about what you know in your bones, what you know matters deeply to you. The inner you, heart/soul, says this takes priority over that. For example, deciding to have and raise a child is sacred work, to be of service is sacred work. When we cannot do both, which is it to be?

So there's something about the present-moment choice that means you can't listen to all the "shoulds" and "oughts" from outside or inside. You're just one woman with a limited amount of energy and all kinds of goodwill and all kinds of wanting to make a difference in the world. And it comes down to individual choice, but who makes the choice matters tremendously. It's not easy. I mean, we all do juggle work.

Nina Simons: One of the things that I've wrestled with for a long time has been reconciling a false dichotomy between self and service. I grew up believing that service was good and service was how I was going to get my strokes and prove my worth, and so I spent a lot of years serving things outside myself that I knew were important. In the last ten years something has changed, through a lot of teaching that included some guidance to pay exquisite attention internally, to see what made my flame grow brighter. I practiced really noticing what my specific assignment was and is. I've been discovering that there is absolute ecstasy in service that's connected to what makes your flame grow brighter, and that there's no dichotomy after all. It turns out that what is really my assignment is the most joyous work I know to do.

I believe part of what we've lost in this plowing-under of the feminine is respect for the work of cultivating our inner gardens, and doing our inner work. For a time around our house, we called the folks who do inner work to the exclusion of outer work "the navel academy," because we saw it as navel gazing. But there is immense power in connecting up our inner work with the call to serve what so greatly needs us out there.

So for me, it's about noticing where your flame grows brighter and seeing how you connect up what you most love with what's most needed out there, because so much *is* needed. We each offer an abundance of creativity and uniqueness, and each of us has our own very specific contribution to make. Now's certainly the time to bring it on.

Joanna Macy: Yes to all that. Service. Finding your passion. Doing what's right in front of you. The voice that every person needs to hear is the voice inside of them. I would add to that counsel the importance of opening our awareness to the larger context of time.

I have just returned from thirty days on a wild stretch of the Oregon coast with sixty people. We called our retreat "Seeds for the Future, an immersion in deep time." Now, those who took part were already up to their elbows, even over their heads, in projects for the healing of our world—and like the rest of us, driven by haste and urgency.

We were deliberately stopping to look at the larger context in which we live. We looked at our culture's peculiar and, I believe, unprecedented experience of time, which is fragmented, speedy, and accelerating. Given market forces and nanotechnology, we're in such a rush we hardly have time to think a thought two inches long. So in this retreat we explored spiritual teachings, especially Buddhist practices, that not only help slow the tempo, but also expand our context to include past and future generations.

To observe your activities within a frame that is larger than your own lifetime is liberating. It's sort of like a poor man's enlightenment, because it frees you from needing to see the results of your own actions. Furthermore, the ancestors and the future ones become more real, and you can feel them supporting you in your work for Earth.

Sister Rosalie Bertell, a scientist focusing on radioactive contamination, says: "Every being who will ever live on Earth is here now." Where? In our ovaries and in our gonads and in our DNA. The choices that we make now, and often under mounting pressure from industry and governmental bureaucracies, directly affect their chances to be born of sound mind and body.

So that wider timeframe gives a sense of buoyancy and of communion across the centuries. Furthermore, it helps us act our age. Having evolved with our planet Gaia, you can think of your true age as being approximately four billion years. But then consider that every particle in every atom of your body goes back to the beginning of space-time. Given this, isn't it time for us to act with the full authority of our fourteen billion years?

Akaya Windwood: The line between women and animals has often been drawn to shame us or keep us in line. As we reimagine this world, what is the rightful relationship between women and our animal bodies?

Alice Walker: For me, the journey lately has been about getting closer to the other animals and understanding that as a path in itself. About a year ago, it occurred to me that I've been in many long relationships with people, but I had only truly started to feel married with my dog and my cat. I decided that I wanted to make it official. So I asked the local priestess to come and all of our friends, with lots of flowers and lots of kitty treats and dog biscuits and German chocolate cake for the rest of us, and we had our wedding.

So that is really how I feel now, that the closer we can get to the other animals, the better for us in that we may then more fully realize that we actually do have these animal bodies. I've learned from my cat and my dog just what it is to really love being alive in the sun, feeling the wind on my face, having really good food, having a nice place to sleep. I'm getting more and more free to feel myself as just another one of the animals on the planet.

Joanna Macy: It is time to celebrate our animal brothers and sisters and our animal bodies. The terrifying thing that is happening to our global culture now is that the instinct for the preservation of life has been cut. We're blocking our base chakra—the *muladhara,* which is our erotic connection with life—to the point where our best-trained minds design weapons that shatter flesh or burn it with a fire that can't be put out, or turn a desert into a radioactive hell for thousands of years.

It makes us crazy when we cut ourselves off from the web of life and all our fellow beings. Chief Seattle warned us of that. He said without the beasts you will perish of a great loneliness. And that isolation leads us to cut ourselves off even more from each other as well as from our own bodies.

Jean Shinoda Bolen: Joanna, I remember about thirty years ago when you introduced a group of women at the first women's solstice camp to keening, and what you did was you read a list of the animals and birds that are now extinct, and after each short list, we keened, and then we learned that the U.N. desk that used to keep track of such things has been put out of business. Today, nobody is keeping track of the life that is extinct. And it occurs to me that for people to be whole, they need to be able to grieve what is wounded and what is lost. When they don't, they get cut off from feeling, and they do addictive things instead of grieving.

Akaya Windwood: What lies under your despair, and what wisdom can you offer us from that place?

Joanna Macy: When young women tell me they are losing hope, I tell them not to be afraid. Losing hope is just a feeling. Just keep breathing. If you're not afraid of losing your hope, then the next minute you'll see something very beautiful. It's when we resist a feeling that we're stuck with it. We're always stuck with what we don't let ourselves accept.

The work that I do in groups originally was called despair work, despair and empowerment. Then it was called deep ecology work, because we found that by honoring our despair and not trying to suppress it or pave it over as some personal pathology, we open a gateway into our full vitality and to our connection with all of life.

So, beneath what I call our "pain for the world," which includes sorrow and outrage and dread, is the instinct for the preservation of life. When we are unafraid of the suffering of our world, and brave enough to sustain the gaze and speak out, there is a redemptive sanity at work.

The other side of that pain for our world is a love for our world. That love is bigger than you would ever guess from what our consumer society conditions us to want. It's a love so raw, so ancient, so deep that if you get in touch with it, you can just ride it; you can just be there and it doesn't matter. Then nothing can stop you. But to get to that, you have to stop being afraid of hurting. The price of reaching that is tears and outrage, because the tears and the power to keep on going, they come from the same source. It's two sides of the same coin.

Nina Simons: I'm reminded of lessons that I've learned from several of you about the value of grieving and darkness. It's come to be a real guidepost for me to help me orient myself toward the places that are painful and difficult. I read an interview with Alice where she said that when we encourage ourselves to go deeper, we expand our capacity for joy at the same time. Part of reinventing how we understand ourselves to be human is to expand our capacity at both ends.

We all have the disease of modern American culture, which lets us think that our minds are so smart. I've been struggling to find my own voice in writing and speaking, and one of my favorite teachers keeps telling me that if I stop trying to sound like a smart white man I'll be fine. I realize how scary it is to me to believe that I have within me already all that I need. So I think that part of us reimagining the world is to know that we have within us everything we need. Some of that is about recognizing the wisdom that's in our bodies and that's in our hearts and our spirits, and not imagining that our minds have to solve it all, because they can't and they won't. Our overreliance on our minds is part of the disease, not part of the solution.

Alice Walker: What I find underneath my despair is actually ecstasy, because I am so incredibly happy that I'm here now, not in the future, not in the past, but somehow lucky enough to be born just right now. It's such a gift. Because the despair for me is that mile-thick covering of ice that Al Gore, in his film, tells us is melting. When I think of our planet, which is so glorious and so alive and so colorful and so warm, with so many birds and all kinds of things, when I think of all that, I feel such sadness, it's almost unbearable. But the joy to somehow have made it here, I feel very intensely at times, when I allow myself the space to experience eternity.

We actually have eternity. We can have it in our lifetime. It's not something in the future. It is in the moment. So when I rest enough to give eternity back to myself, having foolishly squandered it by looking at my watch, then I know that it's really okay. Ultimately, Mother has all the time there is. She will melt this ice ball many times. I'm very sorry that seems to be the future of the planet, but I also feel that she will be fine. She will be fine, and she has somehow managed to leave me here now, to have me witness her magnificence, her beauty, her generosity, and her grace. That's the ecstasy.

Jean Shinoda Bolen: I'm often asked, "Do you have hope?" which is different than love, especially at this time. Like Alice, I think that this is a wonderful time to be here, because what we do now really matters. I like to be in a place or time when I can tilt a situation to make it better. Right now, I think we may have only two decades to stop the destructive course humanity is on. While it is still possible to make a difference, here we are: a generation of women who came of age with the women's movement or were beneficiaries of it, who exist in great numbers, live longer, and have had opportunities, resources, and responsibilities far beyond what women have ever had in the known history of the world, and at midlife or menopause could have thirty, forty, or more good years left to do something together to make a difference Then there are all the men who have also been influenced by the women's movement, as well as the children who are adults now.

I think there's grace in the synchronicities that happen as soon as we feel deeply that what we do here matters and do it from our heart and soul. Amazing synchronicities and connections happen that give us immediate feedback that our particular path is supported. We meet others who are committed to making a difference and find that ideas, inspiration, and energy are generated. They are soul-friends. This is an exciting time. I have a sense that we are at a tilting point and that what we do here will shift what will happen next.

Jean Shinoda Bolen, M.D. (www.jeanbolen.com), is a psychiatrist, Jungian analyst, clinical professor of psychiatry at UCSF, Distinguished Life Fellow of the American Psychiatric Association, and author of *The Tao of Psychology; Goddesses in Everywoman; Gods in Everyman; Ring of Power; Crossing to Avalon; Close to the Bone; The Millionth Circle; Goddesses in Older Women; Crones Don't Whine;* and *Urgent Message from Mother.* She is a major advocate for a U.N. Fifth World Conference on Women (www.5wcw.org), and she inspired the Millionth Circle Initiative (www.millionthcircle.org).

Joanna Macy (www.joannamacy.net), a renowned Buddhist teacher, ecophilosopher, systems theorist, and scholar, is a longtime activist in the peace, justice, and ecology movements. Her wide-ranging work spans Eastern and Western thought and seeks to bring the perspectives of other life-forms to human consciousness and past and future generations. Macy's experiential group work, known to activists around the world as the Work That Reconnects, seeks to convey the extraordinary opportunity of being alive now to serve the survival of life on Earth. Macy's many seminal books include *Despair*

and Personal Power in the Nuclear Age; Dharma and Development; Thinking Like a Mountain; Coming Back to Life: Practices to Reconnect Our Lives, Our World; Widening Circles; and, most recently, *World as Lover, World as Self.*

Nina Simons, the editor of this book with Anneke Campbell, is a social entrepreneur experienced in both the nonprofit and corporate worlds. In 1990, she cofounded Bioneers (www.bioneers.org) and is currently co-CEO. From 1989 to 1994 she worked for the entrepreneurial start-up company Seeds of Change, initially as its marketing director and subsequently as its president. From 1995 to 1997, Nina was director of strategic marketing at Odwalla, the fresh juice company. Nina's current work with Bioneers focuses largely on writing and teaching about women's leadership, nature, and restoring the feminine in all of us.

Alice Walker is one of the most important writers of our time, known for her literary fiction, including the Pulitzer Prize–winning *The Color Purple,* her many volumes of poetry, and her powerful nonfiction collections. Her most recent nonfiction work includes *We Are the Ones We Have Been Waiting For: Inner Light in a Time of Darkness* and *Why War Is Never a Good Idea,* as well as the children's book *There Is a Flower at the Tip of My Nose Smelling Me.*

Akaya Windwood (www.rockwoodleadership.org) is president of the Rockwood Leadership Institute. Having spent over forty years as an activist working for change, she is committed to social and economic justice and to building a compelling vision for effectiveness and collaboration within the nonprofit and social benefit sectors. A longtime resident of the Bay Area, she loves the richness of living and working with diversity and is committed to joy, laughter, and healthy, safe communities.

3

Standing in Relationship to Myself and Nature

Gloria Flora

Gloria Flora's soft voice and gentle manner, combined with the strength of her caring and the power of her will, helped her to achieve tremendous change within the Forest Service. Her clear and determined purpose to serve the common good as a public servant and defender of wild lands gave her the strength to go up against the system that had trained her. I believe it's the integrity of her internal compass, supported by her authenticity, clarity, and love of nature, that makes her so effective.

NINA SIMONS

> *Women tend to use relationships as a measure of the quality of their lives.*

Not long ago, I got up in the morning, pretty upset. I was feeling overwhelmed with all the things I needed to do. I'm starting a national organization to support biochar* and coordinating a groundbreaking

---

*Biochar, a fine-grained, highly porous charcoal made from agricultural and forest waste, helps soils retain nutrients and water. It's been used as a soil enhancer for two thousand years, and as a modern application it could boost food security and discourage deforestation.

35

workshop to optimize natural carbon sequestration. I am also, at the same time, trying to keep my nonprofit thriving; the list goes on and on. But instead of getting up and rushing to my office, I went to the kitchen and cleaned it thoroughly, then called a girlfriend and talked for a little bit. A couple of hours passed, but I then felt calm and centered and ready to face my tasks. And right there in my e-mail was an article on a study about how women respond to stress. It appears that when we women respond to stressful situations, we do not just fight or flee, we also lower our own stress by tending and nurturing, which is exactly what I did that morning. This delay allowed me to face the day calmly, and I kicked butt!

We women pay attention to our setting and surroundings, and we also value connecting with other people and nurturing those relationships. In addition to this heightened relational context, we have a heightened temporal context, as we tend to think well beyond our life spans and ourselves. I believe in part it may be because historically we have been held back, and so we dream of all the possibilities, of all the things that we could do and are fully capable of accomplishing. Perhaps we extend those hopes and dreams to our children and our grandchildren. We know if we keep working and carving space for full self-realization, then our children may have even greater opportunity. So we often operate within a multigenerational frame of reference.

We also have a desire for continuity. When I look at the women gardeners I know, we all seem to be yearning for continuous growth over time, building neighborhoods of diverse plants. We plant perennials, herbs, vegetables, and flowers, dreaming about how they will all grow together, rather than trying to get the biggest vegetables or the most vegetables just for that year. I call that the don't-goose-the-garden technique. We're content to just have it keep producing and evolving over time instead of forcing it to maximize. Companies like Monsanto and ADM, they're goosing the garden. I don't think there's ever been a woman CEO in charge of any of them.

I became a leader in a culture where I was told that leading with emotion or with intuition was inherently weak. When I joined the "tribe" of the U.S. Forest Service, there had never been a woman in a decision-making position—ever. The cult of macho men, marching to the same beat, did not include thinking from the heart, or at least letting anyone know you might be. I didn't see anything weak about intuition. Consider the elephants. Research has shown that the intuition of their leaders is prescient and important to the survival of the group.

I made many decisions based on intuition, even when that meant doing something very different than the norm. And I can't think of a single major intuitive decision I made that I would have done differently. I will give you a good example of one. It occurred when I was the forest supervisor of the Lewis and Clark National Forest in north-central Montana. We had been spending several years on an analysis of the potential for oil and gas leasing in the forest, and trying to determine, if we were to lease, what stipulations would be required to protect the land.

Part of the forest is the Rocky Mountain Front. This is a stretch of a hundred miles of landscape that is largely undeveloped, where the Great Plains slam into the limestone ramparts of the Rocky Mountains. Cliffs soar up thousands of feet from the rolling grasslands in majestic beauty. Here you have the largest herd of elk in the United States, the second-largest herd of bighorn sheep, and the largest winter gathering of mule deer. You have every large charismatic carnivore you could possibly want: grizzly bear, wolf, lynx, wolverine—you name it, it's here. Indeed, every plant and animal species—with the exception of the free-roaming bison that were present at the time of Lewis and Clark—are thriving on the Rocky Mountain Front today.

We studied the ecology and the physical aspects of this stunning landscape, but we also looked at the human dimension. We conducted private and public meetings with citizens, organizations, politicians, and members of industry, trying to understand what people wanted from this landscape and what they thought about its future.

In the end, I signed a decision that did not allow leasing on the Rocky Mountain Front. It was far too important, ecologically and culturally, to risk developing for short-term gain. Even though that decision was very contrary to business as usual, I was clear about exactly why I had made the decision. One motivating factor was the profound ecological and historical significance of that landscape; the second was people's attachment to the place. People's love for that landscape and their profound connection to it resonated on a heart level. There was no way I could allow it to be damaged.

To my knowledge, that was the first and only time that people's sense of place figured prominently in a significant decision made by the Forest Service. I say that not as a brag but as a lament. Why are we not using our sense of place as an important criterion in making decisions about these lands that belong to all of us? We know intuitively that the ability to find peace, meaning, and solitude in the natural world replenishes our souls in a way that little else can. Who are we, as managers of public lands, to deny that and to justify our ignorance behind a veil of numbers? Who are we to value economy over our emotional and spiritual connection to our lands?

I hope in the future people look at this decision and say, "Well, that was a no-brainer. Why would you allow leasing on such an incredible landscape?" But making that decision was one of the greatest challenges in my position with the Forest Service to date. It was frightening, because I was going to depart from "the tribe." I was going to make a decision that the tribe would not approve of, and not only that, it was stemming from honoring people's feelings and emotions, honoring our sense of place rather than more measurable concerns.

I worried that I would be shunned, possibly shipped off to some remote location or hidden in the bowels of a regional office somewhere. But then immediately on the heels of articulating that feeling, I said to myself, "Excuse me, do you think that your little personal life, your career, is more important than sustaining this landscape for generations? I think not." Intuitively I knew that my decision was the correct one, but I puzzled over how to present it in such a compelling way that everyone would understand. So I used my intuition again and simply told the truth: This landscape is too precious and important to develop, so we're not going to do that. Period.

The response was powerful, supportive, and overwhelming. People were ecstatic. And the ensuing legal maneuverings and protests from the oil industry were unable to overturn the decision. Instead of being sentenced to the career equivalent of Siberia, I was honored; and, to this day, I am still blessed to have people express their support for what I did.

 Gloria Flora (www.s-o-solutions.org) works for public land sustainability through her organization, Sustainable Obtainable Solutions, which focuses on large landscape conservation, climate change solutions, and the sustainable production and use of biochar (www.biochar-us.org). An exemplary public servant and steward in her twenty-three years with the U.S. Forest Service, she served as the forest supervisor for two national forests. She made a landmark decision to prohibit oil and gas leasing on the Rocky Mountain Front and established the human dimension as a component of ecosystem management decision-making. She has won multiple awards for her leadership, courage, and integrity.

4

We Got Issues

Rha Goddess

Meeting Rha Goddess, I was struck by her fearlessness, her powerful presence, and her absolute willingness to meet any of the young women she worked with anywhere they chose to go. Her life path explores issues central to her personal inquiry—from hip-hop to mental health to self-esteem to money—and in so doing, she translates her exploration into performance art and teaching to effect change. She writes, performs, and mentors young women in multicultural collaborations, teaching and developing communications essential to informing, equipping, and unleashing their leadership, creativity, and inner authority.

NINA SIMONS

So, who's got next? Or, as we say in hip-hop, who got next? If you had told me fifteen years ago that I would be a full-time activist and social entrepreneur—working at the intersection of art, social justice, and transformation—I would have told you that you were crazy. As the first in my family to enter the corporate ranks of an American Fortune 50 company I had every intention of shattering the glass ceiling, making a whole lot of money, rescuing my peeps from cyclical poverty consciousness, and riding off into the sunset. But the universe had other plans for me.

As I look at my life now, I wonder how my work could have ever been about anything but the celebration, empowerment, healing, and transformation of humanity through uplifting the hearts, minds, and souls of young women. Now, don't get it twisted—I came kicking and screaming. Because not a day goes by that I do not get tired just thinking about how much work we have to do.

Believe me, I am intimately related to what lies before us. As a black woman, born into a country that would just as easily have written me off long before I ever drew breath, I am profoundly aware of the great divides that exist in our society. And there is not a day that goes by that I am not reminded of these orchestrated disparities. But all that ain't got nothing to do with me.

Because it is not up to America whether I live or die, nor is it up to the so-called leadership of this nation whether I thrive or prosper. And the moment that I decide that my fate is governed by what America thinks of me, I give up my power, and my life becomes about the struggle for validation, recognition, and entitlement—on America's terms.

And *that* struggle has nothing to do with me and it has nothing to do with my sisters.

Often I am asked about our work and what it is exactly that we do. The best way I can describe it in this moment is to say that the mission of the Next Wave women's movement and our first initiative, "We Got Issues!" is to hold powerful space so that young women can: get still and hear what is calling them; think strategically and holistically about how to answer that call; and cleanse, heal, purge, and disengage from anything that stands in the way of fulfilling all the above.

We at Next Wave are in the business of travel, and the journey is from victim to vision: we transport souls on the underground, like Harriet did, to freedom.

Our work is necessary because the culture of this society works overtime to cultivate and nurture insecurity, and young women have proven to be easy prey. America has given its daughters an identity crisis, an inferiority complex, a preoccupation with unattainable perfection that leaves many of them—many of us—silenced in the wake of not being anything *enough*.

Yes. We got issues!

Unlike our male counterparts who act out in retaliation, we as women tend to act in and self-destruct through physical and emotional neglect, dysfunctional eating habits, and toxic relationships. We at Next Wave have found that these issues cut across race, class, ethnicity, and geographical location, hence our commitment to all young women between the ages of eighteen and thirty-five. I assert that the most crucial game that each of us can play to bring about transformation in the sociopolitical and environmental movement is the game called "Go Within."

We have come to know that this is the most vital journey young women in America can take right now. As members of a global community, we must consider the restoring of our mental, spiritual, and emotional gardens just as necessary and important to the sociopolitical movement as rallying in the streets and registering to vote. We cannot demand rights that we do not believe, deep down inside, we are entitled to and then expect to receive them. Moreover, the minute we decide that our rights to life and liberty are up to someone else, we have orchestrated a losing battle.

Next Wave women know that the next revolution is about responsibility and accountability to ourselves and to our universal family, and this responsibility begins with honoring who we really are and through the cultivation of our talents and gifts, bringing forth what we have been called to bring forth. If the experience of Hurricane Katrina has taught us anything, it is that this is our America, and we can no longer afford to stand by while those in charge figure out whether they can fix it. As we take responsibility for who we are, we reclaim our rightful place as citizens and work to restore the possibility of fulfilling the dream of a true democracy. So my answer to the question, "Who's got next?" is, "We do."

So, what of this global hip-hop era? And where do we stand in relation to the feminist movement? Since we are in an age of capitalistic market branding and nonprofits are not exempt . . . how are our brand and our movement different? As we watch Lil' Kim aspire to be the next Martha Stewart, a.k.a. jailhouse diva, we get to bear witness to the affliction of striving for fabulousness as the latest distorted outgrowth of the feminist movement. You-go-girl-gone-awry has turned a once-inspiring mantra for personal achievement into a fiercely competitive landscape that challenges feminine kinship, perpetuates gross gender inequality in leadership, and leaves most of us overextended, out of touch, and, frankly, out of breath. Many of this generation's daughters are in over their heads and living way over the edge because we are driven by the overburdening need to have it all, be it all, and do it all—in half the time.

What this creates is a scattered sense of being, a perpetual state of confusion and dissatisfaction, hamster-wheel disorientation, and very little progress. We are so busy and dizzy running around trying to prove we are up to and about something that at the end of the day, when I ask most young women the question, "Where are you at, really?" they are hard pressed to find an answer. We are not grounded, and when we are not grounded we say yes to things—with no idea why—and then become slaves to these obligations that ultimately put us last on our own list.

Next Wave women know that sometimes opportunity is really distraction in a very fly dress. And we must treat it like crack and "just say no." Focus is our friend. Multitasking is just a great marketing scheme that has us feeling fabulous while we run around with our tongues hanging out. This distorted epidemic has flung us way out of balance. What we have seen in our work is a fundamental crisis: as women we have an inability to know ourselves beyond what we do and give to others. And what this has created is a fundamental breakdown in our ability to get still, listen, and receive.

When we define ourselves from a place of reactionary codependence and victimhood, we put resistance in the center of our identity, and it becomes easy to block the good that wants to come our way.

Next Wave women understand universal flow and know that it is through the grounding of vision, purpose, and the growing edge that we are able to discern what is divinely for us: right person, right knowledge, right timing, right me, right medium, right now.

Yes. We got issues.

Another distorted outgrowth of this feminist movement is the belief that our feminine gender automatically makes us more compassionate, understanding, and inclusively nurturing in leadership. This is a myth. We have swum in the same contaminated water as our male counterparts and therefore must do the same deep excavation work in order to bring such (inherent) attributes to bear. A skirt in the chair does not guarantee anything. We cannot take our womanhood for granted, nor can we assume that we have been immune to the constant conditioning and corrupting messages in this society that define success and power.

Next Wave women know that we must challenge these existing notions as a daily practice, and we must think long and hard about who we aspire to be and how we intend to have our feminine-centered values reflected in our leadership. We must be willing to get still and come face to face with our shadow selves. We must get to know our demons real well so that we can bring awareness to when we are in vision and when we are just straight-up trippin'!

Please do not misunderstand me. As a woman, I am deeply thankful for the opportunity to think, live, and dream from an expansive place, and I know that the mothers, grandmothers, and great-grandmothers of the feminist movement made that possible. But I would be remiss as a black woman if I did not speak the truth about the great race, age, and class divides that continue to permeate the modern women's movement. Somehow, despite our best efforts, we continue to have our activism and our representation be disproportionately related to those who can afford to financially underwrite the cause.

That just leaves too many of us on the outside looking in, or at the mercy of others' benevolence for survival. As Next Wave women we commit to self-determination and working across culture, race, and class as a deliberate testimony to the power of collaboration among the underserved and the underengaged. And you would be surprised to find who fits underneath those headings. We work eyeball to eyeball mentoring, nurturing, and challenging one another from a place of deep love, esteem, and investment. This is not like rescuing, nor charity, nor guilt-ridden obligation, but more like universal sisterhood in the making.

Yes. We got issues.

And we got lots of work to do—and Goddess knows, I do get tired just thinking about it. But I trust in a very deep place that as we fortify our souls and our spirit, the universe will line up beside us, and we will be given everything we need to go the distance. After all, what we are calling the state of our world is simply a reflection and a projection of our internal afflictions being played out on the global stage.

Next Wave women understand this, and we dedicate ourselves to sustainability, and we hold our centers like we hold each other. Together we hold the planet—rocking the world back into balance, humbly and sacredly, one soul, one voice, one woman at a time.

Rha Goddess (www.rhaworld.com) is an internationally renowned performance artist, activist, and social entrepreneur. As CEO of Divine Dime Entertainment, Ltd., she was the first woman in hip-hop to independently market and commercially distribute her music worldwide. Her activist work includes founding and executive-producing the young women's performance movement We Got Issues!, the Hip Hop Mental Health Project, and *LOW: Meditations Trilogy Part 1*. She is a 2008 recipient of the National Museum for Voting Rights Freedom Flame Award for her outstanding work in the field of arts and civic engagement.

5

How Art Can Heal Broken Places

Lily Yeh

Lily Yeh is an artist who creates community art projects that transform and heal. When she realized that creating beautiful art wouldn't fulfill her sense of purpose, she connected with people and communities to engage them in the alchemy of transformation. Later, she formed Barefoot Artists to bring healing art to some of the world's most battered and war-torn places. By making collaborative mosaics, she brings wholeness, color, and joy to people who have lived through trauma, violence, and desolation. Doing what she feels born to do, with quiet dignity and by following her inner instructions, causes her light to be regenerative, contagious, and transformational.

NINA SIMONS

I was born in Kueizhou, China, and went to Taiwan during the Communist takeover. My father loved Chinese painting. So when I was fifteen, he took me to an art teacher, and I started painting in the traditional landscape style. It turned out that painting became the passion of my life.

I came to the United States in the '60s. I have a sense of deep rootedness in the Chinese culture because of my study of Chinese painting and because of the things we were taught—Confucianism and Taoism. But my education in Taiwan was very rigid, so coming to the United States helped free me of many cultural limitations. It also thrust me into an alien society where the question was: how could I be me, an Oriental woman with a different sense of value and artistic sensitivity, and at the same time be contemporary, relevant, and able to make my life meaningful?

People can take comfort in me because I'm slow and it took me so long to find my path. I graduated, got a good job, and taught at the University of the Arts in Philadelphia for many years. I had a family, and I did all the normal things. I was creating, having shows. But my heart was yearning for something I could not quite define.

In 1986, I was invited by the late Arthur Hall, an internationally acclaimed African American dancer/choreographer, to create a park on an abandoned lot next to his building in the inner city of North Philadelphia, and this began my journey. Like many places in inner cities, it was a place traumatized by decades of neglect and racial and economic discrimination. The neighborhood reflected the brutal reality of poverty; trash and shards of broken glass were strewn across vacant land, and streets were marred with torn-down houses, which looked like broken teeth. It is called the Badlands.

So I asked people for advice, because I didn't know what to do on this land. I only knew how to paint. I was told, "Don't go in; the kids will destroy everything you create. It's an African American community. They don't like outsiders, and besides, you don't have enough money, a drop in the bucket." The Pennsylvania Council on the Arts gave me $2,500. Somebody said, "Do a feasibility study and forget about the rest." Yet somehow I knew that this project might be the gateway that would lead me to my path.

I was scared and reluctant, and I almost chickened out. At that moment, wanting to withdraw, my inner voice spoke to me in a fragile but clear voice. It said, "If you don't rise to the occasion, the best of you will die and the rest will not amount to anything."

It's almost like what you read in myths: you get the calling on your journey and if you're brave enough, if you're serious enough to respond, then you get to meet your guide. My guide was an African American man by the name of Joseph Williams.

Everybody called him Jojo. He was like a lion, always roaring and angry and wearing his bandanas, and wearing his hammers and knives hanging out and dangling around his belt. He lived in a dilapidated house next to the big abandoned lot on which I was supposed to work. I went to his house. He had heard word on the street and didn't want to have anything to do with a crazy Chinese woman. But I was desperate to get some help, so I went again, and he was tying his shoelaces.

I said, "Jojo, you have to talk to me." I shared with him my dream to create an art park and asked for his help. This simple request disarmed him. Jojo was a feared person in the neighborhood, and I came to realize that maybe he acted the way he did because the world had been trying to put him down. He fought hard to protect his manhood. This Asian woman coming to ask him for help made him feel different.

Human beings are so frail. We don't want to lose face. We often have a false sense of dignity and want to hide our imperfections. That's why broken places hold so much power, because there we are laid bare. We can't hide, and so it's possible for violence to happen, but it's also possible to make a deep and direct connection with people.

One way to equalize is to expose one's weaknesses. My weakness became his strength; that was how we started to work together on equal footing. I offered him an opportunity to work; he helped me with the work. Because of him, children came. Boys, especially, admired him because he was the strong man in the neighborhood. When we were poking around on the lot trying to figure out what to do, kids showed up, also wanting to help. I had shovels and spades waiting. That was how we got started.

No school, no degree can help one design a park that is truly for the community. This abandoned lot felt chaotic even though there was nothing in it. It was chaotic because it had no sense of orientation. I knew that to become a place it had to have a center, and so I picked up a stick from the ground and I drew a big circle. I said, We start from here. The kids were so happy, digging, shoveling, and doing all kinds of things. We found a lot of bricks, some of them perfect, and I realized that these could be our building materials. That's how we learned to use recycled materials. We used broken glass too. And more children came.

I said, Let's not look at our problems, let's look at what we can do together. Here the men were all on drugs. Big Man James Maxton was a drug user and seller and had been a destructive force in the community for twenty years. Now he was making mosaics, and when you make a mosaic, every piece of it looks beautiful. People passing him said: "This pattern is beautiful. You did that for us? Great." This positive feedback was like raindrops to a parched heart, and piece by piece his life began to be restored. He said, "This feels good. If Lily comes back next year, I will give up drugs." And he did. Because of Big Man, the village started to host Narcotics Anonymous meetings.

Together we made mosaic angels. Big Man was suffering such pain with diabetes. We were creating angels, huge, big, majestic, Ethiopian angels. That inspired him to get up every morning. When the art helped restore him, he became the embodiment of love, which affected the whole community. Because he had descended so low, he had the capacity to understand other people's mistakes. When people felt sad and broken down, they came to his shoulder to cry. Big Man passed away in 2004.

Because of Jojo and the children, the project was rooted in the community from the very beginning. For three years my crew consisted of children from three-and-a-half to thirteen years old. They came, eager and wanting to make things. That was how we gained the trust of the adults, who had had their dreams and promises broken so many times. But because they could see that this woman came back in the hottest summertime to work with the children to build something, gradually the adults joined in also. With the adults, we constructed Meditation Park, with its gentle undulating walls enclosing a courtyard completely covered with multicolored mosaic patterns. On one of its walls stood the tree of life filled with white blossoms against a deep azure background. I designed the park with the intention to create a place where one could retreat, reflect, reconnect, and recenter.

When the city blessed us with permission to use another abandoned lot, we transformed it into a park named Garden of the Cosmic Night. Its ninety-by-thirty-five-foot mural hosted gigantic flowers, two stories high, blooming through their multihued petals against a pitch-black sky bedecked with innumerable galaxies and stars. Lo and behold, this is the sky of the twenty-first century, with a spaceship and rocket traveling through the stars.

This is how the project began organically for a woman who didn't know anything about community-building, and who did not particularly want to work with children. Through the process, my weakness became my strength. Then when the adults came, they needed jobs. They needed training. The right person came and helped us. Stephen Sayer is a builder and an educator with a degree in law. He assisted us in turning our summer art project into a nonprofit arts organization, which we named the Village of Arts and Humanities. Working together with neighborhood adults like Jojo, Big Man, and many others, we renovated an abandoned three-story building next to the park into the headquarters of our new organization. This gave us the capacity to launch a year-round after-school program, an adult learning program, and an array of other programs over time.

Then we built houses, and with the help of our dear friend Ken Kolodziej, we turned two acres of abandoned industrial land into a tree farm, a little microbusiness. It just went on and on. That was how an art project grew into a village.

We turned two hundred abandoned lots into seventeen beautiful parks and gardens and many green spaces. The core of the village is a ten-block area. We worked with the schools. We worked with public housing, and we did job training for youths and adults. We began producing crafts, and we published pamphlets and books. We created a youth theater. We created a Rites of Passage program, where the teens spoke, and then youths began to travel and perform in other cities.

Jefferson University worked with us on health issues, and a farmers' market imported fresh produce to us.

We made vegetable gardens, and we even built houses. We renovated six dilapidated buildings on our own. We worked with the city to build six new three-story homes for the lower-income first-time home buyers in the neighborhood. Subsequent to that, the struggling business community came to us for help. So, in 2004, we got a big planning grant. We accomplished this by mobilizing interested businesses and residents, living in the ninety-nine-square-block area near the village neighborhood, to imagine a development that would benefit all participants. We call our vision the Shared Prosperity. The plan that we completed after one year's hard work became the blueprint for the area's future development.

In Taoist thinking, the darkest moment of the night or the most devastating place is the time or place most ready for transformation. No one knew quite how to deal with the inner-city problem; that was why it remained broken. But if a person wants to learn to be creative, to be innovative, go to the heart of the problem—go to broken places. They offer some of the best opportunities for finding solutions. In this broken but open space, people can bring their seeds of creativity as offerings. When people start to share their talents and work with each other, there is cross-fertilization, and the more people share with each other, the more people connect at the heart level. When people do things based on this heart connection, it's unstoppable. That primal source of energy begins to nurture people in a deep way. When we are nurtured, we nurture the things we do, we nurture our environment, and things begin to grow.

I believe this happens more easily through art, poetry, music, and dance than through more intellectual and technically oriented endeavors. It's like hardware and software: we can set up wonderful systems to save lives, and we need to do that too, but we need to take care of the soul. We need to take care of the heart so that our technological capacity falls into the light and not into the dark. We human beings are capable of so much destruction, and now we have the technology to destroy ourselves. Thus I believe that the most urgent issue is working on our human transformation, and art is a powerful vehicle for transformation in part because it is not confrontational. Art is about beauty and authenticity, and it gives us an effective way to improve human relationships and bring people together. This gives us hope.

In 2004, I left the Village of Arts and Humanities. I was at an international conference where I heard a presentation by Jean Bosco Musana Rukirande from Rwanda. His voice describing the suffering of his people touched me deeply. My heart moved and I responded. I said, "Wait for me at the airport, I am coming." I visited him on a summer day in July 2004.

Jean Bosco took me to the village of genocide survivors in the Rugerero Sector near Gisenyi. There I saw no beauty, no smiles, and no colors. I did see one hundred families and two faucets—and sometimes the faucets broke down. The villagers had to walk two or three miles to get water from a polluted river. And there was the mass grave. My heart sank.

I always felt so scared when I began a project. I would ask myself: Why did I put myself here? I did this to myself. These broken places, they imply danger. And there *were* real physical dangers that I encountered. But nothing compares to the depth of what I feel, that sense of deep fulfillment. I am willing to take the risk for this depth of connection, this depth of impact, and this depth of meaning in my own life. I feel that if I do this, then I can die well.

It's a terrible genocide that happened in Rwanda. But it can happen anywhere if all of us don't look inward and take care to balance the light and the darkness. I became so aware of my own imperfection and my own darkness when I was in Rwanda. That awareness is good because we're all human. We are fallible. That's what genocide teaches. When we are in greed, wanting other people's things, desiring other people's wives or husbands, and we don't check that, it begins to create a climate. Then tyrants speak everyone's unconscious desires. I can only check mine and be aware of my *own* shortcomings. When I learn to forgive myself, then I'm able to forgive other people. When we're aware of our own darkness, we are more able to forgive the other and understand the other, and that's the beginning of peace.

When I came to Rwanda, I had $5,000. The survivors asked me, "Can you bury our dead properly by interring their bones in a tomb underground?" I was very frightened by the suggestion because it meant technology, ventilation, aeration—otherwise bones would become soft. Still, I wanted to try my best to fulfill their wishes. To do this, we needed professional help. I was looking for the services of a contractor. Someone told me that the China Road and Bridge Construction Company had a base up the road. I met their impressive young manager, who understood the importance of the project. He said, "Go and raise your money. We're going to help you build it."

We started digging into the ground; we built the bone chamber. Then everything that I feared would happen did, because the cement was porous and absorbed moisture. The bones threatened to become soft, and I became frantic. What to do? Yes, mosaic. I taught the villagers the art of making mosaics. Together we covered the whole memorial monument with beautiful tiled mosaics, and we protected the bones.

The people in the survivors' village had just been thrown together there. Before the art project, they didn't know each other. They mourned in their silence and in their solitude. The art project brought people together. Bedecking the Rugerero Genocide Memorial Monument with mosaics was most appropriate, because we are all broken in one way or another, especially in Rwanda. But through our imagination and creative action together, we transformed brokenness into wholeness. Yes, let's make art, then comes beauty and joy, and then together we will create our future.

In dedication, people brought the newly collected bones together. They placed the bones in caskets, which they brought to the bone chamber. Everywhere you saw purple, the color of mourning in Rwanda. In 2007, the monument was completed. We held a big celebration to give the monument to the people and the government for its safekeeping.

Looking at my original design, this memorial monument site actually resembles the figure of a Neolithic Mother Goddess. This year, the

1994 genocide was commemorated for the fifteenth time. Thousands of people came out to commemorate it. They opened up the bone chamber; they walked in. They opened up the caskets and looked at the bones. Even fifteen years later, the grief was still so intense that it was too much to bear and many people collapsed.

The building of the genocide memorial reflects my understanding that we must look at the difficult, the destruction, the death, the human greed, and the violence. We must address the difficult fact of genocide. We must confront our fear and bigotry. The light and the dark are the embracing pair as in the diagram of the Tao. They represent the essence of life in its eternal conflict and complementary duality. Attention and awareness are like light. They can dispel darkness and ignorance.

While dealing with the dead, we must look at what struggles the living are facing. So I brought volunteers, we got colors, and we got children to paint. That's how we started when there was no common language or history. I showed the children beauty and possibilities. I put the best of their work on the wall. In this way, art is not imposed but rooted in the community with honor and respect. Before, this was just a place where they temporarily stayed. Now it has character. They identify with this painted village now. It is their home.

The community continued to paint their dreams—computers, cars, motorcycles, and goats—and sometimes dreams come true. Every family now has a goat. My friends in Philadelphia at Christmastime asked, "What can we give?" They gave goats, and now those goats have given birth to little goats and created resources for the villagers. This is one way culture creates assets. In the survivors' village, they had nothing at the beginning. Now they have goats and goat milk.

The women aged forty-five years and older said, "We need help. We want to learn traditional basket-weaving." Sponsored by Barefoot Artists, these women learned to harvest yucca, beat and scrape the leaves, wash them in soap, dry them, and weave them into lovely baskets. When one builds a project, it's never linear. One has to respond to people's needs to make it sustainable. Most of the women have bad eyesight. How could they weave? We invited the eye doctor to come, and now everybody has nice eyes and glasses so they can see. When they weave together, they bond in Sisterhood. They support each other and have hope for the future.

A group of young orphans, whose parents were killed when they were three to ten years old, were destitute with no way to make a living. They decided they wanted to learn sewing, and now they sew beautiful things. Barefoot Artists was able to help them start a business. All the orphans now have sewing machines so they can make a living and provide for their families.

Most recently we managed to sponsor a solar energy engineer by the name of Richard Komp. He came and taught solar energy and the making of solar panels. In a three-week period, he trained thirty-seven solar engineers. When you go inside some of the homes in the survivors' village, there is not even a table or chairs, no mats, no bed, but they have solar energy and light. There is solar light for the sewing group so they can sew day and night to make money to send their children to school. In the community parade this year, people marched with the solar panels, which were not imported from America or Europe; they were produced right here in the survivors' village in Rwanda.

I often find it hard to define what I do as an artist, but I've come to realize that broken places are my canvases. People's stories are the pigments, and their talents, the tools. Together we weave something magical, organic, and sustainable. I call it the living social sculpture. Its center is compassion, and its goal is peace and a shared prosperity.

People say, Oh, you bring social change. But one cannot impose change on other people. It is just like nature. If we want rain to come, we must plant trees. We change the quality of the soil. We bring organic materials into it. We make things grow, and slowly the rain will come. So I see myself as a rainmaker, and broken places are our new frontiers.

Ultimately the work is about the light and the goodness in the human heart.

Lily Yeh (www.barefootartists.org) is an internationally celebrated artist whose work has taken her to communities throughout the world. As founder and executive director of the Village of Arts and Humanities in North Philadelphia from 1968 to 2004, she helped create a national model of community-building through the arts. In 2004, Yeh pursued her work internationally, founding Barefoot Artists, Inc., to bring the transformative power of art to impoverished communities around the globe through participatory, multifaceted projects that foster community empowerment, improve the physical environment, promote economic development, and preserve indigenous art and culture.

6

The Open Space of Democracy

Terry Tempest Williams

Motivated by the depth and breadth of her love, the connections Terry Tempest Williams makes among nature, people, art, and spirit enrich how so many of us understand the world. She has taught me the power of communicating vulnerability and strength together, by revealing how they can move people toward greater empathic awareness, compassion, and connection. As a down-winder and longtime activist, she translates that love into action. As a writer, she marries poetry, memoir, spirit, and narrative to create courageous new forms. The perseverance of her inner inquiry to understand her place in the world has opened pathways for me to understand the inextricable interdependence of our inner world with our outer actions and leadership.

NINA SIMONS

The Arctic. I cannot sleep and so I slip from the comfort of our tent to face the low, diffuse glow of midnight. All colors bow to the gentle arc of light the sun creates as it strolls across the horizon. Green steps become emerald, the river laps, the patch of cotton grass ignites. My eyes catch the illumined wings of a tern, an Arctic tern, fluttering,

57

foraging above the river, the embodiment of grace suspended. The tern animates the vast indifference with its own vibrant intelligence. Black cap, blood-red beak pointed down, white body with black-tipped wings. With my eyes laid bare I witness a bright thought in big country. While everyone is sleeping, the presence of this tern hovering above the river, alive, alert, and engaged, becomes a vision of what is possible. On this night I met the arctic angel and vowed that the 22,000 miles of her migratory path, between the Arctic and Antarctica, would not be in vain. I will remember her.

No creature on Earth has spent more time in daylight than this species. No creature on Earth has shunned darkness in the same way as the Arctic tern. No creature carries the strength and delicacy of determination on its back like this slight bird. If air is the medium of the spirit, then the Arctic tern is its messenger. What I know is this: When one hungers for light, it is only because one's knowledge of the dark is so deep.

Here is my question: What might a different kind of power look like and feel like, and can power be distributed equitably among ourselves even beyond our own species?

"We can only attain harmony and stability by consulting ensemble," writes Walt Whitman. This is my definition of community, and community interaction is the white-hot center of a democracy that burns bright.

We are growing and we are evolving this community of ours, committed to social change and ecological consciousness. We are discovering our strengths through our questions, our frustration, our despair, and our joy as we dare to see ourselves as a community of conscience and consequence.

I met Wangari Maathai, the first environmental recipient of a Nobel Prize, when I was twenty-nine years old at the U.N. Decade for Women, and she made me believe that a passionate voice mattered as she taught us how African women were carrying deforestation on their backs as they would search eight to ten hours a day for fire fuel to feed their children. Wangari Maathai changed my life, and twenty years later, last spring, I had the deep privilege of welcoming Wangari to our home in Castle Valley, Utah. When I first met her, she had been forty-four. She was now sixty-four, and you could see what those twenty years had brought to her heart, to her face. Over dinner I asked, "Wangari, what have you learned in these twenty years?" Without even a pause, she said, "Patience." Patience. The patience of trees, the patience of stones . . . what we all know on our own home ground.

I do not believe we can look for leadership beyond ourselves and wait for someone or something to save us from our global predicaments and obligations. I need to look in the mirror and ask myself, If I am committed to seeing the direction of our country change, how must I change myself?

I recall a day, March 8, 2003, in Washington, D.C., when I marched with CODEPINK and thousands of women, children, and men on the eve of war. We walked from Martin Luther King Park down to Lafayette Square only to find that the square was blocked, lined with D.C. police dressed in combat gear. Medea Benjamin, cofounder of CODEPINK, began a very serious conversation with the police, asking them why we were not allowed to proceed onto public space. Rachel Bagby, singer, farmer, and lawyer, with one of the most God-given voices I know, focused her attention elsewhere, on one policeman in particular, and she began to sing to him, "All we are saying is give peace a chance. All we are saying is give peace a chance."

Other voices joined with hers. Like her, this policeman she was singing to was African American, and in that moment of witnessing I realized that neither one of them would be who they were or where they were had it not been for the civil dissents of their parents, their parents' parents before them, and their parents' parents' parents before them. In that moment the policeman stepped to the side, creating the open space of democracy that we walked through.

My brother Steve was diagnosed one year ago with lymphoma. He was sitting at the family dinner table after he had gone through a very intensive cycle of chemotherapy that left his body ravaged and weak. At the table were Steve's wife and their daughters, my husband Brooke and I, my other brother, and our father. We had all gathered together to hear what Steve had learned at Commonweal's cancer retreat in Bolinas, California.

He spoke of healing, not cure. He spoke of gratitude for his life and his desire to be true to the integrity of his own voice. He brought each of us back a stone and passed around the bowl of stones he had gathered. He talked about how when he was walking at Point Reyes, he only picked up stones that had a hole in them, and he said, "I know we have had a hole in our hearts. We can look at this hole in our hearts as a wound or we can see it as a window. May we vow tonight as a family to see it as a window"—another open space.

Shortly after the CODEPINK action, I was invited to speak at the University of Utah in Salt Lake City, my alma mater, to deliver the commencement address. My niece Callie was graduating. It was about family and community, but we were at war. George W. Bush had just stepped onto the aircraft carrier U.S.S. *Abraham Lincoln*, announcing with great bravado, "Mission Accomplished." The graduation took place the following day, and at it, I thought that if I didn't have the courage to speak my own thoughts at this point in time to my own people, my own family, and my own community at my own school, then I had no business being there. I gave a very short talk titled "The Open Space of Democracy." This is a place where there is room for dissent, a place where community is defined as the well-being of all species, not just our own. I urged the students to question, stand, speak, and act. This talk was met with equal boos and applause. As I looked up at the audience, I saw the split within our own country. How do we have civil dialogue when we are not even civil to each other?

After the talk, my senator, Bob Bennett (and it's always complicated in Utah: he's also our neighbor, and more complicated still, my former Mormon bishop), came up to me and said, "Terry, I just want to register my extreme dissent to what you said today." We talked; it was spirited, and then he said: "You've inspired me to write you a letter." And I would like to share with you an excerpt of his letter and my response to it, because I think it has everything to do with how we bypass this political rhetoric that has diminished all of us in this country and find that point of humanity, our deeper selves.

> Dear Terry, as I listened to you outline things that are important to you, an interesting question popped into my mind: "What would she be willing to die for?" Waging war always creates the risk of dying, so any discussion of war raises that issue. Then I asked myself, "What would I be willing to die for?" The answers that came were predictable. At the front end, family, certainly, followed by church, protection of the community, and yes, finally the cause of freedom, for others as well as my own family and friends.

Senator Bennett went on to outline his concerns and thoughts. It was an incredibly thoughtful, provocative letter—a four-page, single-spaced letter, not on official senatorial letterhead, but on his own personal stationery.

I'm embarrassed to tell you that I was not able to answer his letter for months. I was haunted by what he had asked me. What am I willing to die for? I realized that for me that wasn't the question. It's not what I'm willing to die for, but what I'm willing to give my life to. Here is an excerpt of my response:

> Dear Senator Bennett, you asked me a critical question in your letter, one I have pondered for months. What am I willing to die for? Before the war in Iraq, thousands of Americans turned to poetry to voice their opposition to the invasion, creating the largest written protest in the history of this country; 11,000 poems were presented to Congress. The words I contributed were simple ones: "The erosion of speech is the buildup of war. Silence no longer supports prayers but lives inside the mouths of the dead." After much thought, Senator Bennett, what I would be willing to die for and give my life to is freedom of speech. It is the open door to all other freedoms. We are a nation at war with ourselves. Until we can turn to one another and offer our sincere words as to why we feel the way

we do with an honest commitment to hear what others have to say, we will continue to project our anger on the world in true, unconscious acts of terror.

Democracy invites us to take risks. It asks that we vacate the comfortable seat of certitude, remain pliable, and act ultimately on behalf of the common good. Democracy's only agenda is that we participate. If we cannot engage in respectful listening, there can be no civil dialogue, and without civil dialogue, we the people will simply become bullies and brutes, deaf to the truth that we are standing on the edge of a political chasm that is beginning to crumble. We all stand to lose ground. Democracy is an insecure landscape.

Two weeks ago, democracy felt even a bit more insecure when I received a call from the president of Florida Gulf Coast University informing me that the freshman convocation I had been invited to speak at much earlier was being postponed until after the election. The university's president made this decision because I had criticized George W. Bush in print. He said: "If a hurricane is threatening my university, then I'm going to shut it down." I replied: "But what if it's only a tempest?" He didn't think that was funny. We had a long conversation, and, to his credit, he was very candid. He said, "Let me be very clear: the board of regents and my board of trustees are all appointees of Governor Jeb Bush and supporters of the Bush brothers."

That same night, our family gathered in Salt Lake City to learn that my brother Steve's lymphoma was progressing and that he was no longer eligible for the stem-cell transplant we had all been praying for. With silence and with stillness, with sorrow and with love, we embraced the moment and each other and stood in the center of sacred time. "Life," as T. S. Eliot says, "turning shadow into transient beauty."

Despair shows us the limit of our own imagination. Imaginations shared create collaboration, collaboration creates community, and community inspires social change. The experience of the Florida Gulf Coast University has been a painful one, but it has taught me that this is not personal. This story is not about me. This story is about what frightens us; it is a story about freedom of speech in a country increasingly bent on control. We are all characters in this ongoing theater of democracy. The students and faculty protested, stating that their education and their right to think for themselves were being compromised.

Subsequent to that, the president and I joined the students and the faculty in a discussion about how to keep this open space exactly that. What is most threatening to the status quo is dialogue, because honest dialogue and deep listening require us to consider the views contrary to our own. Dialogue offers us the possibility to change, to give up the rigidity of our opinions for the sacred heart of stories where we remember who we are and who we are not and what binds us together rather than what tears us apart.

My brother has shared with us that his cancer is teaching him to act and speak from a place of honesty and to follow what he loves, what he feels and believes. His responsibility is to his integrity of soul, not just external obligations and what other people expect from him. If you would have told me one year ago that my brother, who is a pipeline contractor, would be advocating for a labyrinth to be placed in the center of this new international, intermountain healthcare facility for cancer patients, I would not have believed you. For him, the labyrinth has become both practical and metaphorical. It is exercise and symbol of how we walk the path of our lives. If you had told me that, alongside his Mormon scriptures, he is now reading Emerson and Thoreau and Rachel Naomi Remen, I would not have believed it. The other day he said to me, "Terry, we are all terminal."

How do you want to spend your one beautiful life?

MARY OLIVER

Meanwhile, my father has undergone his own transformation. He is a fourth-generation pipeline contractor who wears cowboy boots that could kill spiders in corners and has a shrine to Ronald Reagan. About a month ago, I told him with all the love in my heart: "We can no longer talk about politics; I'm sorry, but it's too painful." I did not know how to find dialogue. When I was prevented from addressing the freshman convocation in Florida, I warned my father about it, and I apologized because this was not a good time for controversy in our family. We were broken open with Steve, but he said to me, "Do not apologize; this matters." When he found out that I had not been allowed to speak, but that the students had insisted and invited me to come back and participate in a forum on free speech, he said, "I want to come with you."

How close does it have to get before we're willing to change? For my father, it was seeing his beloved son, another down-winder (of the nuclear tests in the 1950s that affected southern Utah), ravaged by cancer. He hadn't been able to acknowledge this truth earlier when his wife, our mother, faced her own cancer. He has acknowledged it now. And when his daughter was not allowed to speak, he saw the Bush-Cheney effect on democracy and an open society. It had to be that close. How close does it have to get before we make the changes required for a full transformation of who we are as human beings?

The human heart is the first home of democracy. It is where we embrace our questions: Can we be equitable? Can we be generous? Can we listen with our whole beings, not just our minds, and offer our attention rather than our opinions? Do we have enough resolve in our hearts to act courageously, relentlessly, without giving up, trusting our fellow citizens to join us in our determined pursuit of a living democracy? The heart is the house of empathy whose door opens when we receive the pain of others. This is where bravery lives, where we find our mettle to give and receive, to love and be loved, to stand in the center of uncertainty with strength not fear, understanding that this is all there is.

The heart is the path to wisdom because it dares to be vulnerable in the presence of power, and power lies in our love of our homelands.

Terry Tempest Williams (www.coyoteclan.com), one of the nation's most celebrated writers, is the author of *Refuge; Leap; Red: Passion and Patience in the Desert;* and, most recently, *The Open Space of Democracy.* Recipient of both a Guggenheim Fellowship and a Lannan Literary Fellowship, she is an active voice on behalf of social and environmental issues. She lives in Castle Valley, Utah, with her husband, Brooke Williams.

PART TWO

Leadership Sourced from Inner Authority

7

Direct Action on Behalf of the Earth

Julia Butterfly Hill

It may be a cliché, but Julia Butterfly Hill really is a force of nature. She first spoke at Bioneers when she was still living in the old-growth redwood tree she named Luna. As people crowded around a speaker, her voice rang out with all the love, anger, pain, reverence, and commitment that coursed through her. When she described her first foray into the old-growth forest and how sacred it was to her, everyone's cheeks were wet with tears. Years later, when she came to Bioneers and spoke in person, she noticed that very few young people were at the conference, and she called for action that helped create Bioneers' youth program. Thanks to her commitment and persistence, this book is published on 100 percent recycled and chlorine-free paper. Julia embodies the power of trusting her own inner voice with integrity and love, and the spiritual authority that arises from it.

NINA SIMONS

When I entered the ancient redwoods for the first time, I saw beauty and power that touched me in a way that traveling from church to church to church with my preacher father had never touched me, and it changed me forever.

A few weeks later I saw destruction that ripped my heart out and threw it on the ground and stomped on it and destroyed the naïveté that I had been living with my whole life. I thought, Oh, my God! How could we have allowed 97 percent of the ancient redwoods to go for good? We can't grow back two-thousand-year-old trees in the million-year-old forest that they're a part of. How can we be allowing them to take seven-foot chainsaws into the forest and mow these ancient treasures into the ground and then follow it up by lighting the clear-cut on fire with diesel fuel or napalm, destroying everything, including the microorganisms in the soil? And then following it up by spraying herbicide to get rid of unwanted trees and weeds, so that they can grow a tree farm? When I found all this out, something reached inside of me and said: "Julia, you must act."

This was not a calling I could sit and chew on and decide upon. It was something that ripped my gut out. If your child's life is threatened, do you stop to ask a politician if it's legal to save your child's life? Do you stop to ask a scientist if it's scientifically possible for you, as one person, to stand up and save your child's life? No. Something instinctual touches you at the core of your humanity and reaches out and compels you to act.

I knew I had to do something. A message came to me over and over like a mantra in my mind during that time. I struggled, because committing myself to the redwoods, when I really wanted to travel around the world, was not exactly my plan for my life. The message I couldn't avoid was this: "Julia, your inactions are as much a part of shaping the world as the actions of others."

Our society trains us to give our power away. Our society trains us to give our power away to name brands on our clothes, to jewelry, to cars, to houses, to makeup, to social status, to politicians, to science, to teachers. We are trained to give our power away all the time, and we are made fun of if we stand up in our power. Maybe I am a little bit quirky, a little bit crazy. But why aren't we standing up and pointing out how really crazy it is that corporations have been allowed to destroy 97 percent of the ancient redwoods and continue to destroy the environment? It is absolutely insane. Maybe it's time we got a little crazy too.

The power that we have as people comes with responsibility. Sometimes the people who come up to me don't want that responsibility, so they're trying to give it over to me, or sometimes their hearts are pure in their intention, and they don't realize what they're doing, but I can feel it. They're giving me their power, and all I want to say is: "No." I don't claim to be an expert. I only claim to follow my heart. I am the leading expert on my heart. I feel compelled to follow it when it tells me, "Julia, get up, go climb a tree and try to save it." And that's what I did. I went up into the tree and stayed there for 738 days, and I saved that tree.

As much as I appreciate the gratitude I receive for doing that, the best thanks people can give me is to say: "I want you to know that you've inspired me to work harder, love more, and laugh with all that I have within me and never give up in defense of this beautiful planet that takes care of us." Direct action is not just about frontline protest. It takes many forms; it's about taking action that has an impact. I'm just asking that we all challenge ourselves, because for me, challenging myself is what helps me learn every single day.

Sometimes I feel like I'm hitting my head against a brick wall. This happens, for instance, when I show up at conferences and look at how many people are taking notes on virgin paper. I look at the lunch being served in plastic containers. And I wonder: What are we thinking? The reality is, we're not thinking. The average American consumes fourteen generations' worth, in a single generation, of the earth's resources. Most of that is called disposable. Most of that is called waste. Everything in the world comes from the earth, including my computer, and the lights in this room, and the seat I'm sitting in. So, if it's coming from the earth, what in the world are we doing calling it disposable? What are we doing stealing from fourteen generations ahead of us and then throwing it away?

We have to begin in every moment to challenge ourselves. Gandhi said, "We must be the change we wish to see in the world." How can we point at what's wrong in the world if we're not living what is right? I was sitting in that tree and looking down at the clear-cuts, watching helicopters swarm around me, lighting the clear-cuts on fire with napalm and having to breathe it through a wet cloth for two weeks until I was so weak I couldn't even sit up. I was looking at the Pacific Lumber mill that takes these ancient forests and turns them into lumber, looking at all these things and getting angry and thinking, How dare they? How dare they? I had to stop and ask, Okay, where do I fit into this equation? Because whether we like it or not—and oftentimes it's not—we all share the planet together.

A lot of people confront me when I talk about these small everyday things. They say, "The world is in a state of chaos. It takes a lot more than the small things to shift the course of the world." Yes, it does. There are some who are feeling compelled to take the front line, but the reality is, our strength on the front lines is the last line of defense, and it's only as good as all of you who are holding that line behind us. If we are not working on this together—living the solutions every moment of every day—before too long we're all going to be plowed under together.

We have to shift the way we look at direct action. But also we have to realize there is no such thing as a nonaction. By not doing anything, we're absolutely shaping the way the world is becoming. Everything we do and say, our inactions, and even our thoughts change the world.

I'm sharing what I've learned by looking down at the earth for two years, and not being able to touch it, by sitting in a tree and not having modern-day conveniences. The first three months in that tree nearly killed me. I climbed up in the worst winter in the recorded history of California, but more than that, I climbed up into an active logging plan, which is the deepest pain I've ever felt in my life. All the time the press asked me, "What was the worst time? What was the worst thing?" They always expected me to say things like, "I didn't have a shower." When I go to other parts of the world or to low-income places where people don't take things like showers for granted, they never ask that question. They think about the down-and-dirty survival things like, "How did you get your food?" and "How did you keep going?" Because a lot of them are struggling with how to keep going in a world that's annihilating their cultures, their histories, their roots, and all our abilities to sustain a healthy and beautiful life on this planet.

Sitting up there in that tree, planning to be there only two to three weeks to a month, I was completely unprepared for anything. My feet have since recovered from the frostbite that was one of the most excruciatingly physically painful things I've experienced. Luckily, I wasn't blown out of the tree by the Pacific Lumber Maxxam Corporation–contracted helicopter. Luckily, I survived the ten-day siege when they tried to cut off my supplies and starve me down. This was only possible because of the help of unbelievably committed Earth First! activists, composed of young people, some grandmothers, and all the heroic members of their support teams.

Sitting through an active logging plan was a pain that has shaped me and will be with me for the rest of my life. Because every day I heard the roar of the chainsaw, over and over until it was like a screeching in my mind. And then I would listen as they'd take the last thread that holds a tree to its roots, and they'd slam a metal wedge into it. When that happens, the tree screams like an animal in pain. That tree screams out as it comes crashing down to the earth. Everything shakes and shatters. All its babies and the life underneath are destroyed. I felt I was being destroyed with it.

I want people to know that I didn't learn the power of love and sacred spirituality through some new-age experience: I learned it through the school of hard knocks. I learned it through the school of pain, because I was eaten alive by that pain, and I became angry. It's important to be angry. Everyone in the world should be absolutely angry at the corporations and the governments and what we're allowing to happen on this planet. But do we do what we do for the world out of our anger? Or do we do what we do out of love? It has to be love.

Anger is a candle that burns at both ends. It will consume you. I'm speaking from experience, because those first three months I was consumed by the anger, an anger that came from sadness. I hurt so deeply that my automatic response was that I wanted to obliterate the loggers. I wanted to obliterate Pacific Lumber Maxxam Corporation. But in the process, I was obliterating myself. Because life is sacred in every one of its forms, even if some people have lost their connection to that sacredness. Yes, the people in Pacific Lumber Maxxam Corporation are really far away from their sacred source, but I swear it's in them, because I don't believe creation messed up. That's where the love component comes in. It is when we look at all of life and we feel that sacred connection that we begin to change how we live in the world. As a result, it will begin to change how others live in the world.

Of course we get frustrated and we get overwhelmed, because we see so much going on in the world that we cannot change. You can bet after six months in that tree I was thinking: Okay, can we save this area already? We have that desire and attachment to outcome. I love to use the example of these women who blessed me and honored me, and blessed and honored the world, with this project they called the Boise Peace Quilt Project. They're a group of wonderful women, some of whom were active in the anti–Vietnam War movement. They ended up having children and raising families, and they couldn't be on the front lines anymore. So they started making quilts. What they do is, they pick an action or a person that represents things that they care about in their world and they quilt a picture of it. Their motto is, "Stitch by stitch, the difference is in the doing." Every action, every word, every thought is the difference.

I honor everyone in the world who is willing to take a stand for what he or she believes in, who is willing to live for what he or she believes in, and who is willing to die for what he or she believes in; not because we should have to, but because when we are willing to, then we learn a whole new way to live. That's one of the biggest lessons I learned in the tree, during a storm in which I almost died. When I let go of my attachment to my very existence, to my actual life, I learned how to live in a way that could never have been taught to me in a schoolroom. I learned life in its purest form.

Julia Butterfly Hill (juliabutterflyhill.wordpress.com; www.whatsyourtree.org) gained international notoriety in 1997 when she climbed up into Luna, an ancient redwood tree slated for logging. Withstanding death threats and gale-force winds, Hill lived on a tiny platform for 738 days, which resulted in a successful negotiation to save Luna and a three-acre buffer zone around the tree, in perpetuity. In so doing, she brought international attention to the plight of our dwindling redwoods. She became an international speaker and wrote a bestselling book, *The Legacy of Luna,* available in eleven languages, and an environmental handbook, *One Makes the Difference.*

8

Joy

A Midwife's Story

Anneke Campbell

Anneke Campbell is an activist, a midwife, a producer, a teacher, and an author. She has an unerring instinct for seeking out important stories, good work, and great activists, and with her intuition and relational warmth she finds effective and creative ways to support them. As a writer and producer, and as my editor and collaborator on this book, her insights in identifying essence and paring away what is unnecessary proved to be invaluable. The rigor and clarity of her attention, honed by her years as a midwife, enable her to be supportive of others' experience and leadership and she savors the empowerment she engenders.

NINA SIMONS

Giving birth opened me up to my self and my sense of purpose. I was a shy and puny child, born by C-section to a mother who had serious health and self-esteem issues, and I was well on my way to accepting her relationship to her body and self as my own. When I became pregnant, the doctors told me they might not be able to deliver my baby naturally. Some instinct or innate wisdom inside me did not want to accept their opinion, and so I prepared to give birth as if it were an initiation rite. I learned to tune in to my body, to appreciate its strength and nurture its functioning. I learned to recognize my fears and meet them.

I feared pain. I was the kid who ran away to hide when facing an injection or a dentist visit. Now I sought out information, as knowledge can be an antidote to fear. I practiced breath control and focus. I learned that when spoken out loud and fully acknowledged by another, my fears lessened and became manageable.

I had grown up in the Netherlands, where midwives and home birth were common, but my adopted country offered no such options. The best I could find in New York City was a medical center where they had just started allowing fathers in the delivery room. The doctors smiled skeptically at my announcement that I wanted to have a natural birth. A lot of women say they do, they implied, but you'll think better of it.

Once labor started, I found an ability to actively surrender to the contractions and to ride the pain like a wave. It was exhilarating. I felt the wisdom of eons of natural evolution powering my body. I felt connected to the women in my lineage, and to mothers all over the world who shared this experience in the most profound way. I was overcome by an extraordinary sense of joy.

As I was readying to push, I reached my hand over my draped belly to pat the baby within. The doctor, concerned for his sterile field, said: Get your hands out of there or I'll tie them down. On both sides of the delivery table were leather hand straps, evidence of the manner in which many women had given birth before me—immobilized, held down.

Later, holding my daughter in my arms, I knew I wanted to help other women be similarly empowered by their birth experiences. And I also felt committed to making sure it was women who determined their manner of giving birth and not the whim or convenience of the doctor or hospital.

This was the early 1970s, and reproductive rights were about to take a leap forward when abortion became legal. It was clear to me that for women to be equal, and to hold the reins of their own lives, they needed to be in charge of their bodies. We needed choice in the matter of whether to have children, and if so, when and how we did so.

There were very few midwives practicing in the United States, and only a few schools, which required that you become a registered nurse first. This was unlike the Dutch system, which sees midwives as autonomous agents serving the birthing woman and protecting the process of birthing from unnecessary medical intervention. I did not want to learn this model that treated birth as a medical problem, to be treated only in hospitals and by doctors. In the United States at that time, with rare exceptions, the only alternative to a hospital birth was provided by the "underground" midwife, and so I found one to apprentice with.

Later I did go to nursing school, in order to be exposed to as many births as possible and to gain nursing skills. My training in labor and delivery was eye-opening. While the nurses did most of the actual work of assisting women, it was the doctors who rushed in at the last minute and received credit and gratitude. Every woman gave birth on her back, fighting gravity instead of engaging gravity and the best angle of her pelvis to push the baby out. The birth process was treated mechanically, with routine procedures that might or might not be necessary. Women had to beg to have their human needs and desires even considered.

Since the 1970s, the importance of bonding immediately after birth for both baby and mother has been well established, but at that time women had to fight to be allowed to hold their babies for more than a few moments before they were whisked away. The obstetric community was tone-deaf when it came to the desires of women to have a say in their experience, to have their individual needs respected, and to have their babies welcomed into the family in a manner that honored emotional and spiritual connections as well as physical safety.

I continued to study, finding a naturopathic doctor out of state who had delivered thousands of babies at home, including all sorts of complicated births with beautiful outcomes. His innate reverence for the natural process reinforced my inner knowing. So also I was strengthened by the scholarship of people like Barbara Ehrenreich and Deirdre English, as well as Suzanne Arms, women who taught me that I was joining in a long lineage of women healers and midwives who have been a threat to the power of the medical establishment since the Middle Ages. In Tennessee, Ina May Gaskin was blazing the trail for other lay midwives with her groundbreaking book *Spiritual Midwifery.*

Back home I partnered with a brave feminist doctor to provide a home-birth service alongside her hospital practice. After a year, the medical establishment took away her hospital privileges to punish her, and she left town. By then I had developed a following, and I decided to go ahead and practice illegally, as the only midwife in the state as far as I knew. My clients would get prenatal tests and care from a number of different doctors, as we wanted to make sure there was backup should a complication occur. Thus the obstetrical community knew what I was doing, and they were not pleased. Not having a license to practice, I was legally vulnerable, but the intense joy I experienced in my work and the profound connection with my clients more than compensated for this problem.

I began meeting with parents wanting birth alternatives, and we organized educational events as a group. We put pressure on the hospital to offer a more family-centered birth experience. Quite naturally I started serving as a leader for this group, and eventually a number of obstetricians invited me to a meeting to discuss the situation.

The meeting devolved into an argument. I tried to explain that supported home birth was safe and named the superior statistics of countries that embrace the practice. I told them that the infant mortality rates in the United States do not compare favorably to those in countries where midwives commonly practice. They said if something goes wrong at home, then the mother herself is responsible. When I asked if that weren't the case in the hospital too, they looked blank. They saw themselves as in charge of the bodies of their patients, rather than in partnership with the whole person. No wonder they were being sued so often.

I brought up the prevalence of infections in the hospital nursery, and the ever-increasing rate of C-sections, which lead to more and more complications. They told me that the only reason women wanted to have their babies at home was because they were selfish and immature and had problems with authority figures.

This did not describe the women I was attending, who included a variety of professional women, including nurses, and even a professor of nursing, as well as artists and rebels, conservative Christians and yogis, and back-to-nature types. I took offense. My approach was too confrontational to gain their cooperation and support, and I didn't know how to speak to our common goal, which was for women to enter motherhood feeling both supported and strong.

I kept practicing, but going up against the medical power structure took its toll. As more women pressured them, the doctors became angrier. If one of our births became complicated and we needed medical help, instead of a supportive backup, we faced an increasingly punitive encounter. It dawned on me that in this obstructive relationship between the medical community and myself, my clients were not being served in the best way, and this forced me to reexamine my methods.

Yes, I loved the hands-on experience of delivering babies, but I was totally exhausted. My underlying passion was for women being empowered through their experience of their bodies, and the joy happened in those moments when a woman's eyes lit up with an expanded sense of herself. These moments occurred in childbirth classes, they happened during prenatal care, in the process of labor, or even a month later when the new mother realized that she felt a newfound confidence in herself. Clearly, such moments were not necessarily dependent on where the birth took place. I realized I needed to rethink how to accomplish my purpose.

In the community, my beloved colleague Patricia, whose baby I had delivered and who subsequently apprenticed with me, took over my practice. I decided that I would shift my focus to fighting for women's rights to be in charge of their bodies and to working to spread the word about the transformative power of birth in other ways, through activism and writing.

Thirty years later there are many midwives practicing in this country. The home-birth movement put pressure on the doctors and hospitals, which resulted in the growth of a true alternative: birthing centers. In some areas women have access to midwives in hospitals. Childbirth classes and the use of doulas have exploded, as have other birth support organizations. There are still illegal or "direct-entry" midwives practicing, and many states are in the process of changing their laws so as to license these practitioners.

Ironically, more women than ever choose to see pain in childbirth as something to avoid rather than to make use of as a tool for growth and self-awareness. As a result, because of early epidurals and other interventions, the C-section rate continues to rise while the infant mortality and morbidity rates remain a national disgrace. And sadly, our reproductive rights continue to be debated and decided by experts and politicians because women are still not the ones writing the laws.

Over the years, I have realized that my vision and purpose shone brightly, but they far outpaced my leadership abilities at that time. I was only beginning to gain skill in speaking for the needs and aspirations of the women I served. Also I was unwittingly following a model of leadership that required self-sacrifice, which proved unsustainable. I honor my years as a midwife. They taught me much about myself and showed me the importance of having support. They also taught me that any movement for change requires patience and the ability to constantly reassess one's strategies.

I will always know joy as the touchstone that I am serving my purpose in the world. And when I run into one of my clients from long ago, and we fall into an embrace, I also know that at its core, my work was about love.

Anneke Campbell was born in Holland. She has worked as a midwife, a practical nurse, a masseuse, a prenatal yoga teacher, and a college teacher of creative writing and English literature. She has published award-winning poetry and articles and has scripted and produced a number of documentaries, including the television series *The Freedom Files,* based on ACLU cases, as well as an Emmy Award–winning drama, *A Day with the Concord Writers.* Her first novel, *Mary of Bellingham,* came out in 2004. The manual for activists she co-wrote with Thomas Linzey, *Be the Change: How to Get What You Want in Your Community,* was launched at Bioneers in 2008.

9

Pushing Hope's Edge

Anna Lappé and Frances Moore Lappé

Anna and Frankie Lappé may be the most remarkable mother-daughter team I've ever encountered. Their partnership in researching and writing Hope's Edge *led them to understand how people survive hardship and transform themselves and consequently, their cultures. Both Frankie and Anna are driven by a personal inquiry and informed by their own vision and guidance, yet together they yield a brilliantly astute and articulate analysis. Here their individual stories are offered up as one, in a generous, respectful, loving, and collaborative way.*

NINA SIMONS

Anna Lappé: I'm twenty-seven years old, the age my mother was when she first published *Diet for a Small Planet.* Two years ago my brother and I sat her down in a bar in New York City and said, "Mom, it's time that you write a follow-up to *Diet for a Small Planet.*"

We told her we were scared about what we were not hearing: the real reasons behind environmental devastation, growing inequality, food scarcity. But maybe even worse, we were frustrated that we were not hearing the stories about what's emerging that is positive, that is hopeful, that proves other paths are possible. In the face of all this, it was becoming harder and harder for so many of us to make sense of the world, let alone have a clue as to what to do.

So together we agreed to write a sequel that would take off where the original *Diet for a Small Planet* left off. (I would start out as research assistant and move to coauthor. Though, as my friends like to remind me, getting promoted by your mother is not that impressive.)

Early on in the book-writing process, I knew the person telling many of us how to make sense of the world was Thomas Friedman, author of the bestselling *The Lexus and the Olive Tree*. A two-time Pulitzer Prize winner and *New York Times* journalist, Friedman's explanation of globalization was being listened to not just by influential Washington types, but by a lot of the rest of us too.

A quick skim and his thesis is clear. The economic system we've got here in the United States, which is now spreading globally, is the best there is. Friedman put it this way: "There is no more chocolate chip, there is no more strawberry swirl, no more lemon lime, there is only plain vanilla and North Korea." In other words, he was saying, relax, we've got plain vanilla: corporate globalization. We don't have to worry about other choices, because there are none. I mean, who would choose North Korea?

I knew that I didn't agree with Friedman's take that corporate globalization was the only path for development and was being readily embraced around the world. But I didn't know what ground I could stand on to argue with him. At the time I was just a twenty-seven-year-old graduate student; he was on the *New York Times* payroll.

We began the journey that became the book *Hope's Edge*. We sat in homes in Brazil, Kenya, India, Bangladesh, Poland, France, California, and Wisconsin, and I learned firsthand how wrong Friedman was.

In Brazil we met members of the Landless Workers Movement, or the MST (the acronym for its name in Portuguese), the largest social movement in South America. The MST emerged in the mid-'80s at the end of Brazil's long military dictatorship, when Brazilians were writing a new constitution. Even urban people were so fed up with the landed elite—1 percent controlling half the land, while using only a fraction of it—that the new constitution says, essentially, Use it or lose it. The government must transfer unused land to serve a "social function." But with the government beholden to the wealthy, not much would have really changed if the MST had not stepped in with civil disobedience to push the government to make this constitutional right a reality.

Thanks to these efforts, one quarter of a million landless families now live, farm, and send their kids to school in communities they've created on seventeen million acres of otherwise idle land. Thirty years ago my mother would have been considered delusional for suggesting land reform was possible in Brazil. For centuries any attempt at land reform had been snuffed out with peasant blood.

In Brazil we talked about the struggle for land reform with MST members in their homes, sitting with them in shacks of black plastic crinkling against the winter wind.

I'll never forget one woman who told us, "Before I joined the MST, I was not just landless, I was everything-less. At first we thought it was about getting land," she said, "but then we realized, land was just the beginning. We realized we had to ask, 'What kind of communities do we want? What kind of food do we want to grow? And how do we want to grow it?'"

My mother and I knew that many of these landless people had become sick from pesticides they were exposed to when they worked on other people's land. So when we heard that many of them had chosen to grow food using organic practices, we assumed it was to keep themselves healthy. They seemed shocked at our assumption. "Do you think we'd go through all of this, risk our lives for this land, only to grow food that could make somebody else sick?" So we were not surprised when they told us that the MST had created the first line of organic seeds in Brazil.

What became clear to us is that when people are creating their own future, it's natural for them to think through their choices, and it's natural to see the ripples of their actions. "We had land, we had farms, we started thinking about schools," they said. "We had to start asking, what do we want our children to learn? We want them to learn that the rural life is a good life. So we started teaching philosophy, even to our grade-school kids."

At the end of our time in Brazil, we got to talk with one of the founders of the MST, João Pedro Stédile. He told us what he considered the MST's greatest achievement. He said, "It actually may not be in lowering infant mortality, nor tripling the wages of our members. No," he said, "our greatest contribution is the creation of citizens. People with choices. Our people," he said, "are going from 'Yes, sir' to 'I think that . . .'"

I reflect on all the MST has done: a quarter of a million landless families settled, two thousand schools created, dozens of cooperatives formed, and on and on, but I also must remind you that it has not been easy. More landless members have been killed in the struggle by landlords with government cooperation than "disappeared" during the entire two decades of Brazil's military dictatorship.

Friedman argues that there is no alternative to plain vanilla and yet here in Brazil is a social movement that proves otherwise. And he was the journalist being trusted to help us make sense of our world? Not anymore.

Frances Moore Lappé: Thirty years ago, the newspaper headlines were screaming at us that we had simply run out of food to feed people. When I was Anna's age, my intuition was that food could unlock the mysteries of the economic and political order, and if I could just understand why people were hungry in the world, I could somehow make sense of it all. So I sat in the U.C.–Berkeley Ag library and developed a research technique, which I've continued to hone for thirty years. I call it following my nose: I let one question lead to the next question, which leads to the next question, and I learned what would forever change my life. Not only is there enough food in the world to feed us all, there is actually enough food to make us all chubby. But because poor people don't have money to make their needs felt in the market, grain is artificially cheap, so it made, and still makes, economic sense to feed one-third of it to livestock.

But when *Diet for a Small Planet* was released, I was terrified, absolutely terrified. I thought, What if I misplaced a decimal point and the whole thing was wrong? But I hadn't, and so my critics tried other tactics to discredit me. The National Cattlemen's Association set a whole team of cooks on the case, trying to prove that the recipes in my book were not edible—at least not edible by human beings. It was during this period that I came to realize, for the first time, that it was because I wasn't trained as a development economist or nutritionist that I could write that book. I began to see the power of beginner eyes. Today, after my kids challenged me to write a sequel to *Diet for a Small Planet,* I looked at this same world again and realized with sadness that more, not less, grain is going to feed livestock.

I also came to see that we are doing with fish what we have done with cattle. We are turning them into protein disposals as well. By taking what they call junk fish like sardines and grinding them into a meal that is fed to expensive fish, like salmon, we are shrinking the world food supply even more.

So thirty years ago, my adulthood began with one realization: we human beings are creating the very scarcity we say we fear. Back then, my question, Why hunger? grew quickly to: Why hunger in a world of plenty? But over these three decades it's continued to swell, to get bigger and bigger, and to encompass an even more puzzling question: How can it be that we as societies create what we as individuals abhor? Not one of us would get up in the morning and say, "My job today is to make sure that a few thousand children around the world starve to death." None of us would get up in the morning and say, "Well, my agenda this morning is to see how many dozens of species I can wipe out before the day is done." None of us would.

So what could be powerful enough to allow us to be creating a world that we cannot recognize as our own? I've come to see that there's only one thing that powerful. And it is the power of ideas. Erich Fromm helped me a lot in this. In *The Anatomy of Human Destructiveness,* he writes one line I shall never forget: "It is man's humanity that makes him so inhumane." What Erich Fromm is referring to is our unique capacity to create, to construct ideas about reality, that then snuff out our deepest sensibilities and even our common sense. Human beings cannot survive in a meaning void. So we create what Fromm calls a "framework of orientation" that literally determines what we *can* see. Thomas Friedman acknowledged it himself, actually, in the beginning of that book, when he wrote: "Every journalist has a super-story."

Einstein himself wrote in 1926 to Heisenberg, "It is theory that determines what we can observe." In *Hope's Edge,* Anna and I call it our mental map. So what is the dominant map that has locked us onto a planetary death march?

Anna has already captured one of these idea-maps in Thomas Friedman's notion that global corporate capitalism is the end of the road. But the second thought-trap is closely linked: We've reached that end of the road, because finally we've evolved a social system that reflects our true nature. We human beings are after all simply selfish little accumulators.

Now, there are many problems with this shabby caricature of human beings. One big problem is that it denies two deep aspects of human nature, deep needs that we all share. First is our need to connect with others in genuine community, and second is our need to affect the world beyond our immediate families. So we live in denial. We live in denial of our deepest needs, and therefore we live in a world driven by fear: fear of expressing who we really are. Nonetheless, on our journey, we met people breaking through their fear. And expressing these twin needs to affect and to connect. We heard it in Hindi, we heard it in Punjabi, we heard it in Portuguese, in Swahili, in Kikiyu, in French, in German, in Dutch. We heard it and we heard it.

Let me now jump back to Brazil, to the fourth-largest city in Brazil, which is Belo Horizonte. In 1993, the citizens of Belo declared food as a right of citizenship. That simple shift in perception unleashed dozens and dozens of social innovations. One was to let organic small farmers use unused plots of public land right in the center of town as long as they kept that organic produce within the reach of the poor. It meant things like taking the thirteen cents that the federal government supplies for each school lunch, and instead of buying corporate food with it, buying local organic food with an increased nutritional content. At the end of the day we asked the facilitator, "Adrianna, do you understand how out of step you are?" What she said made her start to cry. "It's not being out of step that makes me cry," she said. "It is that we know how to end hunger, and it's so easy." I think what she was getting at is that it is doable if we have the courage to shift our perceptions and act.

My last story is about Kenya, where we met Wangari Maathai, who, when she saw the desert encroaching in 1977, planted seven trees. She realized the only way to stop deforestation in Kenya would be for villagers throughout Kenya to plant trees. The government foresters said, "No, it takes foresters to plant trees." That was twenty million trees ago, all of which were planted by unschooled village women.

Anna Lappé: Throughout our journey, I saw how this dominant mental map we described, this global corporate culture, the culture of plain vanilla, is everywhere. Challenging this culture is scary as hell, even for those of us who don't face death threats like our friends in Brazil or Kenya. So how do we face this fear? Now, when I ask myself that question, I think of one moment. It was our last night in Nairobi, and we were sitting together in the Green Belt Movement guesthouse. Wangari Maathai brought her friend Reverend Timothy Njoya to talk with us.

He sat back in a deep armchair and told us the story of his life: the life of a radical priest. He told us about being defrocked for questioning the dictatorship in Kenya. President Daniel arap Moi had been in power since 1978 and had declared opposition parties illegal; criticizing him was a crime.

"I was finally defrocked as reverend," Njoya said, "as if I would not go on criticizing the government."

He had a choice: He knew if he gave one more sermon criticizing Moi, he could face death. He gave the sermon.

"I went home that night," he told us, "and I waited to die. I heard a knock at my door and I saw four men standing there. The first man hit me across my right arm," and then he jumped up from his chair to show us how another man came in and knocked him to the floor. And he fell back onto the ground and lifted his legs up. It looked like a father playing airplane with his kid. He showed us how he lifted his legs to block his attacker. So there Njoya was with his legs up in the air telling us this story about how this man is attacking him with a spear. He had been cut across the stomach and several of his fingers had been severed, but Njoya said to his attacker, "I'm sorry, I've hit you with my legs."

Something happened in that moment. Maybe he became human to his attackers. They stopped.

One said, "We're sorry, we didn't realize you were such a good man. The people who sent us did not tell us this truth." They decided to help Reverend Njoya.

"I thought I was dead already," Njoya continued. "So I started giving away my treasures. I said, 'You take my books, you take my favorite Bible.'"

He woke up three days later in a hospital, alive.

After this story, stunned as we were, my mom asked: "Reverend Njoya, how are you so fearless? Fear is instinctive, we all feel it. How are you able to overcome your fear?" Reverend Njoya smiled and actually jumped up again and said, "It's like the lion." He crouched down and continued: "When the lion senses his prey, he doesn't just pounce, he backs off first, he gathers up his energy, and then he lunges. That's what we each can do," he said. "We think of fear as something out there, but it comes from inside of us, it's neutral. Fear energy is just like any other energy. And so, like all energy, we can harness it. We can take that raw energy," he said, "and, like the lion, transform it into courage."

Frances Moore Lappé: So what Anna and I have learned this year is a lot about hope. We've learned that it's not about stacking up the evidence and concluding that there are grounds for hope. We don't *find* hope, we make the grounds for hope. Hope became for us more verb than noun. We don't seek it, we *become* it.

We also learned a lot about fear. We learned that it's impossible to get over fear. Rather, what we understand now is the fearlessness of an expanding heart. One big enough to hold it all, like the people in Brazil, who have lost over a thousand of their compatriots. They've seen them murdered. And yet they are still creating new curricula. They're growing organic food. They're singing.

The courage of an expanding heart means learning to sing and cry at the same time. It also means what Reverend Njoya said to us, that we can take that pure energy and transform it into courage. Not to become better people, but simply so that none of us misses the opportunity to break through the deadly thought-traps of this era and to simply be fully ourselves in this extraordinary time of loss and suffering and transformative possibilities.

Anna Lappé (www.smallplanet.org, www.takeabite .cc, www.smallplanetfund.org) is a Brooklyn-based author, public speaker, and cofounder of the Small Planet Institute and Small Planet Fund. Her most recent book is *Diet for a Hot Planet: The Climate Crisis at the End of Your Fork and What You Can Do About It* (Bloomsbury, 2010). She coauthored the national bestseller *Hope's Edge* with her mother, Frances Moore Lappé, and is also the author, with eco-chef Bryant Terry, of *Grub: Ideas for an Urban Organic Kitchen*.

Frances Moore Lappé (www.smallplanet.org) is the author or coauthor of eighteen books, including the highly influential 1971 bestseller *Diet for a Small Planet*. Her newest book, *Getting a Grip 2: Clarity, Creativity and Courage for the World We Really Want* (revised edition, 2010), describes an emergent "living democracy" embracing economic and social as well as political life. A founder of two important national organizations focused on food and the roots of democracy, Lappé also created the American News Service (1995–2000), which placed solutions-oriented news stories in over three hundred newspapers nationwide. Her upcoming book is *Liberation Ecology: Reframing Six Disempowering Ideas That Keep Us from Aligning with Nature— Even Our Own*.

10

The Looks-Within Place

Leslie Gray, Ph.D.

Leslie Gray's window on the world, informed in part by her traditional indigenous culture, is striking in its originality and common sense. A psychologist whose worldview is shaped by a profound inquiry into how people become who they are and what helps them to change, she offers a uniquely dimensional vision that seems to encompass past, present, and future. Since reinventing leadership involves reclaiming the value of the unseen or inner worlds as well as reconsidering what power means, Leslie's story has particular value in showing how to honor our inner knowing.

NINA SIMONS

One morning in 1997 I woke up, sat upright in bed, and spoke the words "reciprocal transformation" out loud. I heard myself do this and then realized I was awake. I had the distinct sense that this phrase was a solution arrived at from a dream. The following year I started an organization called Woodfish Institute with the purpose of promoting and fostering "reciprocal transformation" by means of educational programs and charitable projects.

I am a clinical psychologist with a private practice in which I have integrated indigenous healing methodologies into what I consider the best of my Western psychotherapy training. After I got my Ph.D., I focused on learning techniques from traditional shamans and medicine people and then devised ways to practice them in an office setting such that they could be readily integrated into modern, urban daily life. This also allowed me to include in my work my own Native background, as well as my experience teaching Native American psychology and cross-cultural healing at various universities.

Seeing the healing effects of incorporating indigenous teachings into my practice led me to first conceive of their application on a societal level, and then to create an organization to do just that. An overarching goal of this work has been to awaken in people an empathic identification with the earth. Indigenous teachings contain insights and practices that have the potential to greatly benefit the entire planet, especially the advanced countries, which enjoy extraordinary advantages but sadly destroy their own life-support systems.

It is possible for the interaction between indigenous and technological worldviews to be mutually enhancing and generate solutions to many of our world's current grave dilemmas. We demonstrate this annually when the Woodfish Prize is awarded to two people from different cultural worldviews who cocreate a social-action project in which they are mutually transformed.

Right now in history we have all the economic, technological, and legal "fixes" we need to alter our calamitous trajectory. But solutions simply won't come to pass unless people care. Indigenous cultures have always understood that a caring relationship with the environment has to be taught. Therefore, they devised ingeniously effective methods of instruction to generate in the individual a strong sense of personal connection to the vital universe and to reinforce these teachings over the life span. Such teachings are still available to us.

Psychotherapy patients exist in a context, and the past decade—according to a recent issue of *Time* magazine*—is a front runner for the worst decade in history. The Hopi elders spoke several years ago about

---

*See the November 24, 2009, issue for "The '00s: Goodbye (at Last) to the Decade from Hell," by Andrew Serwer. It can be referenced by going to www.time.com and doing a search for "Serwer."

the times we are living in, and their message has become even more relevant in the era of the Great Recession. I first heard the elders' prophecy about seven years ago, and it gave me a model of resiliency that prepared me for the difficult times we are in now. At the same time, I see both friends and patients suffer greatly from the lack of any concept of how to navigate the current turmoil.

"You have been telling people that this is the Eleventh Hour," the elders said. "Now you must go back and tell the people that this is the Hour, and there are things to be considered. Where are you living? What are you doing? Are you in right relation? Where is your water? Know your garden. It is time to speak your truth. Create your community. Be good to each other. And do not look outside yourself for the leader."*

Then the elders said something unexpected: "This could be a good time! There is a river flowing now very fast that is so great and swift that there are those who will be afraid. They will try to hold onto the shore. They will feel they are being torn apart and they will suffer greatly. Know that the river has its destination."

The elders went on to say that we must "let go of the shore, push off into the middle of the river, keep our eyes open and our heads above the water, see who is there with us and celebrate. At this time in history, we are to take nothing personally, least of all ourselves. The moment that we do, our spiritual growth and journey come to a halt. The time of the lone wolf is over. Gather yourselves. Banish the word 'struggle' from your attitude and your vocabulary. All that we do now must be done in a sacred manner and in celebration."

The inspiration for my life work has come from medicine people, seers, healers, and shamans—many of whom were real crackpots. That's a comfort. Their model has allowed me to operate from a place of not knowing. The direction WEST on the Native American medicine wheel is called the "Looks-Within Place." It is the place of dreams and

---

*This prophecy relies on oral tradition. I first heard it from a Plains Indian sweatlodge leader in 2002. I also accessed this prophecy under the title "Hopi Elders Speak, Oraibi Arizona" on December 2, 2009, at the following URLs: www.communityworks.info/hopi .htm; www.spiritofmaat.com/messages/oct28/hopi.htm; www.matrixmasters.com/take-charge/hopi-prophecy.html.

daydreams. It is the dark cave. It is the place Bear goes to sleep in order to survive the harshest season. So, the healing power of WEST is that we do not know. Surely, that is one place we can dwell in honesty. By seeking and trusting answers from the Looks-Within Place, I have personally arrived at ways to turn apparently hopeless situations around while operating from what seems to be a powerless position.

For example, I once worked as a low-level member of the therapeutic staff of a ward in a large mental hospital. The director of that ward was particularly disingenuous. He announced that we had a "democratic process," and that we were all—staff and patients—to sit in a circle each morning, and that "everybody" would share openly. But it was only the patients who were expected to disclose personal information in that morning circle. Staff members were told privately that their role was just to confront patients who did not speak up. Also, the (heavily medicated) patients were told it was an "open ward" and they were "free to leave." But a staff person sat at the exit and, when a patient tried to leave, read aloud to the patient intimidating excerpts from his or her chart. I found the whole setup horrifying. I knew some other staff felt deeply dispirited by the Kafkaesque atmosphere of the ward. It just wrenched all the love of healing—which was why we had gone into the profession in the first place—out of us. But I saw no way out without being terminated.

From my powerless position, I could not see any direct way that I could change the situation, so I sought an answer from the Looks-Within Place and received a nonlinear solution. I solemnly vowed that I would never say a word unless spoken to during my entire rotation on the unit.

By following this advice, I was then freed up to employ every wordless psychological technique I knew. (I'd previously written a paper on interactive nonverbal behavior during psychotherapy.) So, without attracting the attention of the director, I was still able to be a healing presence. If someone said something that accurately described the circle, I would move my eyes, my whole body, toward them. I encouraged them with subtle gestures to trust their own experience until they began to shift ever so slightly into saying just the thing that would both protect them and allow them to heal. I sat in that circle for six months, and by the end, whenever the director would utter one of his mendacious and crazy-making pronouncements, everybody would turn their heads to "check it out" with me. I never said a word, but through subtle movements I pointed the way around a verbal bully. I even ended up with a little gesture for "You can give him a break now."

We all have people like this to deal with. Indigenous elders have taught me that these sorts of dilemmas are best resolved by seeking solutions outside of our ordinary thinking. And this approach can apply to both personal and planetary dilemmas.

Many current domestic and global predicaments indeed appear unsolvable. Nevertheless, creative solutions may lie in realms where apparently contradictory elements unite. This is what Einstein meant when he said that imagination is more important than knowledge.

Visionary problem-solving is, paradoxically, a relaxed endeavor. It is dreamlike. It involves a quality of consciousness that is only hindered by desperate clutching. To release our death grip on what is not working, it helps to have a little humility. A benefit of operating from indigenous models is the calmer perspective that comes from understanding one's place in the world. This is the perspective required for long-range problem-solving, and it's sorely needed in the decision-making of our technologically advanced civilization. It helps to remind ourselves that we are not going to get rid of life. Mother Earth will take a few million years to shake off her skirts and start all over again.

Leslie Gray (www.woodfish.org) is a clinical psychologist who maintains a private practice in San Francisco while teaching ecopsychology and Native American studies at local and international universities. Gray's work blending ancient and modern healing modalities has been featured in numerous publications, including the Sierra Club Books anthology *Ecological Medicine: Healing the Earth, Healing Ourselves*. She is a member of the Society of Indian Psychologists and an associate of the Milton Erickson Institute. In 1998 she founded Woodfish Institute to promote ecological education grounded in indigenous wisdom.

11

Applying Science for Social Change

Riki Ott, Ph.D.

*Riki Ott may be the most accessible, down-to-earth scientist I've ever encoun-
tered, and one of the most effective change-makers as well. The story of her
own call to action describes the energy and authority her outrage conferred
upon her leadership. After many years as a working fisherwoman, she was
called back to biology and activism by the* Exxon Valdez *oil spill, which
occurred near her beloved home in southern Alaska. As is so often the case,
without knowing exactly how, she knew she had to act, and she has since
become a teacher, writer, and activist working to preserve and protect the
health and sanctity of the natural world.*

NINA SIMONS

On March 24, 1989, I flew over the wreck of the *Exxon Valdez*
aground on Bligh Reef in Prince William Sound. It was surreal. The
snowfields on Chugach Range glowed pink in the early morning sun.
The ocean surface was calm and drop-dead gorgeous. And there on
the water sat a blood-red tanker in the middle of an inky-black oil
slick stretching like an amoeba with the tide. A bluish cloud of hydro-
carbons boiled off the surface of the oil slick. It was ten hours after

the grounding, yet none of the promised cleanup equipment had been deployed.

I knew that it was just a matter of time before this oil spread throughout the sound. I felt devastated. A question formed in my mind: I know enough to make a difference, but do I care enough? This is the story of why I was driven to ask that question, and how my life has become the answer since that fateful day.

When that question flashed into my mind, an odd thing happened. Suddenly I felt like I was back in Wisconsin in the late 1960s and I was thirteen years old. Robins were falling out of trees. Even a thirteen-year-old knows that something is wrong when robins are falling out of trees, landing with a plop at your feet, and dying. I went to my father, who could answer everything, and asked why—why was this happening? I discovered there were some things that couldn't be comforted by my father's hug. He gave me a dying robin. I held it in my hands as he explained about the neurotoxin DDT. My dad then went on to fix the problem: He sued the state of Wisconsin over the use of DDT because he cared. He cared about his children and the birds, and he knew enough to make a difference. Wisconsin was the first state to ban DDT—because of my father and his friends.

This legal campaign was staged out of our home. We three kids were crammed into one bedroom so that the Environmental Defense Fund's sole staff biologist and sole staff attorney could stay in our house. They worked at our dining table with yellow legal pads (because computers weren't commonplace then) and amassed a tremendous amount of information into legal briefs. I would race home every day after school to watch things unfold.

Then my father gave me Rachel Carson's *Silent Spring*. I read that book, perched in the sugar maple tree in our backyard. I decided that I wanted to write books like Rachel Carson, books to motivate people like my father—who was a paper salesman and thus an ordinary person in my mind—to make the world a better place.

When scientists can write so that ordinary people can hear and act on this new information, that's when social change happens. My father's lawsuit was successful. The state of Wisconsin banned DDT in 1971, and the rest of the nation followed suit in 1972. America's sky was safe once again for robins, peregrine falcons, eagles, brown pelicans, and other birds—and children.

After reading Rachel Carson's other books, I decided to become a marine biologist like my new mentor. In 1972 I left Wisconsin to go find an ocean. After thirteen years of higher education and tromping around the world's oceans, I decided to take a summer off before I put my Ph.D. in marine toxicology to use.

I spent that summer of 1985 in Cordova, Alaska, which is a commercial fishing village. I was totally captivated by the rugged beauty of the landscape, the strong sense of community, and the friendly, can-do spirit of the people. I decided to stay. I became a commercial "fisherma'am." My father gracefully made the switch from "my-daughter-the-scientist" to "my-daughter-the-fisherma'am."

I quickly learned there are ways of seeing and interpreting the world other than through the prism of my beloved Western science. One way was that of the commercial fishermen, whose knowledge was based on years and years and years of experience, of hands-on work. When what they saw in the sound didn't match what the scientists were telling them, they would challenge the scientists. Another way of knowing the world is the indigenous worldview. Some of this worldview I learned from the last living speaker of the Eyak people, Chief Marie Smith Jones, who passed away in 2008, along with my father. The indigenous worldview is based on eons of experience, and it's passed along through teaching the young the traditional ways of celebrating, harvesting, and sharing wild foods. As with the fishermen, if what the Western scientists were saying didn't match the Eyak experience, the Native people would also challenge the Western worldview.

I had come to love the area and its people and their way of seeing the world. So on that March day in 1989, I saw how the events of my life had arranged to put me in this place, with my openness to these other ways of knowing about the effects of an oil spill. And I decided I did care; I cared more than enough to cast my lot with the Natives and the fishermen.

And I knew that this decision would probably guide the rest of my life.

Following in Rachel Carson's footsteps, I put my academic training to use, and I began documenting exactly what was happening; I began writing books. The *Exxon Valdez* oil spill was the worst in our nation's history. It was closer to 35 million gallons than Exxon's self-reported low-end estimate of 11 million gallons, a figure often repeated by the press. This spill also killed more wildlife than any other spill in the world. The fishermen and Native people asked what would happen to the fisheries, not in that year of 1989, but the following year and years after that, because the pink salmon and herring spawn on intertidal beaches that were now plastered with oil. They asked: Will these babies that have been exposed to this toxic substance be able to survive, and if they do survive, will they be able to reproduce?

We had to wait four years for answers—and the answers came from Prince William Sound, not the scientists. Our fish populations collapsed in 1992 and again in 1993, which totally trashed the economy. The fishermen and Native people sensed the connection between the oil buried under the beaches and the delayed ecosystem collapse. But the scientists were still saying they expected no long-term effects from the oil spill, because in the 1970s, when the Clean Air Act and the Clean Water Act passed, the science demonstrated only short-term harm from oil. By then the press was long gone, so they did not see the collapse of the herring and the pink salmon. They did not report how the wrecked environment in turn wrecked subsistence cultures and economies throughout the whole region.

To get the attention of the media and the scientists, I organized a blockade of Valdez Narrows. Our entire seine fishing fleet blockaded this geologic bottleneck, and we held up oil tanker traffic. The U.S. Department of Energy freaked out and sent in the FBI. The FBI made it as far as Valdez, but they didn't have any boats—we had all the boats. So the Department of Energy ordered gunboats up from Seattle. We knew it would take them four days to arrive, so we held firm. President Clinton finally asked Interior Secretary Bruce Babbitt to meet with us to find out what we wanted. We demanded ecosystem studies. We demanded that the scientists get *out* of the laboratory and get *in* Prince William Sound and quit looking at a little dot of birds here and a little dot of mammals there. We demanded that they connect the dots!

So they conducted four ecosystem studies over eight years. They looked at food-web interactions, habitat interactions, and generational interactions. Scientists learned that the baby pink salmon that *did* survive their oil bath could not reproduce as adults. Scientists also proved that most of the oiled young herring simply did not survive, and the ones that did suffered a damaged immune system that made them sickly and diseased. The killing did not stop in 1989. The end result of all these studies was that by 1999 the scientific community realized that oil is a thousand times more toxic than we thought it was in the 1970s.

The scientists validated the fishermen and Natives' view: low levels of oil *do* cause long-term harm to ecosystems. This was a paradigm shift in science.

After the spill there was litigation. One lawsuit focused on the destruction of public resources—wild lands and wildlife held in trust for us, the public, by the federal and state governments. Exxon settled that lawsuit in 1991 with the feds and the state. The $900 million settlement funded the ecosystem studies and other studies as well.

I wrote a grant to the Environmental Defense Fund, proposing to gather together the scientists who conducted the ecosystem studies, so that they could write a paper to explain the complex science to the public. This happened, and the peer-reviewed paper was published in *Science* in December 2003.

In the meantime, it took me longer than expected to publish my first book, *Sound Truth and Corporate Myths,* because I stumbled onto another cover-up by Exxon. It turns out there was a splash-back effect from the use of the high-pressure hot-water hoses in the cleanup that made thousands of workers sick. Exxon hid its own clinical records, which revealed that 6,722 claims of upper respiratory damage were reported. Two out of three cleanup workers on the beaches were affected. This chemical poisoning epidemic went unreported. I took this opportunity to document Exxon's *three* cover-ups in *Sound Truth and Corporate Myths:* how much oil really had been spilled; the fact that the spill caused long-term harm to wildlife; and the fact that the cleanup made workers sick.

New findings in medical science were also being unveiled while the ecosystem studies were being conducted. We now know that the same oil compounds that made the sea otters sick made the cleanup workers sick with occupational asthma. These same oil compounds are coming out of the tailpipes of our automobiles in the form of ultrafine particles and are manifesting as asthma in children and adults, premature death, hardened arteries, and genetic (DNA) damage.

We have to get off oil. I describe an idea for how to get off oil in my second book on the spill, *Not One Drop,* that deals with the social, emotional, and legal fallout from the *Exxon Valdez*—what breaks when a community goes through a man-made disaster and how to heal this trauma. Getting off oil is not so much a matter of technology as it is about political will and healing community dysfunction. *Not One Drop* also discusses how our legal system is broken and what we need to do to fix it. My book exposes a fundamental problem in our democracy—that corporations have more power than people. It also shows how we can fix this crisis with an amendment to the U.S. Constitution to affirm that only real persons (human beings) have constitutional rights, not non-living "persons" such as corporations.

Riki Ott, Ph.D., shares her personal story of transformation from scientist to democracy activist in *Not One Drop* (Chelsea Green Publishing, 2008), her second book on the *Exxon Valdez* oil spill. Ott has appeared in numerous documentaries, including the award-winning feature film *Black Wave* (Macumba International). She is currently working with national democracy activists on the Campaign to Legalize Democracy (www.ultimatecivics.org), which posts material for educators from fifth grade through university.

12

The Color of Sustainability

LaDonna Redmond

LaDonna Redmond's life prompted her to become a priestess, community organizer, and food activist. Motivated to learn voraciously when confronted with her son's illness, she experienced firsthand how inaccessible healthy food was in her inner-city neighborhood, and she became determined to change this. The power of that fierce determination fueled by her maternal love is indomitable. She has since established a farmers' market that accepts food stamps, and has gone on to become one of the food system's foremost activists and spokespersons for food justice. In so doing, she brings an awareness of history, race, and class to the conversation, while educating people about the need for fair, affordable, accessible, and healthy food for everyone.

NINA SIMONS

> *An African proverb says, "If we stand strong, it is because we stand on the shoulders of those who have come before us."*

From the time I was a child, I have wondered why I was born and what I was supposed to do with my life. It seemed clear that my life had a purpose—not just one calling but perhaps several that evolved over time. Over the years, following these callings has led me to do different things at different times as a community activist and a concerned citizen. I worked at Operation Push as a youth organizer, and I got a chance to see how community change actually does occur when Chicago elected its first African American mayor, Harold Washington, in 1983. Later, after sustaining my own recovery from substance abuse, I led in the creation of a women's halfway house called Sister House.

I care deeply about being part of the solution to the issues—such as violence, and inadequate housing and jobs—that impact my community. But no previous calling could have prepared me for my life as a mother, although my journey with my first child would require all the skills and more that I learned in my life as a community organizer.

During my pregnancy, I would lie awake at night and wonder what I could do to protect my son. There was a lot to be concerned about: African American men are more than twice as likely to be unemployed as white males, and they earn less. They are nearly seven times more likely to be incarcerated, and between the ages of fifteen and nineteen they die from homicide at forty-six times the rate of white males in that age range. African American girls are disproportionately affected by HIV/AIDS, sexually transmitted diseases (STDs), and unintended pregnancy. The death rate of children in Chicago is approximately twenty-four deaths a year. Given this, Chicago's children are being killed at twenty-four times the rate that soldiers from Chicago are being killed in Iraq. Some may say that these things that happen to black youth happen accidentally on purpose. Whatever the case may be, the question remained: What could I do to protect the potential of my son?

My son's birth was marked by a naming ceremony. His name is Wade Cameron Redmond—he is a child of Obatala, the deity that I praise, and he is named after the oldest male relative on my mother's side of the family. Through consultation with a priest we found out that Wade needed to avoid meat. Since I was breast-feeding and we were vegetarians at the time, this presented no problem.

It turned out that my son was born with severe food allergies. One day when we went out for breakfast, I gave him a little bit of milk with some cereal. I watched as his face swelled up, his eyes swelled shut, and his face filled with tears. As we raced to the hospital, I wondered if my son was going to die. At the hospital I wanted answers. I wanted to know not only how this had happened, but how could we stop it from happening again. But no answers were forthcoming. Doctors are not always the smartest people, despite their many years of education.

My husband and I repeated that scenario at least six or seven more times over the next several months. An allergic reaction would cause my son to wheeze, the wheezing could not be controlled unless we took him to the emergency room, and then he would be hospitalized for at least a week. The last time this happened, the medication to control his wheezing did not work quickly enough and the doctors transferred my baby boy to an intensive care unit. I had only one prayer: "Sweet Orisha, please, please let him live." On that day when I saw my son on a breathing machine, I made a promise that if he lived we would never, ever be back there again.

Skin tests showed that Wade was allergic to eggs, all dairy products, peanuts, and shellfish. I realized very quickly that I knew nothing about how to prepare healthy food for my family. I had no idea that there was such a thing as a food system. I determined to learn all that I could about food and about how to feed my baby. So I did what I do best: I read. I read everything I could on food and food production, ecology and the environment, land and land stewardship.

My study introduced me to books and essays by Wendell Berry, Michael Ableman, and Andrew Pollack. I read the *New York Times* and Michael Pollan's articles. I searched the Internet, and I found the Organic Consumers Association website to be a very helpful resource. And I have to admit, I watched a lot of food TV.

But there was something missing: the story of my ancestors and their connection to the land. As the Africans who were brought to this country as slaves to work the land, surely we had a relationship to it. It always trips me out when I go to a meeting and there's a group of farmers, none of them people of color, and they turn around and look at me and say, "Exactly when did you (black folks) get interested in farming?"

Our collective memory is way, way too short.

I hungered for the African American story as it relates to the land, and ecology, and the environment. Our story is one that must include the trauma that Africans have faced when forced to work the land, and then, after they were freed, when being chased off the land. Outside of a few stories written by Alice Walker and bell hooks, I couldn't find a thing.

For all this, I still needed a practical way to get the best food available on the table. I found out that my son needed a diet that avoided highly processed, prepackaged foods, basically because they contained his allergens. My journey to feed my son turned into quite a chore. Pregnant with my second child, I would drive all over the city of Chicago to find organic food, and I found myself at some very interesting places. I visited co-op stores that I never knew existed and an expensive national chain store that we jokingly called "Whole Paycheck." This store did, however, help me reeducate my taste buds.

All I wanted was fresh food—produce without harmful pesticides and meat without antibiotics. But living on the West Side of Chicago meant I had to leave my community, and shopping trips were expensive, not only in terms of the cost of the food I bought, but the gas I used and the time I spent. Given this, the community organizer in me wanted to learn more about the organic food movement. I began attending local organizing meetings. Most times I was the only person of color in the room.

I would raise issues about food access, and the conversation would immediately turn to food stamps and food vouchers, as if the only way that black people could afford food is if somebody gave it to us. Some folks would suggest, "Well, people in your neighborhood don't buy organic food, do they?" Some folks would offer, "Well, we could come and teach people over there about growing food and gardening. Do you think that would help?"—not realizing that African Americans come from the South, where most of us grew up on farms and grew food organically. We did this not because we were trying to supply organic foods to a niche market, but because it was the only way we could grow food. We couldn't afford fertilizers or pesticides.

Too often the food access issue was treated as if it were some sort of social service issue, one that could be solved by government programs or food donations. And yet in my neighborhood, I can buy designer gym shoes, every kind of fast food, every kind of junk food, all kinds of malt liquor and illegal drugs, and maybe even a semiautomatic weapon, but I cannot purchase an organic tomato.

In other communities, the same food access issue is looked upon as a profitable business opportunity. If we are truly going to develop sustainable food systems, then everyone must be included as a potential end user of that system. If we want sustainable communities, then we must talk to everyone about how this will occur. Diversity is critical to sustainability.

At this point, access to organic foods is not the focal point of my activism. As long as organic food is priced only for wealthy people, it just isn't a viable solution to the health needs of my community. So we are working to develop local solutions to the issue of food access. To achieve that end, my husband and I formed a nonprofit organization, and we obtained several vacant lots. We converted those lots to urban farm sites, and we hired people from the community to work on those sites. Also involved are universities and community groups that have formed the Chicago Food Systems Collaborative. Together we are building a grocery store that will provide access to food in our community.

We each have to return to our ancestral roots in order to feed ourselves. I envision a place where we invite community members and others from outside to come together to prepare and eat the food we grow; over dinner, we can have practical conversations about the food system.

We need diversity in the discussion to be able to create solutions for all our communities. When we expand the dialogue in the sustainability movement, all our stories can be told. These include stories of the undocumented immigrants who are growing much of our food, the black farmers who still can't get the money they are owed from the USDA,* and stories from urban farmers as well as the new breed of organic farmers in this country.

This year we launched a small pilot project, called Graffiti and Grub, to deliver food in a grocery-store format for members of the hip-hop generation, who face many health challenges. They are the first generation to have shorter life spans than their parents because of chronic diet-related disease. According to the CDC, 81 percent of African American women today are overweight or obese. Obesity and other chronic diseases such as diabetes can be controlled through diet. We need to expand awareness about these issues, as well as create access to better food for the African-American community.

Introducing all these concerns to the African American culture, making upcoming generations familiar with them, and helping find solutions for them is a calling that I am responding to with all my heart.

LaDonna Redmond, the founder/president of the Institute for Community Resource Development in Chicago, Illinois, is a longtime community organizer in the Chicago area with deep experience in setting up and sustaining a wide range of urban community programs. She is also a journalist and columnist and a mother of two. She is dedicated to healing the earth through cooking and growing delicious food.

---

*See the following for more information on this issue: http://afgen.com/blk_farmers _usda.html.

13

A Fierce and Tender Heart

Jodie Evans

Jodie Evans's life has led her through politics to entrepreneurship and bridged family and activism. Her leadership reconciles the apparent opposites of fierce commitment and tenderness, and this combination confers an inner authority upon her that is both joyful and effective. As a cofounder of CODEPINK: Women for Peace, she helps invent and produce direct actions that call media and public attention to political manipulations and deceit—with an overarching agenda to end war. She supports women's voices in diverse nations, organizations, and projects in myriad ways, and still manages to live in the joy of her life and family while persistently working toward progressive social change.

NINA SIMONS

I had no intention of creating an organization. In fact, I didn't know what I was going to do when I got off the plane in Washington, D.C. I'd heard President Bush was about to give Congress a resolution for a preemptive strike on Iraq, and the violation and insanity of that act was ricocheting inside my body. I knew I had to get there and do something. CODEPINK: Women for Peace began from this intimate need to manage a sense of powerlessness in the face of insanity.

So I gathered with my friends Medea Benjamin, Diane Wilson, and

Starhawk, and, determined not to be ignored, we went from hanging a banner at the White House to the steps of Congress, took off our shirts, pinned doves of peace on our bras, and wrote READ MY TITS, NO WAR IN IRAQ on our bellies. Our spectacle on the steps gave us an opportunity to tell many members of Congress to vote against the resolution, gaining commitments to a "No" vote from then-Minority Whip Nancy Pelosi and Senator Paul Wellstone.

We dashed to be first in line at the House hearing for the resolution. When we sat down, all the cameras were on us, having heard about our afternoon on the steps of Congress. As I sat and listened to the lies and justifications coming out of the congressional members' mouths, I remember feeling myself shake—both with fury at the distortion and with my own fear that I would be unable to meet it with words that mattered. What would I say to the audience behind those cameras that could effectively counter these crazy-making arguments? What would happen to me after I did? I stood and unfurled a giant banner and yelled, "The world does not want this war. Let the inspections work." The police dragged us out.

That night I dreamed of thousands of women creating a beautiful camp with pink tents of music, dancing, knitting circles, joy, and laughter across the street from those beating the drums of war at the White House. Dreams live somewhere inside what can be a painful reality. Tents are not allowed in such close proximity to the White House, nor can you sit down or have signs bigger than fifteen-by-twenty-five inches. Regardless, women began to join our vigil in Lafayette Park. The first to come were from our intimate circles, and then came strangers who had read about us or heard us on Amy Goodman's broadcast *Democracy Now*. Women from D.C. organizations would spend their lunch hour with us or take over for a day while we disrupted weapons-of-mass-destruction panels at a local think tank.

We decided to embrace Caroline Casey's call of Code Hot Pink in response to Bush's color-coded alerts of orange, red, and yellow that were used to frighten the American public into going to war. Since then, CODEPINK has become a group of talented, vibrant, passionate, heart-centered, stubborn, creative, strategic, and outrageously hot-pink whistle-blowers against a foreign policy gone wrong. The women who joined us in D.C. would go home and create vigils of their own until there came to be hundreds of vigils in communities all across the country. They needed to act together with others as an antidote to the powerlessness that threatened to silence and oppress them. They did it because, as Grace Paley says, "the only recognizable characteristic of hope is action." Over the last seven years we have grown to 200,000 strong. All of us receive weekly alerts about specific calls to action, because every week another opportunity to be dragged under by hope-lessness seems to present itself.

My cofounder Medea Benjamin and I found ourselves creating a container for women around the country to act in concert for peace across the world. CODEPINK and the pink messages we wore became how we stood out in the crowd, how we could provoke conversations in checkout lines and airplanes about the lies our media was feeding us. We started to understand the power of the provocative. Much of what we deal with in trying to stop war is how people are used by their fears. To make these fears conscious and break their spell, our actions, costumes, and chants have a touch of the foolish that can liberate and ultimately empower. The intense seriousness of the issue seems to demand an expression molded by audacity, wit, playfulness, boldness, and improvisation.

We need enormous discipline in the face of what our actions stir, and yet our actions must remain spontaneous so as to be true and unpredictable in relation to the power structure they are aimed to affect.

Medea and I would write an alert each week to educate, inspire, and activate our list. A woman outside an Army base in the South could feel the hands of a group of women in New York City. The voices of women in Minnesota were strengthening those in the warmonger state of Florida. We would tell stories from our vigils and give information that simply couldn't be found in the mainstream media. Once a woman came to a vigil, she felt emboldened and connected and wanted more, because when we act, we escape the disempowerment and depression that insane responses engender.

To speak truth into the lies is never a pleasant first step. From the beginning there were many, some even our closest friends, who were uncomfortable with what we were doing. Rejection in some form is immediate, but we don't shy away from our discomfort or that of others. We must speak out because we are surrounded by lies. From the start I knew I must cut through the confusion to get to the person whose gut tells them it doesn't feel right. When we stand with a sign that speaks in direct contradiction to what is being said in a hearing room, for instance, each person can find a resonance with what they know inside; they can believe in what they are feeling and respond to that.

We rented a house in D.C., and twenty-five to thirty women at a time would come to be with us in action in the halls of Congress. Women would first say they were too afraid, or that it felt silly to get in a costume and hold up signs at a congressional hearing with police screaming at them to sit down. Those same women have now gone to jail for speaking up about the lies and speaking truth to the powers-that-be in the halls of power, as did their suffragist sisters many years ago. *The Nation* magazine, which we assumed would be supportive, at first chided us for taking the color pink, yet seven years later they celebrated CODEPINK as the most valuable organization of the whole Bush-Cheney era.

Many women have come to the CODEPINK house wanting to participate but feeling tentative and afraid. But once they join us for a day in the halls of Congress and witness another woman, motivated by her own outrage, step beyond her comfort zone, they can palpably feel the energy. Then they can no longer be held back from stretching beyond their own boundaries to express themselves. Once we have engaged, moved beyond our comfort zone into our own power, and tapped into our creativity within a supportive community of shared purpose, we can never turn back.

The community we have created is potent with love and empathy. Each time we act together, a layer of courage, sanity, and, yes, peace is deposited in our hearts. What we do is always collaborative: each person offers her or his ingredient into the soup, and yet no one individual has the responsibility for the whole recipe. As another ten thousand troops are deployed or another enormous check is approved for war, this collaboration provides a constant fountain of nourishment in the creativity and shifting we do daily so that the message remains fresh and so that we can continue to expose and to educate.

Over the years we have come together for marches, for twenty-four-hour vigils outside the White House for Mother's Day, and in support of Cindy Sheehan at Camp Casey. CODEPINKers from across the country came to help her from the minute she had the idea and stayed at her side for the next year. Even though we participate in events such as this, most of our time is spent in our hometowns, where we have found different ways to bring our peace activism home to our communities.

In my own case, I realized very early on that education was an important factor to peace. If Bush could convince all these people in Congress to go to war, we needed more critical thinkers. My response to that was to start an after-school reading program in my neighborhood. In New York City, the group has spent the last five years going to high schools with counter-recruitment education. In Chicago, a program was created to help the Iraqi refugees who, having lost everything, were left to fend for themselves after just a month's worth of housing and food stamps had been provided to them. Our response to the economic collapse last year was to help a mother whose son, a veteran of the war in Iraq, had just died; her house was in foreclosure. CODEPINK responded by donating $50,000 to help her save her home.

So our global actions and local offerings feed each other. Growing out into the larger landscape, act by act, emboldens all of us. Sharing stories and successes continues to strengthen and expand our capacities and nurture them with beauty, joy, inspiration, and laughter. Doing so helps us refine how we work for peace together, and how we embody peace.

We in CODEPINK know that to give away our power is to betray ourselves before we even begin to act. So we will continue to blow our whistles (hot-pink ones, of course), carry our handcuffs for war criminals, and journey to the epicenter of conflict to find the space where peace is sprouting against all odds—the families in pup tents in Gaza, the women under their veils in Afghanistan, the Iraqi refugees living without heat in Chicago, the single moms in foreclosed homes, and others in struggles all across our own country.

Because we dare to believe that another world is possible, day after day we will continue to speak out against the hypocrisies, the immorality and insanity of drone bombers, torture, overseas bases, bloated military expenditures, sanctions that punish innocent civilians, wars, and the occupation of foreign lands. Each time a woman has the courage to act and share her truth, she plants wonderful seeds. Each such seed offers freedom and power to those around her, and in this way we bring the world closer together and closer to peace.

Jodie Evans (www.codepink4peace.org) has been a peace, environmental, women's rights, and social justice activist for forty years. She has traveled extensively to war zones, including Afghanistan, Gaza, and Iraq, promoting and learning about peaceful resolution to conflict. A documentary film producer, she has also published two books, *Stop the Next War Now* and *Twilight of Empire*. She is a cofounder of CODEPINK: Women for Peace and the board chair of the Women's Media Center, and she sits on ten other boards. She is the mother of three.

14

The Pulse of Global Women's Voices Rising

Jensine Larsen

Jensine Larsen's world travels as a young journalist taught her the power of how clearly women saw what was true and how clearly they knew what they needed to say. She also recognized that they had no outlets through which to express their voices or connect with each other. She envisioned creating a global web of connection to strengthen these voices, their leadership, and their activism. She never stopped to wonder if it was possible—she simply knew she had to do it, and do it she did. Employing the best of new media technology, today she continues to fulfill her purpose with vision, tenacity, beauty, humility, and grace. In so doing, her clear voice has made her a compelling leader for our time.

NINA SIMONS

Many people ask me, "What does the 'pulse' in *World Pulse* stand for?" For me, it symbolizes the electric pulse of women's voices rising across the earth, which I feel vibrating in every cell of my body. I believe that the creative potential of young girls and women is the greatest untapped resource on earth. And I believe that we have the potential, right now, to use the power of the media and emerging communications technologies to truly connect and unleash this potential.

I built *World Pulse* from a vision I had at a very young age. Even though I grew up paralyzingly shy, connecting to this network of women around the world has helped me find my own voice. And when I tap deeply into my own voice, this is what I have to say: "It is absolutely urgent that we apply our skills and intelligence to developing a communications infrastructure that can channel the wisdom of those women living in the midst of some of our earth's greatest challenges so that their voices can reach the public and we can hear their needs and their pressing agendas in their own words."

I grew up in rural Wisconsin, and I was homeschooled. My teachers were the forests and fields and streams. I played house in a tree with my Minnie Mouse phone in the crook of some branches and my Fisher Price stove in the crook of another. When I entered public school in the fifth grade, the way that information was taught with superficial multiple-choice and true-and-false questions shocked me, and I began to doubt myself. I started keeping my voice inside, and I became so shy that it was hard for me to raise my hand and ask to go to the bathroom. I could not even get up the courage to correct people who were mispronouncing my name. It took me until high school to break through that, and you can imagine the surprise of my classmates in rural Wisconsin, who after six years with me discovered that they had not been calling me by my real name.

At this point in my young life, I started reading the *New York Times* and the *Economist,* which left me feeling empty inside. I wanted to hear and learn from women leaders, but their voices were absent.

So I decided I needed to get out in the world, and at nineteen, I worked full time, saved some money, and took off for the Amazon. I ended up in Ecuador working with indigenous communities, particularly indigenous women who were struggling to reclaim their native lands in the face of multinational oil contamination. At that time, oil companies, many of them from the United States, had leaked over four times the contamination of the *Exxon Valdez* oil spill onto their lands over the past twenty years. Their children were dying of skin cancer and they were dying of stomach cancer, and they asked me to be their messenger. They told me to take their stories back to the United States, the largest oil-consuming country in the world. This started to awaken me to the possibilities of being a journalist and a messenger.

From Ecuador I went to Burma and then to Thailand, where I worked with Burmese refugees, mostly women who had fled the ethnic cleansing that is still going on to this day. That was when my life changed and I had the vision for *World Pulse*, although it would take many years for that vision to become a reality.

As I interviewed these Burmese women, who had endured the absolutely unthinkable, I found them to be so courageous that all I could do was be in awe of them as I held out the microphone for them to speak into. So many of these young girls and women were being trafficked into underground brothels, where the AIDS infection rate was as high as 80 percent. I thought: What is their future? And yet despite the bleak outlook of their lives, they had this flame of determination in their eyes to bring about democracy; they had this yearning and a vision of the solutions they were intent on creating. I recognized that their voices were like gold, given their potential to show the world that they were innovators, they were poets, they were organizers and educators and tremendous leaders for the world.

I remember waking up in Thailand on one of those hot mornings where you're totally drenched in sweat. I was preparing myself to do more interviews, and I had a vision that there should be a global media source that would broadcast the wisdom of these women. But I was twenty-three years old at that time. I was still really shy and had no publishing experience whatsoever and no resources. I couldn't even go to my family for a hundred dollars. I doubted myself and held my vision inside for another five years.

I finally took the leap when I was twenty-eight years old because the voices of those women wouldn't leave me alone. I would wake up in the middle of the night with my own voice telling me that I needed to act on my dream to create an outlet, a communications portal, for the unheard women of the world. But I also started looking at the data and fully understanding how staggering the gender imbalance is in the global news media. I hadn't known, for example, that women are the focal point of news stories only about 10 percent of the time. Women comprise only 1 percent of the world's editors. This is the media that defines what we feel is possible in the world. Women do two-thirds of the world's work yet make only 10 percent of the world's income and own only 1 percent of the world's financial assets.

So I started building a team, creating a magazine, making networks with journalists around the world, and fund-raising. I raised my first $400,000 from $50 and $100 checks, which took a couple of years. It makes me proud to say that *World Pulse* was born from the grassroots and today is serving grassroots to grassroots.

When the first edition of *World Pulse* magazine came out in 2004, the reaction from our audience helped us define our next steps and shift our business strategy. We were on newsstands across the United States and Canada, and as a result we started getting waves of interest and were deluged from two different factions. Women, primarily from North America, were reading the print magazine, passing it around among their friends, and saying, "Oh, my God, I hadn't heard about the situation in Iraq from these Iraqi women leaders; I didn't realize a holocaust was happening in the Congo, or that there were solutions for the drug war being proposed by women leaders in the United States." They were ringing our phone off the hook because they wanted to do more. More than just write a check, they wanted to connect, to travel, to volunteer, and to donate their resources.

On the other side, we were getting e-mails from remote places where you wouldn't think that there would actually be Internet access: from the heart of the jungles of Colombia and rural parts of Africa, the majority of them from many small educational projects and healthcare clinics across the globe. These women were saying, "Please cover us. We need visibility." But we didn't have the ability to cover all these stories, and that's when we started to conceive of PulseWire.

I felt like a bit of a mad scientist tinkering around in a media laboratory with my team, figuring out how to create the unique infrastructure that was needed. But as the communications revolution started to build, we became aware of the interactive potential of what is now known as Web 2.0 and were able to develop PulseWire, a global women's newswire through which a woman anywhere in the world who may have access to a cell phone, or perhaps an Internet café, can connect to others and speak out for herself.

Today we have women reporting from the ground and speaking out from over 150 countries. We're listening deeply to these women at the grassroots level and publishing their stories. In turn, our readers, when they're inspired, can get online and connect directly to these women—wherever they are in the world.

As we looked out, our decision to go for it strategically was reinforced by three unstoppable trends happening in our world today. The first such trend is the rise of women's leadership. It is undeniable. We're seeing it across all sectors: business, government, and religion. You see President Ellen Johnson Sirleaf in Liberia. You see Michelle Bachelet in Chile. You see it in Rwanda, the very first country where over 50 percent of the parliament is made up of women. In the United States we are lagging a bit behind. Compared to other countries, we are in the sixty-ninth position for political leadership by women—clearly we have some work to do.

The second unstoppable trend is the communications revolution that is galloping across the globe, especially the developing world. We're seeing that even in remote and impoverished villages from Iran to South Africa, women are using their laptops and cell phones and connecting through cybercafés to communicate market information, to build influential movements, to report on violent crimes, and even to access healthcare information.

The third trend is the new consensus that investing in and educating young girls and women is the fastest way to solve global problems. When the U.S. Pentagon, as one benchmark, determines the security of a region by figuring out how many girls' schools are in that area, we know that things are changing. Businesses are starting to wake up because they're realizing that women control 85 percent of consumer spending in North America, thereby controlling market potential. And the *Economist* says, "Forget China, forget technology, it is women who are driving the global economy."

These trends create the perfect time for creating a voice like PulseWire, but this rhetoric is not truly translating yet. The resources getting to women's groups are still a trickle, and there are huge barriers because so many of these women's groups and programs are extremely isolated. At the same time, I think one of the biggest obstacles is our own internalized oppression. When you have experienced so much repression or abuse, particularly physical abuse, when one in three women worldwide have experienced violence or rape in some form, it's really hard for women to believe in their own selves. Not recognizing our own power may be the biggest thing that's holding us back.

As we began to build PulseWire, I thought, we'll empower women around the world. But people thought we were crazy, or, at least, that it was such a big idea that it wouldn't happen. I give huge kudos to our incredible team who kept up in the face of such skepticism. Also, I didn't realize the extent to which we ourselves would become empowered and supported through this process.

Soon after beta-testing (i.e., giving the site a trial run to make sure everything is in working order before going live), I met a woman who changed my life and also helped us think strategically about how Web 2.0 could be an empowering tool for women. Our editors called me over and said, "Jensine, there's a cell phone text message that's just come on, and it's from rural Kenya." It said: "Hello, hello, is anybody there? Please tell me I am not lost." We would go on to learn that this kind of question/need for reassurance is not unusual for many who are coming online for the first time. We welcomed her and asked her to tell her story, and it poured out of her: Leah was forty-three years old, she was HIV-positive, she was living in a very impoverished area, and she had five children. She was a six-foot-tall Amazonian woman who had weighed ninety pounds two years ago. But she had access to antiretroviral drugs and had a burning fire to live. What she wanted was to help all the women of her community, given that she had taken on the caregiving for over seventeen women who were dying of AIDS. She wanted to know how could she access information, how could she become a better leader.

Well, Leah made so many connections on our site that she began to be invited to travel to Mexico and to Canada to speak, as a rural woman, at AIDS conferences about her visions and solutions. She received some training as well as a donated laptop. She began to report on the ground when the election violence broke out in Kenya all around her—replete with gunfire and displaced children seeking refuge in her home when the violence broke families apart. It was a terrible time, reported to us firsthand by her and by other women of Kenya.

In the midst of this, Leah began to give us technical advice, saying, "Please consider sending text messages to our cell phones when someone is commenting on something we have written in PulseWire. Then, we will know we have a message and it's time to go to the cybercafé, because so often we have to walk thirty kilometers or more to get there. Thank you for considering this request on behalf of millions."

I began to realize that Leah had bigger visions for PulseWire than even I did. She would Skype me late at night. She now has 340 Skype contacts, many more than I do. Leah could see that I was up late working, and she would say: "Go to bed, Jensine, zoom off to bed, you must rest. Don't worry, I have the PulseWire flame. I'll carry it for you."

I can't tell you the relief I felt that this woman, who was going to more funerals in a week than I had been to in my whole life, was carrying this dream forward.

I drink my morning coffee with PulseWire, and I read it before I go to bed at night. It's like a sanctuary to me, but it's also like having the electromagnetic field of women's thoughts and minds cranked up in volume. We hear incredible stories from women like Sunita from Nepal, who is implementing microfinance in a village of five hundred. She says, "This is a revolution for me. Yesterday my neighbors didn't want to hear from me. Now the world is waiting for my voice." She is starting to organize women throughout pockets of her country— women whom she has met on our site. She is now meeting them in

Katmandu and mobilizing to create youth programs and build local community.

A group called the Rafiki "Friendship" Club was started by another woman in Uganda; it teaches illiterate women how to read and write by matching them up with pen pals in the United States. She started with twenty women. Now it's spread to two hundred in over four villages, and the women she's matching with from Europe and North America are flying there and meeting with these African women. They are embracing their newfound sisters and are being inducted into the tribes and starting local medical clinics and making films about all of it.

I think the most important component of what we're seeing is the sense of "I am not alone, and there's a community of women out there that can support me, whether I'm writing about my own experience with female genital mutilation or what it is like to stand in line for water at 4:30 every single morning." There's incredible strength in not feeling isolated, in not feeling alone.

When women feel confident and feel free from the shame of rape, they're going to be freed up to stop the rape of the earth. They will be our whistle-blowers. Women building solutions on the ground need massive infusions of resources, and this communications infrastructure will allow us hear where the resources need to go. Yes, the education of women is key, but it is not just about grammar or arithmetic. I'm talking about inner confidence, the leadership that comes from inner power. Once you connect women, they are going to teach each other this. They will empower each other, just as has happened for me.

Women's voices will come out of the shadows, and they will drive their own development and destinies. Global decision-makers will no longer be able to ignore us, and we will become a united and political economic force that will hold corporations accountable, overturn dictatorships, improve the lives of men and boys, and create a culture shift that values life over profit and destruction.

I hear it now. I hear women's voices storming the airwaves and ringing in the halls of Congress. I speak from experience: lifting and connecting women's voices is not about charity. Women's voices are on the rise, and we are on the brink of a volcanic eruption of human potential that will shift the world and empower us all.

Jensine Larsen (www.worldpulse.com), formerly a freelance journalist covering indigenous movements and ethnic cleansing in South America and Southeast Asia, is the founder of World Pulse Media. This global media source covers world issues through women's eyes. Its flagship, *World Pulse* magazine, as well as the interactive global women's newswire PulseWire.net, enables women worldwide to speak up for themselves and to connect to solve global problems.

PART THREE

*Reweaving the Web
of Connection*

15

Becoming a Blessing

Living As If Your Life Makes a Difference

Rachel Naomi Remen, M.D.

Rachel Naomi Remen, who is gifted with the soul of a spiritual leader, the compassion of a great healer, and the storytelling prowess of a sage, tells tales to heal the soul of our species. Transcending all of the false separations that divide us, Rachel's story is one that will stay with you, as its applicability in daily life is ubiquitous, deep, and enduring. She reminds us of just how interconnected we really are, and how mysterious and unforeseeable those connections can be. I learned from her that leadership may take as many forms as there are people to practice it.

NINA SIMONS

I want to share a few of the old wisdom stories about becoming a change agent—the wisdom that's been passed down in stories about how the world is made and how we can make a difference in the world. A good story is like a compass: it points to something true and invites us to orient our own direction according to it and perhaps to live a little better. The best stories remind us of who we are and what matters, of what we can do and what we can be. They help us see ourselves and the world differently.

So I'll start with a story from the fourteenth century. My grandfather told me this story almost sixty-five years ago when I was very small. He was an orthodox rabbi and a student of Kabbalah—the Jewish mystical tradition. So Grandpa was a flaming mystic, and he was also a wonderful storyteller. This is one of my favorite stories, the story Grandpa called "The Birthday of the World."

In the beginning there was only the holy darkness, the source of life. At some point in the history of things, the whole world as we know it, the world of a thousand, thousand things, emerged as a ray of light from the heart of the holy darkness. And then, perhaps because this is a Jewish story, there was an accident. The vessels that contained the wholeness of the world broke open, and the light of the world was scattered into an infinite number of sparks of wholeness that fell into all events, all organizations, all people, where they remain deeply hidden until this very day.

Now, according to my grandfather, the whole human race is a response to this accident. We are all here because we are able to discover the hidden wholeness in all of life's events, in all organizations, and in all people. We can tend it, and strengthen it, and make it visible once again. By doing so we can heal the world back into its original wholeness. In Hebrew this task is called *Tikkun Olam*—Restoring the World. Healing the world is a collective human task that involves everyone who has ever been born, everyone alive, everyone yet to be born. So according to Kabbalah, each one of us is a healer of the world.

Now, Grandpa was talking to a very little girl. I was four at the time, and I wouldn't have understood words like "restore" or "heal," so he used another language, which was a part of his own spiritual tradition. "Neshume-le," he told me, "you can become a blessing. You can bless the life around you." I understood this immediately because my grandfather blessed me all the time.

Every Friday Grandpa would light candles and speak to God. When he was finished talking to God, he would call me to him and place his hands on the top of my head. First he would thank God for making him my grandpa, and then he would tell God something about me that was true. Every week I would wait to find out what that was. If I had failed at something, he would appreciate how hard I had tried. If I had made mistakes during the week, he would mention my honesty in telling the truth. If I had slept for only five minutes without my night light on, he would celebrate my courage for being able to sleep in the dark. These few moments were the only time in my week when I felt safe and at rest.

My family of physicians and health professionals were always struggling to learn more and to be more. Enough was never enough. If I brought home a 98 on a test, my father would ask, "What happened to the other two points?" I pursued those two points relentlessly throughout my childhood. But my grandfather didn't care about such things. For him I was already enough, and when I was with him I knew with absolute certainty that this was so. My grandfather died when I was seven. At first I was afraid that without him to see me and tell God who I was, I might disappear. But slowly over time I came to understand that in some mysterious way, I had learned to see myself through his eyes. And that once we are blessed, we are blessed forever.

Many years later, when, in her extreme old age, my socialistic and agnostic mother began to light candles and talk to God herself, I told her about these blessings and what they meant to me. She smiled at me sadly and said: "I have blessed you every day of your life, Rachel. I just never had the wisdom to do it out loud."

When you bless someone you expand them; you offer them a place of refuge from everything that conspires to diminish them. A place of refuge is an opportunity for self-remembering. Often it is found in a relationship with someone who sees the hidden wholeness in us before we can. The future is determined by the potential of the present, the potential in each one of us. In this critical time in the human story, potential cannot be wasted. Those who uncover the hidden wholeness and potential in others, who are committed to witnessing it, believing in it, and strengthening it, may be the architects of the future of the world.

Here's another wisdom story, an American Indian legend about how change happens. Change depends on the hidden web of connection between us all. This web of connection can only be seen through the open heart. Most of us are so distracted, so busy, so separated from the world around us and the world within us, that we may never have noticed the web of connection between us. We may live so closed-hearted that we think we are alone. It is the responsibility of Grandmother Spider to remind us of the web of connection and strengthen it. I've always thought that she does this by telling us stories.

The web of connection confers great power on each of us to change the world around us. It confers on us the power to become a blessing to total strangers, people whose names we do not even know. Because of this web of connection, each of us has already blessed many more people than we can even imagine.

I have a friend called Elaine who is an expert on domestic violence and spousal abuse. She has saved the lives of hundreds and hundreds of people, mostly women, through her writings and her teachings. I was having dinner with her one night, and I found myself wondering how such a lovely and gentle person had become an expert in abuse and brutality. So I asked her. "Oh, Rachel," she said, "I used to be one of these women."

Then she told me that her first husband had been an abusive and violent man, but he had also been a pillar of the community. In public he had always behaved toward her as a perfect gentleman, so people had actually envied her life and her marriage. No one dreamed that her private life was a living hell. Like many abusers, he had told her the abuse was her own fault because of the stupid things she said and the stupid things she did. Over time she became so ground down that she actually came to believe that she deserved to be treated in this way.

All of this ended abruptly one day on a street corner in New York City, when she and her husband were there as tourists. As they were standing on a corner and waiting for the light to change, she looked across the street and saw a remarkable Art Deco building. Delighted, she turned to him and said, "Honey, look at that beautiful building." He, believing that they were alone, responded in the tone of utter contempt that he reserved for their private conversations. "Oh, that building there?" he said. "The one that anyone with eyes in their head would know is just like any other building on the street? You're such an idiot." She responded by falling silent, as she had done for years when he spoke to her in this way. But a woman standing next to him, a perfect stranger who was also waiting for the light to change, turned to him in disbelief. "What?" she exclaimed. "That's a perfectly beautiful building! She's absolutely right, and you, sir, are a horse's ass!"

Then the light turned green, and this total stranger crossed the street and went on with the rest of her life. But this was the moment that Elaine's whole life changed. In this moment, she suddenly understood that she had never deserved to be treated in this terrible way. In the blink of an eye, she saw what had been happening to her in seven and a half years of marriage, and she felt something completely unfamiliar rise up in her. She described it to me as a kind of certainty. Standing there on that corner, she simply knew that it would take time and planning, but she was going to be able to leave this man.

Now, this isn't a story about Elaine. This is a story about the stranger. Because if we were to go to New York City today and somehow find her and ask, "Excuse me, ma'am, have you ever blessed the life in anyone?" I somehow doubt she would say, "Oh, yes, twenty years ago standing on that corner and waiting for the light . . ." I think probably she'd say something more like, "What? Me bless lives? Do I look like a holy person to you?"

Everyone and everything has in it a dream of itself, a hidden wholeness. According to many of the world's wisdom stories, it is possible to collaborate with that dream, to strengthen it and make it real. This requires developing the eyes to see it and the ears to hear it, and the intention to serve it.

Befriending the hidden wholeness in the world is a way of life. My grandfather taught me a lesson about this when I was small. Grandpa never actually taught me anything. He would simply create the conditions so that I could discover for myself whatever it was he wanted me to learn. When I would run to him with my discoveries, he would seem to be surprised. "How *wonderful*, Neshume-le!" he would tell me. My grandpa wanted me to discover the hidden wholeness in the world for myself and to recognize my power to make a difference.

So one Sunday when he visited me, he brought me a little cup. I was very excited to see what was in it, certain it would be as magical as he was, but when he handed it to me, I saw that the cup was filled with dirt. I wasn't allowed to play with dirt and told him I was disappointed, but he just smiled. Taking me into the kitchen, he showed me how to put a little water into the cup. "Neshume-le," he told me, "if you put a little water into the cup *every day,* something may happen."

Now, this made no sense to me at all. At that time I lived on the sixth floor of an apartment building in New York City, and I had no context for what might happen if you put water on dirt. Yet grown-ups were always telling me things that didn't make sense. Cross on the green, not on the red. Why, when the red was so much prettier? But I loved my grandfather, so I promised him I would put a little bit of water in the cup every day.

The first week was easy. I was excited to see what might happen, but nothing did. So the second week was harder. When he came to see me again on Sunday, I tried to give the cup back to him, but he wouldn't take it. He just smiled and said, "Every day, Neshume-le." The third week was very hard. Sometimes I wouldn't remember to water the cup until after I'd been put to bed, and I'd have to sneak down into the kitchen in the dark and put a little water into the cup. But I didn't miss a single day, and one morning there were two little green leaves in the cup that hadn't been there the night before. I was simply astounded. I could not wait to tell my grandfather, certain that he would be just as surprised as I was. But he wasn't. What he said was, "Ah, Neshume-le, life is everywhere, even in the most ordinary and unexpected places." I was delighted. "And all it needs is water, Grandpa?" I asked. "No, Neshume-le," he told me. "All life needs is your intention and your love."

So perhaps the bottom line is this: We are born with the power to befriend the life around us and the life within us and heal the world. All life needs from us is our intention to care.

Have you noticed that none of these wisdom stories seems to be about anger? Perhaps anger isn't what's needed to change the world. Perhaps wholeness is rarely, if ever, the outcome of anger. Anger is just a demand for change. Often it's our first response when we see something unjust. It gets us involved, but when it becomes a way of life, it limits our power to make a difference. We can never solve the problems of this world by engaging with them at the level of the problems themselves. Or, in Einstein's words: "No problem can be solved from the same level of consciousness that created it." Anger and blame and judgment cannot heal the world or guarantee the future. *Then what is it that will sustain the world? What will allow the world to continue?*

Let me tell you the Jewish wisdom story that answers this very question, the legend of the Lamed Vov, which my grandfather also told me when I was very small. In Hebrew, *lamed vov* is the number thirty-six. "Neshume-le," Grandpa told me, "the world will continue only as long as there is a minimum of thirty-six people alive who are capable of responding to the suffering of strangers, people they don't even know. If at any time there should be fewer than thirty-six such people alive, the world itself will come to an end."

I was impressed. Who were these people? They must be famous people if the whole world depended on them. But no. Grandpa said, "No one knows who these people are, even they themselves don't know who they are. The Lamed Vov don't respond to the suffering of strangers because they know the survival of the world depends on it. They respond to the suffering of strangers simply because the suffering of strangers *matters*. So perhaps you, Neshume-le, are one of the thirty-six on whom the survival of the world depends."

I was an imaginative child, and this story made me worry. How did the Lamed Vov respond? What did I have to do? If the whole world depended on them, it must be something very hard. What if they couldn't do it? What then? "Grandpa," I asked, shaking a little inside, "what is it they're supposed to do? Is it hard?" He laughed and said, "They don't need to do anything, Neshume-le. They respond to the suffering in the world with compassion. Compassion for people whose names you don't even know is the foundation of the survival of the world."

I sometimes think this may be the most profound of the wisdom stories for us today. What if the sustainability of the world depends on each of us recognizing we may be one of the thirty-six? What if our own compassion for people who have a different language, a different way of talking to God, people who share with us only a common humanity, is the key to the future of the world?

Our culture places great emphasis on technology and science to create a better future for us. But the past years have showed us the limitations of science and technology and expertise to create a better world. We have the technology to build buildings that are 110 stories high, the science to make planes and fuel them to fly across the country in six hours and around the world in a single day. We can even enable people who are fleeing for their lives to talk to other people about it on their cell phones. Every one who owns a TV has seen how our expertise has enabled us to unleash incredible destruction on innocent people. It's become clear that our expertise has not made us whole, and it will not make the world whole either.

It's going to take something different to heal the world, something simpler and older and more accessible to us all. The future of the world may depend on each of us remembering to bless the life in others—even total strangers—and blessing people out loud. It may depend on remembering the unseen web of connection between us, and the power this gives us to make a difference in other people's lives. And ultimately it may depend on remembering that everything has hidden in it a dream of itself—that the seeds of wholeness and needed change are already present in all events and all people and every one of us, and that the wholeness of the world can only be restored one heart at a time.

Rachel Naomi Remen, M.D. (www.rachelremen.com), is clinical professor of family and community medicine at the UCSF School of Medicine and a nationally recognized medical reformer and educator who sees the practice of medicine as a spiritual path. Her professional formation course for medical students, The

Healer's Art, is presently taught annually by more than four hundred faculty in sixty-eight medical schools nationally and in Taiwan, Australia, Canada, Israel, and Slovenia. Dr. Remen is a master story-teller, the author of the *New York Times* bestseller *Kitchen Table Wisdom: Stories That Heal* and the bestselling *My Grandfather's Blessings: Stories of Strength, Refuge and Belonging.* She is the author of numerous book chapters and articles in peer-reviewed journals and public media and holds three honorary Ph.D. degrees. Dr. Remen has a fifty-five-year personal history of Crohn's disease, and her work is a unique blend of viewpoints from both the physician and the patient.

16

The Interactive Digital Mural

A Tool for Social Reconciliation from the Local to the Global

Judy Baca

As Judy Baca works with communities to honor and reclaim their histories of place, people, and planet, she creates murals to connect people with each other, with their lineages, and with the land. She masterfully combines her interests in cultural reclamation, ecological restoration, and human and societal healing. Her weaving of art, technology, and social skillfulness with her deep intelligence, heart, and worldview helps her leadership to effectively heal and transform people and communities while reconciling past and present with an inclusive vision for our collective future.

NINA SIMONS

This story begins with a river. The city of Los Angeles was founded on the banks of this river. There the first Tongva villages were formed in the shade of the trees that brought cooling to the arid desert landscape. The river expanded in the winter, contracted in the summer. The Tongva people moved with the river, and they accommodated its receding and expanding waters. Settlements were formed alongside their villages, the first missions and the first Spanish settlements. But in the 1920s, after a particularly bad period of flooding, our city fathers determined that the river had to be tamed. The river had overflowed its allotted space and destroyed valuable real estate, by then Los Angeles's most valuable commodity.

As a child, I watched as the river turned to concrete. I think I can trace the beginnings of my career as a political landscape painter to growing up alongside the Los Angeles River and watching its transition. I remember the moment when I came to the flood-control channel and stood with the Army Corps of Engineers' Aesthetic Recovery Division and looked down at the river. The forty-year-long project was complete: they had constructed a concrete channel for the river to run through for its entire length. The purpose of the new Aesthetic Recovery Division, though short-lived, was to deal with the concrete of the arroyos. They were eyesores. They left dirt belts on either side of the channels, and they divided communities.

The flood-control channels, of course, had many other serious consequences for the land. The concreted river deprived the aquifer of water replenishment through normal ground seepage and carried the runoff swiftly to the ocean, along with all the pollution from the city streets, which affected the Santa Monica Bay. In a sense the concreting of the river represented the hardening of the arteries and created disease in the land. It was apparent to me then, as it is today, that this decision to concrete the Los Angeles River would affect the people of the city for generations to come in subsequent planning and development decisions and a spiritual discord associated with the land.

What I saw was a metaphor. The hundreds of miles of concrete conduits were scars on the land. They were like the scars I'd seen on a young man's body in a Los Angeles barrio in my early work with the gangs of East Los Angeles. Fernando, my friend and mentee, had suffered multiple stab wounds in gang warfare. I asked him how he was feeling after the attack. "My wounds are healing," he said, "but my body is a map of violence." So together, we designed transformative tattoos in an effort to make the ugly marks into something powerful and beautiful. He loved to say he was my greatest artwork.

That day overlooking the channel, I dreamed of a tattoo on the scar where the river once ran, as a metaphor for healing our cities' division of race and class; I proposed the Great Wall of Los Angeles. I dared not speak aloud the words that I'm saying today: that the concreting of the river was an act of violence against the earth, and healing was needed for both the river and the people who lived along its banks.

I began to understand the notion of the land having memory because of my grandmother, Francisca, an indigenous woman who practiced healing in our family. She asked plants for permission before she took a cutting. She could make a dried twig grow. Everything had a place and a purpose in Francisca's world. Even what I thought were weeds growing by the water fountain she turned into exquisite vegetables with frijoles. She taught me that the distance between dreaming and making real is very small. Because of her teaching, I have tried to learn to listen to the land and to imagine for artists and for my students the notion of how we can excavate the land's memory.

Looking at the layers of meaning of the land, we start with its inherent nature. Might a valley site, for example, have been formed by a glacier? What is its current topography? Is it now agricultural fields, shopping malls, housing? All the land has a spirit. It is why every culture believes that it's important to preserve a place where a significant event occurred—in order to understand what happened there. The spirit in each landscape is made up of all its living elements, and that includes people, animals, and plants. As humans, we enter the land late. History does not begin when we come through the door.

For twelve years I worked with four hundred young people on the recovery of their histories, practicing a connection between each other across race, class, and gender differences. We worked to tattoo the scar— where the river once ran in the San Fernando Valley—with images that would remember our dismembered history. Lifelong connections were made there between all of us. The vehicle for this was art, and the result was the longest mural in the world.

I was an initiator as well as a participant. What I realize today is that I wasn't much different than they were. I came from the community surrounding the Great Wall, having grown up in the L.A. city school system not knowing my family's contributions, although I was university educated. I recovered my story along with them.

A relationship exists between the disappearance of the river and the people. If you can cause a river to disappear, how much easier is it to cause the history of the originating people to disappear? We painted 2,700 feet of mural, a half a mile of imagery on the river. We excavated our own stories and those of our families to recover our history, a history that had been left out of the history books. Hundreds of artists and scholars and members of the community contributed time, knowledge, and their own memories in the making of the long wall.

We painted the indigenous plants of the region and the stories of the original Tongva and Chumash people of the region and their relationship to the land, sea, and animals. In giant images we recorded the story of Mrs. Laws, whose refusal to move from her home in Watts changed the black covenants laws that controlled where African Americans and Latinos could live in Los Angeles. We showed the story of the more than half a million Mexican Americans who were deported in sweeps across California during the 1930s repatriations, despite their status as U.S. citizens. More than seventy thousand were deported from Los Angeles alone.

Today, the original children of the Great Wall are grown, and they are returning as alumni to work with another generation of Great Wall youths. I'm proud that the Great Wall has been declared a site of public memory worth preservation by the State of California's cultural and historical endowment. Sometimes we get it right. And they have funded us with $1.2 million in seed money to begin to repair the historic sections, some of which are thirty-three years old. This restoration is now in progress, along with new sections to be added by another generation of children of the Great Wall.

But as important as it is to remember and record the stories, it is equally important to remember the people who produced the work. Ernestine Jimenez is one of the four hundred young people who worked on the production of the mural. At the time, she was fourteen, pregnant, a gang member on drugs. She was what they called a throwaway kid, a person who would not benefit from this experience. I hired Ernestine.

Thirty years later, when she was forty-four, she was interviewed and asked about the meaning of the wall. This is what she had to say:

> The way I grew up, you fight through life. I was raised to believe you don't like nobody but your own race. Sometimes you don't even like your own race. In the beginning there was a lot of tension. I think everybody wanted to fight everybody, just the way they looked or the way they looked at them or the way they dressed. But after a time you just started getting to know that person as an individual instead of knowing them as you were taught to. Everybody became good friends. It took a lot of growing up. Also, I wouldn't have gone back to high school because I wouldn't have had a role model to push me to go. As long as I stayed in school, I could come back and paint the mural. This mural opened my eyes so much. When we painted the mural of the Holocaust, I met the people that had the tattoos on them, and I learned there was another world harder than mine. Now, even when I'm feeling down, I still walk by here and I thank God I did accomplish something in life.

One gang member at a time. Many of our youth's primary identification was affiliations as gang members of defined territories in a neighborhood where crossing a street to another territory could mean being shot by an opposing gang. But in our engagement with the river, we all hailed from the same street.

New segments are being developed today that draw relationships between the healing of the river and the people. Young people born in the '80s are developing a new Interpretive Green Bridge on the Great Wall to bridge the gap that the river has made between two communities. The new Interpretive Green Bridge will be constructed of river debris such as broken glass and plastic and will be lit by photovoltaic lights and solar panels. Visualizing upcoming connections between the history of the river and the people, we are putting another generation to work on reclaiming our history and tattooing the scar where the river once ran.

While my focus has been on healing our relationship to our land by reclaiming our past, my mural work has expanded to include imagining a positive future. For the last ten years I've been inviting other artists to work with us to produce an addition to a world-traveling mural on world peace called "The World Wall: A Vision of the Future Without Fear." Each country to which the work travels produces a ten-by-thirty-foot canvas mural to add to the traveling installation, which assembles into a one-hundred-foot-diameter circle, thus becoming an arena for dialogue. I'm asking artists to participate, not with large amounts of money, not with commissioning capacity, but as one artist to another with the question, "Can we dream together a vision of the future without fear?" What happens when we recover our stories and envision peace?

This traveling mural records the various countries' visions of the future and is now nine panels strong, with work from Israel and Palestine, Mexico, Russia, Finland, and Canada. Our central panel on "peace," painted by my team in Los Angeles, is an image derived from our conversations with Hopi elders. We could not envision peace as anything but the "absence of war" at first. What did peace look like? The elders said, "Peace is simple, Judy. It's about bringing the world into balance, the sun and the moon (male and female), the earth and man, and then maintaining the balance as an action: continually acting in that moment of struggle to maintain balance." In the struggle to achieve a world of peace, metaphors are a powerful path.

Judith F. Baca (www.sparcmurals.org), a world-renowned painter and muralist, community arts pioneer, and scholar has been teaching art in the University of California system (including at UCLA) for twenty years. She was the founder of the first City of Los Angeles Mural Program in 1974, which evolved into the now-legendary thirty-year community arts organization known as the Social and Public Art Resource Center (SPARC) in 1976. She continues to serve as SPARC's artistic director and focuses her artistic energy in the UCLA/SPARC Cesar Chavez Digital/Mural Lab.

17

Women, Plants, and Culture

Kathleen Harrison

Somewhere deep in our bones, or in our lineages, we understood how to commune with the plants, how to read their signals, and how to live in mutuality with them. As an ethnobotanist, Kat Harrison has lived and studied with many cultures, relearning how to bridge the languages of people and plants in time-honored, wise, and sensitive ways that will hopefully inform us as we move forward. As an artist, Kat has learned the great value of stillness and observation, which her leadership style embodies. Her quiet dignity and gentle nature reflect a strength through a softness that's accessible to us all.

NINA SIMONS

I have worked many years in the realm of people, plants, and plant medicines. In the 1970s, I spent quite a while in the Peruvian Amazon working with healers who used a spectrum of plants from the most subtle to the most powerful. Then I came back into my life in California and worked on many other botanical projects while raising a family. It was only in 1993, when I went back to the Amazon, that I completely *got* the idea of plant spirit. In fact, it was no longer an idea; it became a reality and got under my skin and changed my life substantially.

Since 1995, I've been able to spend time most years with a traditional healer's extended family of Mazatec Indians in the mountains of Oaxaca in Mexico. I've also been able to learn more about the indigenous Native Californian relationship to nature and plants. I see wonderful parallels in these nature-based societies in which everything is viewed as animate, and every species is a being. I think we too need to develop an intrinsic perception of this hidden reality to make the medicine that we grow, are given, or even buy more effective. Our culture has become extremely reductionist and materialistic in its worldview, so we need to learn from models that can help us understand spirit in nature and spirit in medicine.

The word *spirit* comes from the Latin for breath, so what we're talking about when we say a plant or a species has a spirit is that it draws energy from the universe and expresses it in a particular form. An ancient notion of many indigenous cultures around the world is that there were primordial beings on Earth before we came along. They interacted and had relationships, love affairs, conflicts, and exchanges of all sorts, and each of those beings became a species.

According to those creation stories, we humans, as complex and differentiated as we may seem, are one being, and each of the plant species that we use as medicine is also one being. I've learned from my native friends to talk to the spirits of those plant species. Whether you're ingesting a plant or growing it in your garden or passing it in the forest, you learn to speak to it as though it were a being you are meeting for the first time, or greeting it in such a way that indicates you know each other already. In its genes and in its form the individual plant carries a constellation of qualities, actions, and ways of interacting with us that we need to speak to. To know about it is a step, but to speak to it and listen to it is really what makes the medicine work, because then we are creating a relationship.

That's why in many parts of the world it is women who carry the knowledge of plants and gather the medicines. Women are good at relationship. As is the case for all female mammals, and most particularly female primates, one of our roles is to be nurturers and doorways for life. When children come through us, they are not ready to be in the world, of course, by themselves. In some species they are, but not in mammals, so we have to give them a deep level of attention and read their needs in a way that goes far beyond the verbal to help them survive and grow and thrive. We women have to be able to sense on all levels the needs of the beings around us.

We have this innate ability, no matter what or who we apply it to. These skills translate well into gathering plants. We can look back through the entire history of hominids and see that we survived and thrived by using our senses of taste, smell, touch, and sight to make clear distinctions between one plant and the next, between safety and danger, between all the different ways that the elements present themselves to us, and it was mostly women who perfected these skills.

I think it's important for women that we recognize and appreciate the inborn skills we have at paying attention to the natural world. These are the skills that allow us to call nature in through our hands to be food, to be medicine, to be magic, to be whatever the many forms of partnership are between the plant world and human women. Language itself can be an obstacle in this quest. It can be a sort of screen we get trapped behind, separating us from the multileveled reality on the other side of it.

I love words, but our culture has bought into the idea that there's an objective reality, and it's important to remember that this very objectivity is, in many ways, a cultural construct. I think we're becoming braver about showing what we know and not being held back by the inner judge that says, "Objectively speaking, that sounds crazy." Women are often more willing to trust their subjective experiences, dreams, and intuitions and are therefore more able to develop a relationship to the plant world that is spontaneous and deeply authentic.

I'm encouraged by what I've been seeing as a teacher. For years I've spoken at herbal conferences and taught at herb schools and in college classes focused on ethnobotany. Perhaps three-quarters of the attendees and students are young women who are studying to be herbalists or are called to work with plants in some way, often seeking a way to heal themselves or others. These young women give me heart because they're starting farther along than many of my generation who had to work through old cultural baggage just to begin to trust our instincts, to begin to know nature, to begin to rediscover that our roots were in the earth too. Now I see many women coming in with the assumption that they have the ability to be healers. I want to encourage this new generation to learn to listen to the ancestors and to the voices of all the species around us, however humble and subtle.

I'm a champion of subtlety. The subtler something is, the more you have to pay attention, and that's a good thing. Remember, it's not always the big, loud species that are the best teachers. Sometimes it's the little, quiet, humble ones.

Plants have the ability to transmit energy. Plants draw in and transform earth and water and nutrients and light and make their bodies out of them. The plant beings are manifestations of these forces being woven together, and we humans have relied on them to sustain us from the beginning of our evolution. In cultures that are close to the earth I see a recognition of the power of plants to hold and draw energy in a situation and to move it along, thereby changing it in a healing way. The plant world is constantly whispering to us, if we can hear it. There's been a long partnership between plants and, significantly, women around the world who know how to take plants with offerings and with prayers, and to use them to move energy. This is part of all our ancient traditions, and we're gradually returning to these ways.

These concepts are rooted in the way that native people—worldwide, those who are still close to the earth—live daily. In relating to the natural world, one of the most basic principles that they abide by is reciprocity. When, for instance, you meet a plant and you wish to take some of its body for medicine, you ask its permission and you explain why you need it, and then you give it something back. On this continent the ritual has long been to give tobacco, the most sacred traditional spiritual plant of the Americas, domesticated thousands of years ago by indigenous early Americans. I've thought about what is most valuable to people in our contemporary culture, and I think it's time.

Time is the thing that we feel we have the least of, that we value, so we can offer a plant our time if we want to ask something of it. The way we can offer it time is to learn about it, sit with it, and maybe grow it. But even if you're just purchasing some of it, try to learn about that plant's world—where it grows naturally, what it looks like, what it's related to. When we use a plant, we're communicating with the entire chain of experience of that species through its evolution.

Medicine, in the traditions I've worked in, is not just about chemistry. It's about that which heals. Many cultures talk about the songs that come through the plants. If you listen well to a plant that you have solicited as medicine, they say that you can learn its song, and that its song will be as effective a medicine as the plant material itself. That's when you've taken in that plant as your deep ally: when you can invoke its medicine without even necessarily touching or finding the plant. At that point you have access to the spirit of the medicine.

It has been part of my work to go to cultures that use sacred visionary plants in Mexico, Ecuador, and Peru and learn their mythology and sometimes their ceremonies. These traditions and these sacred plants have to be met with total respect. I ache when I think of any of these sacred plants becoming mere commodities in our culture. The commodification of spirit is really dangerous territory. We're generally not wise enough and openhearted enough to take that type of medicine on our own, for casual use, without a teacher or a healer who can show us how it really is medicine. But I can certainly grow a beautiful little peyote plant, and it can be a teacher to me, even if I just watch it flower and act as its guardian. A tiny little delicate plant can have a very powerful spirit.

Our culture still has a strange relationship to plants. For example, it's interesting that finally, after a very long period of denouncing cannabis, we've opened the dialogue enough to talk about it again as medicine, as it has been for thousands of years to many people, and little by little money has come forth to do studies. Formal studies have validated thousands of personal anecdotes in concluding that it actually relieves pain. There are so many receptors in the human brain for the active principles in cannabis that it is uncanny. When used with intention and gratitude and awareness, it can be a multifaceted medicine. It is our sister and ally in many ways.

I try to keep my eye on the big picture and observe how cultures vacillate in their appreciation and rejection of powerful plants and how fear and denunciation cycle around again to an appreciation of these plants.

We're in a time of such fierce denunciation of tobacco right now that we find it very hard to talk about its holy and sacramental properties. A plant in itself is not evil or good. Its effect depends upon how we use it and how conscious we are, and that's true of all medicine. Unconscious use of anything is damaging, and conscious use of anything can make it medicine, and this goes for food and all the other substances that we love and hate. Still and all, we seem to go through periods of demonizing aspects of nature that we don't understand.

Chocolate is another fascinating psychoactive plant. Chocolate pods are filled with beans that have been used as offerings; in Mexico they still are. People give them and other plants and seeds to the Virgin Mary or to the spirit of a mountain or the local gods. They give them things that they know will please them, and how could chocolate not please them? Some plants they burn as incense, and some they just lay in sacred places where water wells up out of the ground. They bring not necessarily flowers or spectacular-looking things but often more subtle gifts. You bring nature to nature because it shows that you have paid attention and understand reciprocity. You don't take without giving something, and then you're always grateful for what you get. That's medicine.

Kathleen (Kat) Harrison (www.botanicaldimensions .org) is an ethnobotanist, artist, and writer who researches the relationship between plants and people, with a focus on myth, ritual, and spirituality. She teaches for the California School of Herbal Studies, Arizona State University, and the University of Minnesota, specializing in tropical field courses. She has done recurrent fieldwork in Latin America for the past thirty-five years. As co-founder and director of Botanical Dimensions—a nonprofit foundation devoted to preserving medicinal and shamanic plant knowledge from the Amazon and tropics around the world—Harrison has helped support indigenous projects in Mexico, Peru, Ecuador, and Costa Rica.

18

The Okanagan Way

Jeannette Armstrong, Ph.D.

Jeanette Armstrong has been one of my greatest teachers. In her quiet and unassuming way, she offers traditional ways of relating—to each other, to the land, to the dream world, and to our creativity—that always reveal pathways to wholeness. The depth of her understanding of the interrelatedness of life—among people, plants, place, creatures, and the invisible world—helps me to notice what may be underrepresented or lacking in any collective. The value she places on hearing the dissenting voice is medicine for transforming the polarizing and oppressive structures we face. I believe her worldview has profound implications for transforming our cultural inequities and unjust systems.

NINA SIMONS

I grew up on a remote part of the Penticton Indian reservation in the Okanagan region of British Columbia, Canada, where I was fortunate to be born at home into a traditionalist family. Our first language was Okanagan, and we practiced hunting/gathering traditions on the land. I'm still immersed in that family. Growing up in a small community that was also fractionalized by colonization gave me some valuable insights. I have observed that the relationship we have with each other impacts what we do to the land. In other words, what we do to each other and how we look at each other, how we interact with each other, is reflected in what is happening to the land.

The land that I come from is dry and semiarid. It's considered the northern tip of the Great Basin desert, and the ecosystem there is very fragile, one of the most damaged ecosystems in Canada. Many conservationists and environmentalists are very concerned about the species that are endangered and disappearing in the Okanagan. Over the last century, extirpations have been happening there, some of which I've witnessed myself.

This has been difficult, because we grew up loving the land. We grew up loving each other on the land and loving each plant and each species the way we love our brothers and our sisters. This is the point I want to get across: a proper understanding of the land doesn't just happen as an intellectual process, nor as a result of needing to gather food and needing to sustain your bodies for health. It happens as a result of how we interact with each other in our families and in our extended family units and in our communities and in the networks outward with other people that surround us on the land. Those networks are extremely important parts of how we interact with the land and what happens to the land. The work I have to do in bringing health back to the land cannot be done without creating an understanding of this interrelatedness.

Our people organized themselves in a way that was very different from what I see happening on the outside. We love to go out to the land to gather, which I have done every year of my life and look forward to every year. We gather the foods that have given me life and have given my grandmothers life and have given my great-great-grandmothers life for many, many generations. What our grandparents said is that the land feeds us, but we must feed the land as well. What they meant was that we give our bodies back to the land in a very physical way, but we also do other things to the land. We live on the land and we use the land and we can impact the land; we can destroy the land. Or we can love the land and it can love us back.

In the Okanagan, our understanding of the land is that we're not just *part* of the land, not just part of the vast system that operates on the land, but that *the land is us*. In our language, the word we use for our bodies contains the word for land, so when I say that word, not only are my human abilities to think and to dream present in the word, but the last part of that word also means the land. Every time I say that word and refer to my body, I realize that I am from the land and that my body is the land. So one of the things that I was looking at in the development of our education program was to find a way to teach about how we, as a society, used to interact and to find a way to describe that, and distill that, so that this teaching can help in reconstructing our communities.

In the most basic sense, our use of the land relates to our need for food, for shelter, for clothing, and for many other things. These are things that we all need in order to live and breathe every day. Besides that, we need pleasure. We need to be loved, we need to have the support of our community and the love and care of the people who surround us. If I look around at how the land has been impacted by what I call the Western culture, I see an overuse of the resources by some people and a lack of access for others. There are people who cannot access even the basic things they need for their lives. They have no rights, while some people have an entitlement, a right to more.

When you look at the idea of democracy from that perspective, you can see there's something profoundly wrong with a hierarchical system in which people can exist within the idea that it's okay to have people sitting next to you or next door to you who do not have access to the same things that you have. A profoundly basic principle of our community is that everyone needs to have the same access to the basics and the same access to the enjoyment and pleasure of life.

One of the things I started to observe and understand was that how we interact with the land is also a function of how we approach each other and make decisions as equal human beings. So I examined the construct of how we make decisions. I looked at the traditional Okanagan decision-making process—I'm not saying that it works today—but elements of it are still present and have been carried forward because we are only two generations since colonization began.

One of the things I came to understand is that in our decision-making we have a word, *enowkinwixw,* which demands four things from us, and they all have equal weight. These are the needs of the individual in being an individual, the needs of family in being a family, the needs of community in being a community, and the needs of the living relatives on the land. We use that process continuously in an informal way in our community.

We can also engage this construct in a formal way. *Robert's Rules of Order,** for instance, is thought of as a democratic construct in which the understanding of democracy is that the majority have the decision-making power. From my perspective, embedded in that construct is an adversarial approach. It sets up a construct in which there is always going to be conflict. There are always going to be those people who are in the minority and those people who are in the majority and the subsequent oppression of the minority. I understand that is probably the easiest way to do things. But in terms of looking at what the outcome is in this country and on the land and globally, it seems to me that, systemically, we might want to rethink how that works.

From our native point of view, the minority voice is the most important voice to consider. It is the minority voice that expresses the things that are going wrong, the things that we're not being responsible toward, the things that we're being aggressive about or trying to sweep under the carpet or shove out the door. Our leaders would say that if we ignore the minority voice, it will create conflict in our community, and this conflict will create a breakdown that's going to endanger all of us. This conflict will impede or endanger how we think of ourselves as a cooperative unit, a harmonious unit, a unit that knows how to work together and enjoys being together and loves one another. If that happens, then the things that we need to do on an everyday basis for meeting each of the four needs start to break apart. I can see how that's happening today.

Robert's Rules of Order is the short title of a book containing rules of order intended to be adopted as a parliamentary authority for use by a deliberative assembly. It was first published in February of 1876.

We should be able to find creative ways to meet the needs of the minorities. Is it about economics? Is it about societal access? What are those minorities about? If we think about ourselves as human beings with minds and creativity, we should be able to take into consideration how we meet the needs of those minorities. The Four Societies process that we call *enowkinwixw* asks us to do that and tells us that if we can't do that in our community, our humanity is at stake, our intelligence is at stake. We can't call ourselves Okanagan if we can't provide for the weak and the sick and the hungry and the old and the people who do not have skills.

One component of the decision-making process is reserved for the land. We have people who are called "land speakers." We have a word for them in our language, which describes people who are the voice of the land and what it needs. I've been fortunate to be trained and brought up as a land speaker in my community. We also have people who are trained to be speakers for the children, for the mothers, for the elders, for the medicine people, for the water, for any of the components that make up our existence.

I, in my role as land speaker, have been trained by my elders to think about the land and to speak about the land. What that means is that I don't represent the people's view and I don't think of myself as an expert, but I do consider myself as one person who, continuously, must be responsible for decisions that are made, even the smallest of decisions. I am the one to stand up and ask: How will this impact the land? Usually elders or spiritual leaders are part of this group, and they ask questions like: How is this going to impact our food? How is this going to impact our water? How will a particular decision impact the land in which my children, my grandchildren, my great-grandchildren, will live?

Another part of the process requires people to look at relationships. There are people who stand up and say, "It is my responsibility to see how a decision is going to impact people. For example, how is it going to impact the children?" They are usually women or community policy makers or leaders, and they ask: "What are the children's needs? What are the elders' needs? What are the mothers' needs? What are the working people's needs?"

One part of our community is asked to think about the actions that need to be taken. They are usually men or community service leaders, and they stand up and say, "What are the things that need to be built? What are the things that need to be implemented, and how much is it going to cost?" All those important details need to be questioned and discussed. The actions are going to cause a number of different effects later on down the road. If we overuse something, or if we take too much of a resource, there are people who are asked to stand up to point that out to bring awareness to it and to remedy it.

There's another group of people that we call the visionaries in our community, the creative people. These are the artists, the writers, and the performers whose responsibility it is to bring in the perspective that there are creative approaches, that there are new ways we can look at things. They remind us that we should always make room for newness, because we need to be creative when we come up against something that we can't resolve and that we haven't come up against before.

All four of those components within community participate in a decision-making process. The process then becomes a different process than that of *Robert's Rules,* in terms of a democratic process. The process becomes not only participatory, but inclusive. This gives people a deeper understanding of the variety of components that are required to create harmony within community. When we include the perspective of the land and we include the perspective of human relationships, one of the things that happens is that people in the community actually change. They realize that the material things don't have a lot of meaning, and the desire to secure material wealth and fear of not having "things" to sustain you disappear. When you start realizing that people and community are there to sustain you, this gives the most secure feeling in the world. When you're immersed in that, then the fear starts to leave and you're imbued with hope.

This is the kind of work that I'm involved in at the En'owkin

Centre. I'm talking about reaching all the community, not just those who live in the Okanagan but people whom we reach outside of that. And not just the indigenous people, because at this time in our lives, our elders have said that unless we can Okanaganize those people in their thinking, all of us in the Okanagan are in danger. It sounds very simple, and yet it seems to be an overwhelming task, a huge task.

But I think about an auntie who asked me the other day, "Where are you headed off to now?" I said, "Oh, I'm going to speak at the Bioneers conference." She thought it sounded like a good thing and asked: "How did you get invited to do that?" I told her that I think it happened because I talk about some of the things that seem everyday and simple to us. These things that make sense to us also make complete strangers into loved ones who now are part of my extended community. For me, these people I meet feel the same as that auntie.

I think that's how we need to relate with each other so we can be the way we need to be on the land. Then the material things that seem to overwhelm us with demand—you need a new car, you need lots of money, you need power—will start to lose their hold on us. We won't need material things as our security blanket when we understand that the power is *us*: *we* are our security on the land, and *that* is what's going to sustain us.

We started a program to replant habitat with indigenous foods for some of the endangered species. We've got about ten thousand plants going now, for sustenance of ourselves and of endangered species. We find that the various people—our own community members and those coming from the non-native community, from the multicultural societies, from the senior people's communities—they all love going out there to gather the seeds and pot them and replant habitat. Our young people too are healed by this activity, the young people who are having such a difficult time. Just being together out there on the land has a healing impact.

It is how the land communicates its spirit to us, and it does this in an incredibly profound way.

Jeannette Armstrong, Ph.D. (www.enowkincentre .ca), a member of the Okanagan Syilx Nation, is a Canadian author and artist and executive director of the En'owkin Centre (the culture, language, and arts education institution of the Okanagan Nation) as well as an assistant professor of indigenous studies at the University of British Columbia–Okanagan. She is also a member of the National Aboriginal Traditional Knowledge subcommittee of the Committee on the Status of Endangered Wildlife in Canada, and she has also received a number of honorary doctorates and awards, including EcoTrust USA's Buffett Award for Indigenous Leadership.

19

Changing the World One Heart at a Time

Charlotte Brody, Rachel Naomi Remen, M.D., and Belvie Rooks

Each of these women has a wide-ranging and profound intelligence, and they are informed by the wisdom of their bodies, minds, and souls while leading from their hearts. Their inquiry into what causes people to change offers some surprising insights.

NINA SIMONS

Charlotte Brody: I grew up in Detroit, Michigan, where I was close with a couple named Jessie and Marty Glaberman, who were follow-ers of C. L. R. James.* What Jessie Glaberman, may she rest in peace, taught me is that she learned from this teacher to recognize that we're living in a pre-revolutionary society, and that we all live in the shadow of capitalism, oppression, and greed. So we have to forgive each other for being pre-revolutionary people. It's exactly because we walk around with the hope of the world in us, but buffered and battered and blocked

---

*Cyril Lionel Robert James (1901–1989) was an Afro-Trinidadian historian, journalist, socialist theorist, and essayist influential in the United Kingdom and the United States.

by all of the vestiges of imperialism, racism, capitalism, and all the bad -isms, that we have to forgive each other and really help each other do the best we can. Organizing for social change recognizes the light in each of us and finds ways to connect these lights and give them more brilliance in the world.

Belvie Rooks: We have a profound connection! In the 1970s, I was teaching at Federal City College (now called the University of the District of Columbia) in Washington, D.C., when C. L. R. James came to the United States from London. I was an activist with a daughter and an extra room in my house, and I offered him that room. He accepted, so I had the experience of getting to know a person whose work I had read and admired. His book *The Black Jacobins* is one of the most amazing historical books, a fluid, dialectical history of the Haitian revolution. One of the things he says in the introduction is that great men—and I told him I would have added women—make history, but only such history as is possible to make.

I had the great pleasure of having him grandfather my four-year-old daughter, Noliwe. He treated her with such respect. On the days I had late meetings, she'd come to school and wander up and down the halls, and she would hear Mr. James lecturing. She would hear his voice and would wander into his class, which was packed with two hundred people. Whenever she showed up at the door, he'd say, "Excuse me, ladies and gentlemen, Miss Rooks is gracing us with her presence. Miss Rooks, would you care to come in?" She'd go and sit in the very front row. She would listen to him lecture for about three minutes and get totally bored. He would notice and say, "Thank you so much for joining us. Ladies and gentlemen, Miss Rooks has gotten bored and will be leaving us shortly."

I loved that this man, whom people from all over the world came to see, never let a little girl come into his presence without stopping and acknowledging her. The last time I saw him in London, I let him know that my daughter was in graduate school at the University of Iowa, planning to be a historian. She now teaches at an Ivy League university. Her view of history is, I think, very much shaped by the fact that a person of this intellectual stature always took the time to listen to her and tell her how wonderful she was. This is all synchronicity, because I certainly did not know that Charlotte would begin our panel by talking about C. L. R. James, someone I had not thought about for a while. It's also interesting because earlier today I had been very affected by Rachel's stories about being seen by her grandfather.

Rachel Naomi Remen: In a funny way, the most important person in that classroom all those years ago was your daughter, because she was the one with the greatest potential, more than the older people. She's the one who really belonged to the future.

Belvie Rooks: Your grandfather stories made me think of my grandmother Carrie Kayton, who was raised in the Methodist tradition. She was the first real Christian that I knew. She practiced her faith by taking in women who had been beaten by their husbands and hiding them. I saw her give food and clothes to women and children. She gave little odd jobs to men out of work. All the things that Jesus is said to have talked about, I saw her practice. She had a huge heart and read the Bible constantly. I left that tradition when I was thirteen, but she used to quote a biblical verse (Esther 4:14) to me throughout my life when things got really hard. It says, "But for such a time as this you were born." I think about that a lot now, even though my grandmother has not been with me for over thirty years.

Rachel Naomi Remen: Yes. My grandfather died sixty-two years ago now. There's a great advantage in being a mystic—you can feel people's effect on you and their presence around you if they are no longer alive. In this room right now, thousands and thousands of people are participating even though many are long gone. I think immortality isn't about having your name on a building, but rather that we have had the intent to make a difference kindled in us by those before us, and we're going to pass that forward. A hundred years from now, there'll be a room like this full of people, where no one will know our names, but our intent to make a difference in the world will be as alive in them as it is in us. The lineage of service, which started at the very beginning of the world, goes on forever, as long as there are people. It is passed from hand to hand and from heart to heart.

Charlotte Brody: We're speaking of the web of connection. Let's talk about how we practice reweaving this web. We have lots of expressions for it. I like "I've got your back" as an expression. I like the idea that there are other people whose intention is to protect my intention. I like the idea of solidarity, which is almost an archaic word, but I like that in Jobs with Justice,* the idea is that you sign up to show up for somebody else's struggle, that twice a year you'll show up for someone else's rally, someone else's picket line. I like it in part because it's tactical; it recognizes that occasionally we need more people to be visible than we might organize with every day. But I like it more because if we really can live in the web of connection, then it's okay that I'm not doing everything. I'm not doing health care reform, which I care deeply about, and I'm not working to stop the war in Iraq, which I care deeply about. I can do a piece, knowing I'm part of a web of connection in which other people are also doing a piece. Between all of us, we're moving it all in the same direction.

Rachel Naomi Remen: In a certain way, perhaps we're all profoundly *a part of* the same work. I think we're strengthened by that.

Belvie Rooks: I believe that we're all part of what Martin Luther King Jr. called "the beloved community." A month ago, I attended a small gathering and retreat with about thirty people at Alex Haley's farm in Tennessee, which is now run by the Children's Defense Fund. The intention was to revisit Dr. King's vision of the beloved community and explore its relevance in the context of today's reality. I had an opportunity to sit with people who had been in the civil rights movement and worked directly with Dr. King. There were people like Bernice Johnson Reagon of Sweet Honey in the Rock fame, who started out as a freedom singer for the civil rights movement, and Dr. Vincent Harding, who documented that struggle and was also the principal architect of

---

*Jobs with Justice is a campaign to support the struggles for workers' rights. It can be referenced at www.jwj.org.

Dr. King's famous "Why I Oppose the War in Vietnam" speech. There were also young environmental and social justice activists. We were of every color and description, young and old.

I was able, in that small circle, to give voice to the grief that I've been feeling, due to the fact that I'm working on a film project with a young man from Watts who, in the short two years that I've known him, has been as a peacemaker to more funerals for young people killed in his neighborhood than I have attended in my entire life.

When I was in the retreat, I realized that I was feeling this deep sorrow and sadness for the children of the planet, and I broke down. I started to cry amid a presentation I was to make, and it turned out to be a very important moment in the gathering, because all I could do was cry, and all Bernice Johnson Reagon could do was sing. When Bernice sang these songs from our elders that lift you up, everybody started crying. Afterward, this young man from Detroit came over to me. He was a beautiful dreadlocked African American, and he said: "I want to thank you. I've been to so many funerals and I have not been able to cry for ten years." He had not cried since he was a boy.

Rachel Naomi Remen: I think it's dangerous not to cry. I think it's dangerous to read your newspaper and go on. I think that there are two ways that the heart expresses itself in this world—one is with joy and the other is with sorrow, and both mean that your heart is still alive in you, and it's still responding, in spite of everything. To have you sitting with us with your heart open is inspiring, Belvie. I see you as a kind of role model of what's needed in this world. We need to cry. I think that's where we find the strength of our intention.

Charlotte Brody: Celinda Lake, who is an extraordinary woman from Montana and a pollster who's been doing polling and focus group work for many years, says that for the first time in her polling life, more than half the American people express their concern and fear that their children's lives will be worse than theirs. I think that's worth crying about. I think that part of the organizing we need to do is crying about that and figuring out what in the hell we're going to do about that, one step at a time.

I'm a first-generation American. My parents came over from Europe after World War II, and I lived the American dream. My parents believed it and they made it work and they then tried to pass it on to other people. I'm the first person in my family to go to college. I grew up in Detroit and the United Auto Workers kept tuition at the University of Michigan affordable. My life is better than my parents' lives were, and their lives were better than their parents' lives were, even with the Holocaust.

It is such an important story that people are afraid their children will be less secure, that the economy won't work, that access to healthcare will be even worse than it is now, that the environment is in crisis. It's our job to say, as Belvie did, "Okay, let's all take a deep breath together and live in the sorrow of this, live in the part that isn't about blame, but feel the anger that can help us figure out how to get out of it."

Rachel Naomi Remen: Most people access their feelings in layers. Very often the top feeling, just below the surface, is anger, which is much easier to feel because you can feel pretty self-righteous about it. You can feel that you are a better person than whomever it is that you're angry at. It's an easier feeling for the ego, but it's not as true a feeling as the sorrow, which is the next layer down. Because once you finish expressing your anger, you're going to have to face that sorrow. And under that is usually the most painful feeling of all, fear. Mad, sad, scared. And under that is the intent to act to make a difference.

Anger never really sustains the conviction that says, I stand for X and I will stand for X as long as I live. The anger is not rooted in our very nature and our deepest sense of how life needs to be. Anger is usually *against* something, not *for* something better.

Charlotte Brody: It feels to me like when the identification with injustice that can be anger turns to blame, the truth becomes a lie, because in the self-righteousness, I lose the forgiveness for myself for not being perfect. When it's all "I'm right and you're wrong," it's always a lie, and you can't figure out the strategy out of a complicated, knotted lie.

Belvie Rooks: That's very interesting. When you spoke about blame and judgment and why it was important not to engage in blaming, what came to mind for me was something that Bishop Tutu had said coming out of the truth and reconciliation process in South Africa. He described a very polarized kind of reality based on race. He said that in this process, mostly what people talked about is the reconciliation part, but the part that didn't get talked about as much was the wounded part. In the context of South Africa there was a racial divide, where the white people in South Africa were wanting to get to the reconciliation part, and the black majority, who had suffered tremendously, felt the need to stay with the wound a little longer, to go deeper, so that this wounding could be expressed, heard, and healed. That's a question to live with: How do we hear "the other" in a universe that's alive and interconnected, yet the very idea of "other" is a socially constructed reality that we inherit as part of the air we breathe?

Bishop Tutu said something else insightful in terms of a healing process. Often when a wound scabs over, what is necessary is to go through a painful process of removing the scab and pouring on what he called the healing balm of attention, love, and forgiveness so that the real healing can occur.

Rachel Naomi Remen: And that's where the courage lies, yes. I think that what you're saying is profound, because without the process you're talking about, there is no true healing. If a person experiences his or her wound not as a victim but simply as a witness, then it allows the other person in the relationship to recognize his or her own wound that allowed this to happen. Instead of having a perpetrator and a victim, what we have are two profoundly wounded people. In recognizing that relationship, a true healing and true forgiveness can begin, because we each need to forgive ourselves as well as forgive the other person.

Belvie Rooks: There's something about looking at the shadow side of who we are, in the face, fully and without flinching. It's one of those areas where I lack courage. For instance, I never could look at those photos of lynched black men hanging from trees. I always closed my eyes. Unfortunately, that image is so deeply etched in the American psyche, it's almost iconic. Throughout the South, plantation owners would force black families, often at gunpoint, to view the body the next day while it was still hanging. Even the children were forced to look. The message was a very strong one: this is what could happen to you if you step out of line.

So in a way, I was claiming my own power by my refusal to have that image stamped in my consciousness. But often I would peek, and then feel complicit somehow in the murder just by being an observer. I was always struck by the carnival atmosphere. Often, there's a little girl watching. I would always construct a story about this girl, trying to protect her. What on earth would she, as a child, be thinking? What did it do to her soul?

When I saw the photograph that was taken at Abu Ghraib, of the young woman from Virginia who had these Iraqi men on a rope, the face of that young woman and the face of that young girl in the lynch mob merged for me.

Rachel Naomi Remen: I connect what you are saying to the first story you told of your daughter sitting in the classroom. I believe the most important person in the picture is the little girl. And it's an open question: Does she become the woman holding the Iraqi prisoners on a leash? Or is her soul set on fire? Is she the one who will make a difference?

Charlotte Brody: If she has one person, one family member, one grandfather, one teacher who affirms the holy spark in her, imagine the emotion. Whether you're a four-year-old or you're a grown man in that picture, you're repulsed and shamed and horrified, and you're told that those are emotions you need to diminish. It was a picnic. People baked cakes and came to lynchings. I feel so strongly that we have to tell those stories too. Unless we own our own history and how all of us got here, we'll never reweave the web of connection between us.

Think about that Billie Holliday song, "Strange Fruit." That was a very popular song. So, here it is in the mid-1950s, the era of the gray flannel suit, and here is this profoundly beautiful song about lynching that becomes part of the popular culture. In a way, we've gone backward. The Civil Rights Act passed, we got a little affirmative action, so we don't need to talk about the oppression and the pain of African Americans anymore. We treat history as disposable. Even in social-change networks, we don't tell the story as complicated as it actually was.

Belvie Rooks: Some of us came from Ireland, Russia, the Holocaust, the transatlantic slave trade, the Trail of Tears, the internment camps. We can't ignore the suffering that got us here. We need to create space for the grief and acknowledge that this is not weakness. The operative thing, of course, is that we are here now—together.

Charlotte Brody: In a way, that's what art is for. Art is supposed to find that one little piece of numbness that has a jagged edge and pull. Music, dance, art museums—those people that did all that fabulous work are trying to reach us in our numbness and help us reconnect.

Rachel Naomi Remen: Being numb to suffering doesn't make us happy, it just leaves us numb. I think it is all about practice. It's about building the capacity, the habit of remembering yourself, remembering your heart.

But really, it's the idea that you have to face things alone that makes things intolerable.

Charlotte Brody is a registered nurse and the director of chemicals and green chemistry for the BlueGreen Alliance, a national strategic partnership between labor unions and environmental organizations dedicated to expanding the number and quality of jobs in the green economy. Formerly national field director for Safer Chemicals, Healthy Families, the director of programs for Green for All, and the executive director of Commonweal, Brody was also a founder and executive director of Health Care Without Harm; the organizing director for the Center for Health, Environment, and Justice; the executive director of a Planned Parenthood affiliate in North Carolina; and the coordinator of the Carolina Brown Lung Association.

Rachel Naomi Remen, M.D. (www.rachelremen.com), is clinical professor of family and community medicine at the UCSF School of Medicine and a nationally recognized medical reformer and educator who sees the practice of medicine as a spiritual path. Her professional formation course for medical students, The Healer's Art, is presently taught annually by more than four hundred faculty in sixty-eight medical schools nationally and in Taiwan, Australia, Canada, Israel, and Slovenia. Dr. Remen is a master story-teller, the author of the *New York Times* bestseller *Kitchen Table Wisdom: Stories That Heal* and the bestselling *My Grandfather's Blessings: Stories of Strength, Refuge and Belonging*. She is the author of numerous book chapters and articles in peer-reviewed journals and public media and holds three honorary Ph.D. degrees. Dr. Remen has a fifty-five-year personal history of Crohn's disease, and her work is a unique blend of viewpoints from both the physician and the patient.

Belvie Rooks (greenglobal.heart@gmail.com; www.growingaglobalheart.com) is a writer and educator whose work weaves the worlds of spirituality, feminism, ecology, and social justice. She is cofounder of Growing a Global Heart, a project to plant a million trees along both the West African transatlantic slave route and the Underground Railroad, as a way of combating global warming while honoring and remembering the millions of unnamed, unheralded, and unremembered souls who were lost during the slave trade.

20

Embracing the Other

Cultural Diversity and Resilience

Kate Kendell

Kate Kendell has long been a leader in the LGBT (lesbian, gay, bisexual, and transgendered) community, and she taught me what courage, curiosity, perseverance, resilience, and patience it takes to be effective in a long-term struggle. This lucid story is about her mom, and what it's like to walk in her shoes. She speaks about taking a stand to confront injustice at the most basic human level, and addressing social prejudice and "other-ness" by connecting across differences through practicing empathy, being able to sit with our discomfort, and looking beneath our beliefs and opinions to each other's core humanity in order to collectively create a world that's safe, fair, and equitable for all.

NINA SIMONS

I approach the topic of "embracing the other" from two different perspectives.

The first perspective is as a white woman of European descent, a member of the dominant culture, privileged by class, race, and education, and walking in the world carrying that privilege as an individual committed to social justice. Often many of us who are white progressives embrace the other, particularly our brothers and sisters of color, the way an overzealous aunt embraced us when we were young—a little too forcefully and with an enthusiasm that was not entirely welcome. We knew this aunt loved us, but we wished she would back off just a little bit. But perhaps because of our own guilt, or our own desire to demonstrate our bona fides as antiracist allies, we can often come off, to the recipient of our embrace, as being inauthentic.

My caution for those of us who are white progressives is that this embracing of otherness around race must be motivated by a deeply rooted commitment, regardless of the difficulty, rather than driven by a patronizing sensibility or by guilt or by fear of rejection. Whether it's a one-on-one relationship or part of a broader movement, our commitment to antiracist work has to come from within. Because if we are approaching that relationship from a truly authentic place of trying to dismantle our own racism (having been raised in an absurdly racist culture), our embrace of the other will manifest itself eventually without us feeling we have to prove it.

I think there are many instances where we, as white queer progressives—because this is what I personally know the best—make serious mistakes. For example, when the mayor of San Francisco, Gavin Newsom, began issuing marriage licenses to lesbian and gay couples in San Francisco in 2004, we were right there at ground zero. The mayor's office called our office, the National Center for Lesbian Rights, to tell us they were considering doing this, and it was truly the most emotional, heady, incredible, fascinating time.

It was perhaps the first time I felt part of a true grassroots, community movement, happening right before my eyes. It began on February 12, 2004. When marriage licenses began being issued, couples by the thousands surrounded City Hall. Many stood in the rain for hours. Strangers brought dry socks and coffee and flowers. It came to an end on March 12, 2004, when the California State Supreme Court ordered the city to stop (and the next day we filed a lawsuit to win the right to marry statewide). But over the course of that month, it seemed the entire Bay Area and much of the nation came together and celebrated what was happening: this moment of justice and equality. It was powerful and profound for the folks who were there.

What was reflected in that line of people waiting for licenses at City Hall showed a much greater diversity than what got televised around the country, although not as much as there could have been and should have been had there been a conversation about what marriage means and who it benefits. What ended up in the press were statements from mostly white lesbian or gay couples who were saying things like: "This is what it must have been like when African Americans won the right to vote," or "I feel like Rosa Parks must have felt." Gavin Newsom was compared alternately to Rosa Parks or to Martin Luther King. I read these statements in the press and had to fight the urge to gather all the copies up and destroy them so no one could read them. I knew how these statements would sound to black folks and others who had endured white supremacy and racism.

I understand the impulse to appropriate those images and icons, which have cultural significance and the imprimatur of societal support. The African American civil rights movement was a great thing and is a source of understandable inspiration. But the lesbian, gay, bisexual, and transgendered (LGBT) civil rights movement is not the same as the African American civil rights struggle. Our histories are too disparate and diverse. The history of slavery and Jim Crow are experiences that the LGBT movement has never endured, and appropriation of landmark civil rights leaders is seen too often as dismissive of the depth and damage of racism in this country.

But it is all too easy to make these simplistic comparisons. I have done this myself. After the 2004 election, I was so depressed that it was all I could do to crawl down the stairs into the kitchen to pour myself a cup of coffee. I said to my partner of twelve years, Sandy Holmes, who is African American: "Oh, I can't bear it. We should go to Canada." She looked at me and said, "Hmm, so you think you're the first people this has ever happened to?" Her point was clear: In every fight for justice there are some very bad days, there are defeats, setbacks, attacks. But you don't accept defeat. You pick yourself up and keep fighting. She reminded me of what we're in, and why it's called a struggle. Whether it's queer issues or whether it's immigrants' rights issues or environmental rights issues, we're in a struggle for the soul of this country.

I do think there is much that white people generally and white queer people specifically can do to foster meaningful alliances and ensure that this embrace of the "other" feels more authentic and welcome. But we do have to understand that the interaction will always lack some integrity because of how we're able to move in the world based on our privilege.

Particularly as white LGBT folks, we must always be mindful of our passing privilege. Even though I walk like a linebacker, people usually see me as heterosexual, given that we live in such a heterosexist world. I think there are many white LGBT folks who move in the world in the same way. Most folks we come into contact with don't know of our sexual orientation unless we tell them. This passing privilege is with us all the time, whether we want it or not. On the contrary, most folks of color do not enjoy passing privilege based on their race.

Most LGBT folks never have to deal day to day, in every interaction, with how someone would treat us if they knew we were queer. We get to choose when we're going to disclose our sexual orientation or gender identity and when we're not. That in and of itself undermines our ability to be authentic partners with folks of color. It can never be the same unless you're going to wear a badge on your chest and deal every moment of every day with the dominant culture's reaction to you. But recognizing the responsibility and the fact that it exists is something. In this culture, it might be, some days at least, as much as we can do.

The second perspective that I have on the issue of embracing the other is as a lesbian—a radical feminist lesbian—for many, many years. I talk about it everywhere I go. I get paid for being a lesbian. It's the first thing many people know about me. Given this part of my identity, the "others" in this instance are those who oppose my equality, those who see me and my community as not deserving of full dignity and legal equality.

To use the hugging analogy again, in this instance the embrace of the other can be like hugging a porcupine. The reality is that I don't want to embrace those "others" because those others aren't just like me, and I don't have common ground with them. I'm an environmentalist, they are loggers; I'm committed to racial equality, and they are just idiots and not very thoughtful; or I'm a lesbian, and they say I should not exist and that my identity undermines the fabric of this country. If these "others" could erase me and the people I love and my family out of existence, they would do so. Because it feels so personal, I don't want to embrace them. It feels like they're bad, they're wrong, and they stand for everything I hate.

What I have learned over the course of doing this work for almost ten years now as the executive director of the National Center for Lesbian Rights is that if I live in that place, I'm my own other, and I'm my own worst enemy. If I live in that place, I'm undermining the exact vision that I have for what this world can and should be, my view that people can be different and still valuable and good, and just because they're not there doesn't mean I can't be an example of where they should be.

Where I draw inspiration for trying to hold this vision is from my mother. I was raised Mormon and my mother was devoutly Mormon right up until she died, and yet she was my most ardent champion. When I came out to her, I was nineteen and so afraid of what her response would be. I was afraid she would reject me. Most of all I was afraid I would disappoint her, and she would make that very visible to me and verbalize to me how disappointed she was in me. When I told her, halt-ingly, I paused, and she didn't respond right away. Immediately I wanted to fill the void. I said, "I'm sorry. I'm worried about your reaction. I'm afraid you're going to be so disappointed. I'm really scared to have this conversation." She said, "Honey, I'm not disappointed. I'm not mad. What matters to me more than anything else is that you're happy." She never wavered from that position of unconditional acceptance of me.

Fast-forward to just a couple of years ago. My mother suffered her second stroke in ten years, a very serious stroke. I flew out to Utah. I was worried I wouldn't make it in time. I did, and there followed many, many days and weeks with me flying back and forth, during a pretty arduous recovery. One day while I was there, the speech therapist came to her for speech therapy and asked her what would normally be some very simple questions: "Afton [my mother's name], how many children do you have? How old are your children? Do you have grandchildren? What are their names? Where do they live?" Then she asked: "Tell me what your children do for a living, like Kathy here. Why don't you tell me what Kathy does for a living?" I was thinking that this was going to be fascinating. Keep in mind, my mother struggled through all these answers and got some things right and some things wrong. The stroke affected her ability to verbalize and put it all together. But in answer to this question, she looked at me and looked at the speech therapist and she said, "Oh, what Kathy does is very important. She takes care of all the lesbians and gays in the world."

To which the speech therapist said, "Well, that's an awfully big job."

The legacy of my mother, who died two years ago on October 30, is to embrace the most difficult other, the other that would deny my existence, the other that would make me feel dehumanized and demoralized. Even though I was "other" to her, my mother embraced my otherness in such an authentic and open and committed and inspiring way, the least I can do is to honor her openness and her love by trying to have some measure of such openness to everyone else. In that way, I honor her life, her legacy, and my own vision for what is possible in the world.

 Kate Kendell (www.nclrights.org), a former corporate lawyer, then Utah's first-ever ACLU staff attorney, has since 1996 been the executive director of the San Francisco–based National Center for Lesbian Rights (NCLR), a progressive, feminist, multicultural legal center devoted to advancing the rights and safety of lesbians and their families and other oppressed members of the queer community through direct litigation and advocacy. She has done hundreds of interviews with dozens of the most prominent national print, electronic, and Web media and is very active in fostering alliances among other community and advocacy organizations committed to social justice.

21

From Mourning into Daybreak

Nina Simons

*We've forgotten how to mourn. Lost the art of grieving. No one
keens anymore.*
*Women in Greek tragedies knew how, but these days, we
medicate.*
*We veer away from the depths, and so we rarely ever see the
peaks.*
*Now we have become an unfinished circle—a culture caught
recycling our wounds*
because we don't acknowledge the pain, grieve our losses,
and complete the cycle of mourning.
How will we ever see daybreak without mourning?
*If we don't feel what hurts, surrender to its demands, speak the
wound,*
how can we really begin to heal?
I understand young people's prolific piercings now,
black rings and claw-like ornaments jutting through their skin.
*Wanting to wear some mark of realness, courage, their
willingness to feel pain.*

It's a modern-day sun-dance, dancing to awaken the world.
Proof they are not to be counted among the anesthetized,
among those lulled into false security.
Proof they are unlike those who have been coaxed by conflating
climbing a ladder with being held in a web, or
distracted by the illusory fulfillment of acquisition.
When my father died, I felt the rock I stood on suddenly gone,
    my self in free fall.
I was warned that it might take a year for me to heal.
It was at least that, and it was longer.
I was grateful for the crystalline expanse of time I permitted
    myself.
I entered expanded elastic months of feeling transparent,
of squinting at the striking brightness of colors, line, and light.
I oscillated between emptiness and attunement—
the tenderness of my tears for him always only a breath away.
I was appalled to discover our illiteracy toward death,
and envied the Japanese tradition of wearing a black armband
    for a year
following the loss of a loved one,
so that everyone knows not to treat you in the usual way.
The tattoo I got that summer—permanent art marking my
    impermanent body.
A gift to myself—the pain a strange kind of prayer,
the hand of Botticelli's Venus reminding me of her invisible
    presence,
making good my promise to remember the hand of the feminine
always over my heart, having my back.
A huge crow swoops to meet me, his large beak stuttering open.
He croaks his hello, frog-like.
Perhaps he's drawn by the bones the dogs have left 'round,
    carrion for his dinner.
But it's me he's focused on, coaxing me into dialogue.
When I respond, he flies closer, perches to stare at me.

Beady black eyes glow fiery against shiny indigo feathers.
He caws in clusters of three, his wings inflating with air upon
    each inhale,
Cccaaaawwww, cccaaawwww, ccccaaawwww.
My responding calls intrigue him, and we converse.
An arc of connection cuts through the apple crisp autumn air.
He pauses, turning his head and beak to an improbable angle
to suck water from the pool puddled in the birdbath.
I learned about duality from my father, a man whose lionheart
    was far too tender
for all the deaths his love suffered in its youth.
He was a Jewish man who loaned out his collection of Santa
    Clauses
to a different shopkeeper each year, so that his whole West
    Village neighborhood
could enjoy the wildly diverse and neighborly abundance of
    them.
His voice was always tentative, feelings muffled to lessen
    the risk he took in expressing them—his losses of love
    transformed into fearfulness of losing face.
But felt, his affection was a soothing bath that made everything
    safe,
the sun I basked in when I was small.
Warm arms I could count on—except for those contracted moments
when the shadow of loss overtook him.
Isn't it strange, how unspeakably beautiful life becomes
    whenever death draws near?
It hovers close now, all the time, with extinctions everywhere,
eighteen hundred species disappearing daily—my mind reels at
    it, staggering.
The tundra melting, trees tilting drunkenly as they lose their
    ground,
entire cultures losing their lifeways, the terrain too erratic for
    hunting anymore.

Who mourns these losses?

To enter that one-ness, the kinship of the crow, we must first feel the pain.

When I knew I'd never have a child, I vowed I'd have myself.

I wept with relief when the wise man told me

I had more children to care for in this life than I could if I had my own.

How can we close the circle, complete the cycle, and not go mad with grief?

Afraid I'll start wailing, I rock inwardly and don't stop.

My body moves with the sadness in waves that offer comfort.

Rocking helps to still my chattering mind.

How can we grieve for the vividly colored corals bleached white,

for the elephants brutally hunted for their tusks,

for all those flyers, nesters, and crawlers whose habitats have been logged

to make mail-order catalogs, phonebooks, and newspapers?

The crone within me wants to shake us all awake, screeching: Don't you get it?

This is no time for small talk

This is a time for myth making

This is a time for epic poetry

This is a time to tell the tales of life, love, and resilience

that will become our compass for the days ahead.

A time to remember the grace and celebrate the magic

that infuses and informs this world.

We live on the only planet we know of where the sun and moon appear the same size.

The only planet where an eclipse is possible.

Doesn't that seem like instructions to you?

To awaken from this self-induced slumber, to emerge from this contracted isolation,

we've got to drink down the darkness and dive to our deepest fathoms.

Peel off our fancy garments of presumed protection,
to land at the bottom, naked, cold, and bruised, with nowhere
   to go but up.
Time we shed the venom that got us here, the twisted rage of
   blame and shame,
And choose instead the anger that rises, pure and clean, up
   through our feet,
That draws us to our full height, knowing what must be done,
clear about what has to stop, igniting us to stand for what we
   love.
How else can we begin the healing?
The web that holds our world together is tattered,
And all our hopes and dreams are suspended in it.
No sutures, butterfly closures, or Elmer's glue can fix it.
Only our tears can begin to mend its torn strands,
tears and giving ourselves to feeling, loving, and losing.
Mourning how much is dying, mourning so that the light can
   return.
The revolution must have dancing; women know this.
The music will light our hearts with fire,
the stories will bathe our dreams in honey and fill our bellies
   with stars.
The interlacing of our souls will renew our humanity.
Our rhythms will merge with the heartbeat of the Earth.
What breaks the mourning open for me?
It shines through my connections, my friends, my kin.
Some that are human, and some that are not.
I soar in the sea, glide stealthily among sea turtles,
swoop circles over snowpack, eagle shushing.
I laze lizard-like on warm boulders amid rushing rivers,
slurp oysters gathered fresh from warm, moist sand.
I am lifted by the courageous uprising of women, and girls,
and by the emerging voice of the feminine within us all.
Together, leading from our hearts first,

we may yet restore balance and heal ourselves whole.
And I am strengthened by my kinship with the land,
with the high desert hills of northern New Mexico.
Her mountains first called to me twenty-five years ago,
and we've barely stopped talking since.
She reminds me of a time when her desert landscape
was submerged underneath a shallow sea.
I visit her alluvial fan, a place where her rocky ridges meet a
  flattened plain.
A riverbed splays there, opening her legs to a widened basin.
A great open hand of sand is mounded at this place,
to mark the fertile zone where two ecosystems meet.
Tickled by the magic of landing on this nexus,
This place where differing worlds meet,
I pray for the help of those who came before.
At dusk, I wander down the arroyo by our home.
I am flanked by criss-crossing dogs chasing scents,
and a crow swoops low over my left shoulder, cawing.
I wonder at seeing this old friend,
Is he a bird of sorrow, or a creature of connection?
I know he is both.
At the bottom I stop, standing still on a sandy spit
savoring the dry, clean scent of ponderosa forest.
Near my feet, a perfect white shell catches my eye.
It spirals pristinely, speaking to me in soft and sacred whispers.
Listening closely, I hear stories of its life before,
and of its mother, the sea.
I know the sea as my mother, too.
She holds me softly when I feel empty,
her buoyancy helps me find laughter again.
My awe at the beauty of this world fills the spaciousness within
  me,
and I understand more deeply the crow's complexity.
I realize it is Kali, goddess of death and rebirth.

Within me, I feel the dichotomy of connection and
    disintegration melt away.
I remember how daybreak follows mourning.
Waves and troughs in an ever-changing sea
that together, informed by the moon, mark the tide.

Nina Simons, the editor of this book with Anneke Campbell, is a social entrepreneur experienced in both the nonprofit and corporate worlds. In 1990, she cofounded Bioneers (www.bioneers.org) and is currently co-CEO. From 1989 to 1994 she worked for the entrepreneurial start-up company Seeds of Change, initially as its marketing director and subsequently as its president. From 1995 to 1997, Nina was director of strategic marketing at Odwalla, the fresh juice company. Nina's current work with Bioneers focuses largely on writing and teaching about women's leadership, nature, and restoring the feminine in all of us.

PART FOUR

*Renegotiating Power:
Generosity, Mentorship,
and Respectful Relations*

22

Local Living Economies

Green, Fair, and Fun

Judy Wicks

Judy Wicks is the most joyful and innovative businessperson I know. She brought her full exuberance and celebration to the reinvention of her successful restaurant business, which became a vehicle for education, healing our relationship with the earth, and reknitting the social fabric of community. When she tried something new that worked, she shared it with her competitors in order to better transform the city. She then expanded her purview to become a full-time advocate, educator, and activist. She reminds me that personal fulfillment and pleasure are possible when undertaking a large-scale assignment.

NINA SIMONS

When I get up in the morning and open my closet door, I see a sign that says, GOOD MORNING, BEAUTIFUL BUSINESS. It's a daily reminder to me of just how beautiful business can be when we put our creativity and our energy and our care into producing a service or a product for our community.

Economic exchange can really be one of the most meaningful of human interactions. When I see that sign in the morning, I think about the farmers out in the fields picking fresh fruits and vegetables to bring into the café that day, and I think about the farm animals, the pigs and the cows and the chickens out there in the pasture enjoying fresh air and sunshine. I think about our goat herder, Dougie Newbold, who says that when she kisses her goats' ears, it makes the cheese better. I think of the bakers coming in and putting the cakes and pies in the oven and the maintenance crew making sure everything is clean and prepared before the guests arrive. I think of the Indians down in Chiapas, Mexico, picking the organic fair-trade coffee beans for our morning cup.

Business is about relationships with everyone we buy from and sell to and work with, and about our relationship with Earth itself.

The first time I walked onto the narrow, tree-lined Philadelphia street in 1972 where I live and work today, I was enchanted. Just after I moved into my apartment at 3420 Sansom Street, future home of the White Dog Café, I learned that the entire block was condemned to be torn down to make way for a shopping mall. I eagerly joined the local community group that was organizing to fight the demolition and save our homes and businesses. Ultimately, we prevailed. As part of our strategy, our group developed an alternative proposal to the shopping mall based on the vision of urban activist Jane Jacobs, author of *Death and Life of Great American Cities.*

Jacobs talked about the importance of mixed use, where communities prosper with a diverse mixture of residential and retail, where people can live and work and go to school and find leisure activities in the same walkable communities. She challenged the urban renewal movement of the '50s and '60s, in which neighborhoods were razed and replaced by car-dependent suburbs and work and family life became separate. Studies show that it was at this time in the 1950s when happiness in American society began to decline. It was also the time of increased industrialization of agriculture: farmers began to be forced off their farms by corporate farms and developers, and consumers lost their personal link with the earth and with our food.

Today, most Americans no longer know who grows our food, who bakes our bread, who brews our beer, who sews our clothes, who builds our houses. We've become disconnected from each other and from our places. Without these direct relationships, few of us think of the consequences our economic transactions have on other people, communities, animals, and nature.

Today I live above the shop in the old-fashioned way of the family farm, family inn, and other traditional family businesses. Living and working in the same community has given me not only a stronger sense of place but a different business outlook. Making business decisions in the best interest of the common good comes naturally when those affected are friends, neighbors, and employees in the environment I experience every day.

As a small-business owner, I am more likely to make decisions from the heart. When I first heard of the concept of paying a living wage, I had the typical businessperson's knee-jerk reaction—no one's going to tell me how much to pay my staff! But one day I was down in the kitchen, and, just by coincidence, three young men looked up at me while they were prepping vegetables, and I realized, Of course I want these three young men to make a living wage. How could I think otherwise? For someone who works forty hours a week in the White Dog Café not to be able to buy their food and pay their rent? What had I been thinking?

On another occasion, I was influenced by my direct relationship with nature. I had heard about the problem of global warming and the idea of sustainable energy—principles I understood intellectually. However, I hadn't been moved to act until there was a drought in Pennsylvania about eight years ago.

I had gone up to my special little place in the Poconos, where I like to hike, and found that the leaves were falling off the trees in July, and all the beautiful big ferns were crumpled up like brown tissue paper and the creek was as dry as a bone. Not even the birds were singing, and there was an eerie sense of fire in the air. I thought, This is what it's going to be like with global warming, with droughts and fires in some parts of the world and floods and storms in other areas. I walked over to a large oak tree, put my face against the bark, and promised that I would do something about global warming. So I went back to town and we signed up for alternative energy, and White Dog became the first business in Pennsylvania to purchase 100 percent of its electricity from renewable sources.

When businesses grow larger and larger, the distance between the decision-maker and those affected becomes greater. Yet business schools teach their students to grow or die, that bigger is better, rather than small is beautiful. Also, success in our business world is measured by material gain. We're taught the false premise that economic growth benefits everyone, while in reality continual growth is destroying the planet. The rich get richer while the wealth of the rest is actually declining. With all that material wealth and consumption, studies show that Americans are less happy than we were fifty years ago, and less happy than our European counterparts. We're less healthy as well, with a diet of fats and sugars that has caused an epidemic of obesity.

There was a time when I questioned my success because I didn't have two or three restaurants, but I made a conscious decision to stay small, because I realized that in being one special restaurant, I would be able to maintain what was important to me, which was the authenticity of the relationships I had with my customers and staff and suppliers and community. I came to understand that success could be measured in ways other than growing materially—by increasing knowledge, by expanding our consciousness, by developing our creativity, by deepening relationships, by increasing happiness and well-being and having more fun.

At the White Dog Café, we grow deeper through our many community-based programs. We take our customers on solar house tours and teach them how to conduct energy audits of their homes, how biodiesel works, and where our food comes from. We take them on tours of farms and of prisons and on child-watch tours to witness the lives of inner-city children. We took thirty-five customers and staff down to New Orleans to volunteer after Hurricane Katrina. Some people say that my real profession is using good food to lure innocent customers into social activism!

One of the most important and effective things we do at the White Dog is to buy from local farmers. For many years I knew the importance of buying pastured eggs and chicken, but I had never heard about the atrocities of the factory farming of pigs—social, sentient beings with feelings and emotions like other mammals, like our dogs, like ourselves. It's a betrayal of our sacred duty as stewards of farm animals to treat them in this way—a form of institutionalized cruelty that is destroying our own humanity.

I was horrified to think that the pork I was serving at the White Dog was actually coming from that inhumane system, as almost all pork in our industrialized economy does. So I went into the kitchen and said, "Take all the pork off the menu—the bacon, the pork chops, the ham— we can't serve this until we can find a humane and sustainable farmer." Our chef made an inquiry about this to the man who was bringing in our free-range chickens. We started buying two pigs a week and learned how to use all the parts of the animal.

Next I discovered the terrible way that cattle are raised. Cattle are herbivores; they're supposed to eat grass. But because of the large subsidies of commodity corn growing, it's cheaper to bring the cows inside and feed them corn and ground-up animal parts than to let them have their natural diet of grass. I switched to grass-fed beef, and eventually I looked at my menu and I thought: I'm finished now. We have a cruelty-free menu and no other restaurant in town does this. This can be our market niche.

But then I said to myself, Well, Judy, if you really do care about those pigs, and if you care about the small family farmers who are being driven out of business, if you care about the workers in these horrible factories and slaughterhouses, if you care about the environment that's being polluted by this concentration of manure, and if you care about the consumers who are eating meat that's full of antibiotics and growth hormones, then you would not keep this as your market niche, but you would teach what you know to your competitors.

So it was no longer enough to have the right practices within my company. *I had to move from a competitive mentality to one of coopera-*

tion in order to build a local economy based on humane and sustainable farming. I asked the farmer who was bringing in the pork, "Would you like to grow your business?" He said yes. I asked, "What's holding you back?" He said, "I need $30,000 to buy a refrigerated truck." So I loaned him the $30,000, and then I formed our nonprofit, White Dog Community Enterprises, and hired our first staff person, Ann Karlen, whose job it was, as part of our Fair Food Project, to go around to other restaurants in town and talk them into buying from local farmers.

That's how we began. I started putting 20 percent of my profits into our nonprofit work, which grew to connect hundreds of farmers, restaurants, and stores. With the help of donations from our customers and grants from foundations, we also publish a local food guide, connect midsized farmers to schools, hospitals, and senior centers through our Farm to Institution program, operate the Fair Food Farmstand, and with partners started the Common Market, a local food distribution business.

Two events took place in the fall of 1999 that caused me to direct my full attention to creating a national movement. The first one was the massive protests in Seattle against the World Trade Organization. I didn't know enough back then to go, but my daughter was present, and from her I learned about the danger of corporate rules that override our locally legislated laws that are in place to protect our environment and our workers. I saw that the Seattle demonstrations included the environmentalists, the labor union leaders, the farmers, the teachers, the professors, but there was no clear voice of progressive business owners. So I thought, How can we direct positive energy toward building an alternative to corporate globalization?

Only days after Seattle, I learned that Ben & Jerry's was to be sold to Unilever. Of course, it was a forced buyout. Ben & Jerry's had always been the leader in our socially responsible business movement. It was from Ben & Jerry's that I first learned the concept of a multiple bottom line that measures not just profit but our impact on society.

Nevertheless, since the advent of the responsible business movement, even though much progress was made in the concept of the multiple bottom line, the environmental crisis had worsened, family farms were being put out of business by factory farms and family businesses by chain stores and Wal-Marts, and companies that had been models of social responsibility had been sold to multinationals. This added to the concentration of wealth and power that the movement was organized to combat in the first place. Odwalla Juice, Inc., sold to Coca-Cola, Rhino Records to Time Warner, Cascadian Farm to General Mills, the Body Shop to L'Oreal, and more recently the majority interest of Stonyfield Farm to Groupe Danone and Tom's of Maine to Colgate.

I could see that the socially responsible business movement that I had been part of for years was continuing to use the old paradigm of continual growth to measure our success. In addition, it had been neglecting important issues like a sense of place, appropriate scale, and ownership. Democracy depends on having many owners—the more owners, the more freedom and equality.

Currently the movement for responsible business has two fronts: there are those, such as Ben & Jerry's and Stonyfield, that are bringing reforms to the large corporations, and those that are working to build an alternative to corporate globalization through the local living economy movement.

So that's why six years ago, in the fall of 2001, I cofounded BALLE, the Business Alliance for Local Living Economies. We started with a simple premise: that an environmentally, socially, and financially sustainable global economy needs to be based on a network of sustainable local economies. In living economies, basic needs are produced at home, while what is not available locally is bought through fair-trade relationships, which support the communities where products originate. BALLE is now an alliance of over eighty local business networks in Canada and the United States, comprising over twenty thousand locally owned, community-based businesses.

Building local economies not only reduces carbon emissions, but at the same time it prepares us for a world affected by climate change by reducing our reliance on long-distance corporate supply chains, which are easily interrupted by adverse weather and social upheaval.

The local living economy movement is essentially about decentralization and localization—localizing business ownership to bring economic control back to our communities from faraway boardrooms; localizing energy sources so that we're not dependent on oil from faraway places; and ensuring that every community has access to locally produced renewable energy. It's about localization of our food systems so that we have food security. It also seeks to foster localization and decentralization of communications, promoting independent media that's free of corporate control; localization of culture to protect local cultures from corporate monoculture; localization of politics to align economic development with local business ownership and green regional economies; and localization of leadership so we have many local heroes rather than national icons.

Perhaps most importantly, establishing communities around the world that have local food, water, and energy security creates the foundation for world peace. If poverty is not being able to provide for oneself, then community self-reliance is our greatest wealth, with an economy providing direct access to basic needs. Community self-reliance offers a meeting place for the left and the right, for liberals and conservatives, because it combines the values of self-reliance favored by the right with the values of community and cooperation favored by the left.

As we build this new economy, we can make great strides toward economic justice. It's important that we help those who have been left out of the global industrial economy find ownership opportunities in local living economies. We can do this by directing capital and local government services toward helping minority entrepreneurs start green businesses in their communities—businesses that increase community self-reliance. In our own businesses, we can mentor and hire young people of color. We can develop purchasing partnerships with minority businesses and have sister relationships with minority-owned restaurants, as the White Dog does, or minority-owned health clubs, as BALLE cofounder Laury Hammel has done.

We need money to grow living economies. Many of us put our savings into the stock market, which takes the money out of our communities.

When I realized this, I disinvested even from screened funds and stocks and put my savings entirely in Philadelphia's Reinvestment Fund, where my money is loaned out to locally owned businesses and community organizations in my own region. This fund even provided the money to build the wind turbines in Pennsylvania that produce the wind energy we use at the White Dog. I call this getting a living return, not only a financial return; it also provides the benefit of living in a more sustainable local economy.

During debate about climate change and the need to cut carbon emissions, there's often a focus on the costs and the hardships of moving to a low-carbon economy, but little talk of the benefits to our quality of life. We're not talking about going back to the cave age. Rather, this is about gathering with our good friends and family over delicious and nutritious locally produced food, meals that we share in a warm, well-insulated home, that we get to by riding our bikes or walking along uncongested streets or taking public transportation.

We can also have more fun in our own communities rather than depending on expensive vacations to faraway places. An example of creating collective joy for me is the many block parties at the White Dog, where we dance in the street at Noche Latino or Rum & Reggae. For years we put on a Liberty and Justice for All Ball on the eve of the Fourth of July out in the street. In a skit called "Birth of the Nation," I dressed up as a pregnant Colonial woman with a sign on my back that said, GEORGE WASHINGTON SLEPT HERE! The Revolutionary War drummer would play, and a midwife with her lantern would deliver my two twins, a black woman and a white woman both dressed in red, white, and blue, with banners: one said LIBERTY, the other said JUSTICE. They hopped up onto the stage and tap-danced to "Yankee Doodle Dandy." Then we wheeled out a waitress dressed as the Statue of Liberty, lit our sparklers, and sang "God Bless America."

The local living economy movement is about maximizing relationships, not maximizing profits. It's about growth of consciousness and creativity, not brands and market share; democracy and decentralized ownership, not concentrated wealth; a living return, not the highest return; a fair price, not the lowest price; sharing, not hoarding; simplicity, not gluttony; life-serving, not self-serving; partnership, not domination; cooperation, not competition; win-win exchange, not win-lose exploitation; family farms, not factory farms; biodiversity, not monocrops; cultural diversity, not monoculture; creativity, not conformity; slow food, not fast food; our bucks, not Starbuck's; our mart, not Wal-Mart; valuing life over lifestyle; and, as the Earth Charter says, "being more, not having more."

At its heart, the movement for local living economies is about love. And it's love that can overcome the fear that many may feel in the hard days ahead as we face climate change, resource depletion, and environmental decline. Our power comes from protecting what we love—love of place, love of life, of people, animals, nature, all of life on our beautiful planet Earth. And for the entrepreneurs among us, it's also about a love of business. Business has been corrupted as an instrument of greed rather than one of service to the common good. Yet we know that business is beautiful when we produce a product or service that's needed by our community.

Our materialistic society has desensitized us to the suffering that underlies our industrial economic system. We're also desensitized by a false idea of masculinity based on control and domination over other people and nature. We need a more feminine, nurturing approach to life—to bring forth the goddess in each of us, men and women both, reconnecting with each other, bringing care and compassion to our economy and trust and harmony to our world.

We must open our hearts and eyes and ears—to hear the cry of the pigs in the crates, of a cow for her calf, of animals in laboratories, in the fur industry. To feel the suffering of men, women, and children enslaved in sweatshops, in the rug industry, in diamond and coal mines, and in chocolate production. The suffering of migrant workers in slaughterhouses and pesticide-soaked industrial farms. The suffering of the people of Iraq, of Nigeria, of the rainforest tribes—everywhere there are oil and natural resources to exploit and to fight wars over.

Let us hear the cry of the whales, of the polar bears, of the trees, of the coral reefs, of the natural world that is dying around us. What provides the energy and passion for all we must do in this movement is simply to love and protect what we truly care about and, in so doing, find our place as humans in the family of life, and live in a world at peace.

 Judy Wicks (www.judywicks.com), an international leader in the local living economies movement, cofounded in 2001 the Business Alliance for Local Living Economies (BALLE), comprising over eighty business networks in North America. She is also the founder of the Sustainable Business Network and Fair Food in Philadelphia, which connects local family farms with the urban marketplace. During her forty-year business career, Wicks founded the landmark White Dog Café. As its proprietor for twenty-six years, she gained a national reputation for community involvement, environmental stewardship, and leadership in the local food movement.

23

Girl Power for Social Justice

Lateefah Simon

Lateefah Simon's extraordinary and inspirational work with the Center for Young Women's Development in San Francisco takes young women off the street and teaches them self-esteem, job skills, and even governance. Employing young women to work with young women whom our society has written off, combined with the power of treating one another with dignity, care, and respect, is transformative. It may change how we see and relate to folks who are homeless, imprisoned, or living in poverty or with addiction. More important, what Lateefah reveals in her respect for them is that it's precisely these young women who are and should be leading their own movement for empowerment.

NINA SIMONS

We are living in impossible times. I feel it in my bones. Last night when I was reading my daughter a bedtime story, I thought to myself: I'm weary, but I'm not weak. These times are hard all over the world. Young women are struggling. Young women are dying. Young women are fighting and resisting.

So yes, I'm overwhelmed by the world, and what is coming of this world that we were all born into, yet I remain overjoyed. Before my grandmother died she said to me, "Lateefah, you and me and all that

189

make up our family, we are not supposed to be here because of everything that happened. We were supposed to die. But baby, we are still here and we are still fighting." So I'm overjoyed by the fact that resilience and power are still here among us, and we may be tired but we will rest, and we will get up the next day more fired up.

We have a cadre ready to organize. We have a generation of young people in this country that survived some tumultuous times, the young people that were born in the 1980s. We are millions and millions strong who have lived through the drug war, who have lived through the proliferation of prison building, who have lived through our parents dying from state violence. We have lived through it and we are here, and that's why the Center for Young Women's Development was called forth, because we are taking our space as poor young women of color who—some of us were on the street corner, and some of us are in cages—say to the world, "We are here, we are strong, we are politicized, and we are organized. So take us seriously."

It is time to make room for the folks we want to organize for. It is time to begin making room for them to lead the marches that we're planning, and for them to plan the marches that we will walk behind them in. It is time to make room for all of us who claim that we are part of a movement. So that when we're going to the meeting, we don't walk by the girl on an inner-city street corner, and we don't walk by the young man who has nothing, and we invite them to be leaders in the movement that we are representing. Please make those sisters and brothers a priority, not just because of their brilliance, but because of their frustration, and yes, the anger that they bring, because we so desperately need it.

At twenty-seven years, I feel a little bit old, but I came in at age seventeen to the organization that I've been so humbled to work for. It had only been around for one year. I was hired by a woman who wore Birkenstocks; she was from New York, and she had a Ph.D. But she was revolutionary when no one else wanted to step up, and she created an infrastructure so that ghetto girls like me could take over. Rachel Pfeffer created the Center for Young Women's Development, and she used her privilege and education to create a social structure in which we could get a little bit of assets to begin to hire sisters off the streets. To hire the young women with crack in their hands, to hire young women who were in jail cells and who were waiting to get out, so that when they touched down they had a job, and that job was to be organizers.

This happened eleven and a half years ago in San Francisco when those young women were made a priority only because they were on the receiving end of a social service payment. The thing Rachel Pfeffer did, which I so appreciate, is to flip the model so that the young women who oftentimes receive services, who are dying to survive, would become leaders of their own social movements once again.

So three years after she came into the organization, she left, and over thirty young women had been hired. We were doing street outreach on every corner in San Francisco, talking to young sisters about how beautiful they were, saying: "You may not be able to leave the streets today, but here are some condoms, and please, I want you to live, because we need foot soldiers, so be here. Please be here. And you know what, there are cops around the corner, so go in a store. You should not be arrested because you are trying to pay your rent when some of those johns that are picking you up own the buildings where you are paying rent." Yes, we began to see the contradictions and we began to understand that social service organizations didn't see the power that we could develop because they simply wanted only to serve us. I can get a Pap smear anywhere, but what I really wanted to learn was how to organize a rally.

What we learned when Rachel left was that the organizational structures under that big old 501(c)3, they are a little difficult, but there is nothing more difficult than being sixteen years old and the state takes your baby away as soon as it is born, and you pump your milk from your jail cell, and a foster mother comes to pick it up and you get out and you have nothing, and you can never see your child again. Or being the girl in the next jail cell, who has a felony because she got caught with her man's dope. She comes out of jail but can't move into her mother's house because her mother has Section 8, and if you have a drug felony in this country you cannot live in subsidized housing. So she goes back onto the streets and gets rearrested because she's simply trying to survive.

So we know that we have to organize. We realize that there is no grant that we cannot write. There is no contract that we cannot get. There is no organization that we cannot build. We can hire our own people and we can walk the streets and we can do what they call community mapping. We can do that because we can talk to our own.

We have to break down every single wall that exists because if we can come together, we can hire each other. We can learn how to feed our children and do social justice work together and pay our rent and stay off the streets. Yes, we can continue a job-training program in which we hire young women to be organizers and have them push policy. Yes, we can continue doing street outreach work where we're talking to young sisters to engage them in a struggle that's larger than themselves. Yes, we can go inside Juvenile Hall every day and provide political education to young women on lockdown with no counselors in the room.

Folks say, "Lateefah, how do you know all this stuff? You haven't been to school and you talk about policy?" We all have to understand that we're standing on a lot of people's shoulders. The ancestors are watching. They're watching out for our generation, so we'll just keep on speaking what they're telling us, which is to prize those whom Isaiah prized. Prize those whom Isaiah prized. Understand that the brilliance lies in places that you walk over every single day. At the Center for Young Women's Development we go out on the streets once a year and literally hire sisters and pay them a good wage. Ten-fifty an hour doesn't compete with the $350 a day they make on the streets, but what we can promise in addition is skills and pride and a sisterhood that's irreplaceable. We promise that they will work with young Latina sisters, with black sisters, with Asian sisters, with Native sisters, with young, poor white sisters; they will be challenged to confront their issues with sisters of every hue.

We work it out, and anywhere we come, we come strong and we come fierce, whether we go in front of the city council or to the United States Supreme Court—which we did last week to hear conversations about the constitutionality of the child death penalty. We stood in line with law students and girls from the ghetto waiting to hear arguments in the Supreme Court. We were there at 5:30 in the morning, and we told those sisters on the plane, It's just a building, and like folks say, those buildings can be torn down. So let's prepare ourselves to govern.

That's why we will be taking, hopefully, more than twenty young sisters to South Africa to learn that any repressive situation can actually be overturned. We will go to the townships, and we will talk with young people who have nothing, but they're organized. We will be going to Johannesburg, because we want the young people we work with to feel in their bones that another world is possible. That other world won't come tomorrow, it's not completely perfect in Johannesburg, but the young people there are working to make it so.

We're training young women inside Juvenile Hall. As executive director, I don't have any power in creating programs, and that's why the center is successful, because the sisters on the street do have that creative power. Young women who are parenting inside many institutions in the United States do not have the opportunity to see their children. In San Francisco, in our community mapping, we noticed that the young women who did get to see their children were oftentimes shackled hand and foot during their baby's visit. Our center helped turn that around. This work that we're doing is fierce and it has results.

Young women who were previously incarcerated have organized themselves and are now a project of the Center for Young Women's Development. "Baby Mamas United" are working on a bill of rights for young incarcerated parents to push through the San Francisco probation department and the probation commission. We hope to make this a state model. We are forcing the institutions that say they want to take care of our kids to take care of our kids, and if they don't, then it's our responsibility to shut them down. The Center for Young Women's Development will lead—hopefully in the next ten years—the revolution for young women who are in cages.

We have nineteen sisters on payroll, and another twenty on stipends. We have young women who are feeding their children by doing social justice work. Understand, to make this population a priority, a population so left out, we must make it doable for them to do the work.

We're paying them to train and heal, and to learn about power, and how it really manifests in our souls. They get massage therapy and acupuncture; they are exposed to circles and sweat lodges. We're providing holistic therapy on-site, because that's how we believe you build a movement. We have food in the refrigerator and paychecks come every Thursday. I've been executive director since I was twenty, and what I've learned most in that process is that there's nothing that we cannot do. This year we are almost a million dollars strong. That may be meager compared to what we're fighting, but we know that anything is possible.

Now you can't pay everyone to be in a movement, but what you can do is pay attention to the leadership and make sure that they have what they need. At the Center for Young Women's Development, we place a lot of emphasis on organizing, advocacy, and, yes, service. If we are going to mandate a movement of all, let's *include* all, and let's work extra diligently to ensure that our people can do this work, and be effective, whole people.

Lateefah Simon is the executive director of the Lawyers' Committee for Civil Rights of the San Francisco Bay Area. She is part of a new wave of African American civil rights and community leaders. Born and raised in San Francisco's Western Addition neighborhood, at nineteen Simon was appointed executive director of the Center for Young Women's Development, becoming one of the youngest leaders of a social service agency in the country. She has also led the Reentry Services division at the Office of the San Francisco District Attorney. In addition to a MacArthur (Genius) Fellowship, Simon has received numerous awards, including the Jefferson Award for extraordinary public service in 2007. She has spoken at the United Nations, before the United States Senate, and at countless trainings and conferences around the country.

24

Transforming Philanthropy

Kathy LeMay

Kathy LeMay is a wise, committed, and fearless leader who's re-envisioning the practice of philanthropy to include seeing each of us as having something essential and valuable to offer. She gives counsel to philanthropists, donor activists, foundations, and nonprofits about how to direct their resources to be most aligned with their vision and their values. A dedicated feminist and animal rights activist from a working-class background, Kathy advocates for each of us to recognize and wield our power to effect change by gifting our time, treasure, and talents toward the changes we most deeply value.

NINA SIMONS

Awhile ago, I had a radio interview with a person who asked me: "Do you really consider yourself a philanthropist?" I said, "I'm way more of a philanthropist than Bill Gates, because after he writes his checks in December, he doesn't have to figure out in January how he's going to pay the mortgage." We've been sold a notion of what philanthropy is and what it looks like, which I believe has disempowered the general public from stepping into that space and claiming it as their own. While the current time is being called a new dawn of philanthropy, the way this trend is defined can also be a little harmful. I meet people who say to me: "Warren Buffet just gave $31 billion in something called G-stock. I

195

don't even know what a G-stock is, and it's not like my $25 a month is going to matter now."

I believe we are involved in an expansive redefinition of what it means to be a philanthropist. What I have to say is intended for someone who gave $25 away or $25 million away, someone who volunteers ten hours a month or someone who volunteers forty hours a week. Women's philanthropy is about inclusiveness.

I met a woman in Mexico City who swept sidewalks. She made five pesos a day. She gave one peso from each paycheck to orphanages. On the flip side, I was with a woman who was in high finance in New York City. She gives away $11 million a year. The woman in Mexico felt empowered by her giving; she felt she was making a difference. The woman in New York told me she didn't consider herself a philanthropist and wasn't sure change was happening.

What does it mean when we look at philanthropy in terms of how much we give away rather than our intention in giving money away? What does it mean when we value the amount of the check and not the services offered to an organization or an initiative? At my company, Raising Change—which works to change mind-sets around money and social change and build bridges between progressive nonprofits and donors—our goal is to help donors become more bold and unapologetic in how they give their money away. It's called generosity planning, and the bottom line is this: Every single person in the world can live a generous life. How you define generosity is based on you, your values, your ideals, your passions. Each of us can give our time, treasure, and talents to make the world a better place.

I created my personal generosity plan (what I've called a social action plan) when I was twenty-four. The volunteer work I did in Bosnia during the war was what ignited my work of fund-raising for the women there. As I was preparing to return to the United States, I asked the women I had met: "If I could do anything for you, what would that be?" They said they knew exactly what they needed to do to rebuild their lives; they needed resources to make it happen. I went home and thought: What treasure do I have financially? What's my talent, and in what way will I be taking a stand on rape and on genocide camps in Bosnia? What am I actually going to do about it?

After this trip I wrote a plan for how I would make a difference. I looked back on my giving: at age fourteen I started writing $25 checks. I volunteered where and when I could. I grew up in a mill town in Massachusetts. For four years my mother raised my sisters and me on her own on little income, with help from food stamps. Because of my mother's investment in us, I have been able to earn more money than I ever thought I would and, more importantly, to give away a lot of this money as well as my time and talents to those causes I care most about. Today I believe that I'm one of the most powerful philanthropists in the world because money is a tool that I use to its fullest capacity to serve my vision.

Because I shifted my relationship to money and stopped worrying that I wouldn't have enough, my plan came to life. My plan is powerful, focused, fierce, and bent on making change. And having this voice around money gives me choices. I know what I care about, and that is what I fund. Your cause needs your resources. The best ideas in the world don't move forward fast enough because they don't have money to fuel them.

I want every single person in the world to have a social action plan or generosity plan that is a living, breathing testimony to her vision, values, and hopes for the future. This plan can guide us every day, creates goals for where we want to be eighteen months from now, and looks ahead at what impact we want to have had ten years from now on the areas that mean the most to us. We also do twenty-five-year planning and fifty-year planning, because people may have times where they can't be on a board or volunteer for some years. We want to remove the pressure that we have to do it all today or tomorrow.

When you awaken the bold, unapologetic philanthropist within, you step more confidently and easily into your own unique voice. When you match your time and money with your values and live as generously as you can, you will unleash in you that which you've always felt.

Redefining philanthropy in this way happened through the experience of doing a lot of solicitations. Years ago I was meeting a possible woman donor at a famous restaurant in New York City, the Four Seasons. I got there first, and I looked at the menu and thought, Oh, shoot, bagels are fourteen dollars. I'll just have water and eat later. She and I hadn't met before, and when she came in, she had on a full mink coat, a lot of makeup, and really high heels. She came over to me and said: "Hello, it's a pleasure to meet you, I've reserved a table." She took her coat off and handed it to me as she started to walk away.

I remember thinking, The universe is offering me the most incredible opportunity. I can hang it up, grumble all day long, then go back to the other development officers and say, Guess what happened to me at the Four Seasons, or I can help make social change happen while I'm fundraising. I chose the latter.

As she started to walk away, I took her hand and said: "Can I share something with you?" She nodded. I said to her: "I am a huge animal rights activist, and it would bring me to tears to hang up your mink coat, but how about if I find someone who can hang up both our coats?" She looked at me with tears welling up in her eyes. She said: "All these people told me about who you were. I was so intimidated that I spent all this time getting ready in the hope you would think I was smart and had something to offer. If I don't look perfect, it reflects poorly on my husband."

We stood in the Four Seasons holding each other, crying and laughing. I realized that what it means to be a woman involved in fundraising and in philanthropy is to move past all the things that are being imposed on us around class and status and imposter syndrome and fear, and just connect. It was an amazing breakfast.

By keeping my values front and center—which meant sharing my needs and my truth not just in programmatic work but in my way of fund-raising as well—she and I were able to have a breakthrough. Luckily, she was a fantastic woman who welcomed sharing our truth. I am grateful to her for sharing her heart. I feel that on that day we met in a field where one day all women will meet. She became involved in the organization I was working for and wrote a check in support of its important work.

It's powerful to investigate how we see ourselves in relation to money, and in relation to people who have it or don't have it. What are the opportunities to engage in a new conversation that fund-raising requires us to have? I think money hasn't been adequately distributed, and philanthropy hasn't yet reached its potential to change the world, because we haven't yet had the right conversations. In some ways, I think we have to earn wealth redistribution by being as brave about money, class, and status as we have been about the toughest global issues of our time. These days we can talk about issues like rape, genital mutilation, and violence against women, where it once was taboo to mention such social ills. This can happen with money as well. Let's show each other that a little thing like money won't prevent us from creating the world we all know is possible.

Kathy LeMay (www.raisingchange.com) is the founder, president, and CEO of Raising Change, LLC, which helps organizations raise capital to advance social change agendas worldwide. LeMay, who began her activism in war-torn Yugoslavia, where she worked with women survivors of the siege and rape-genocide camps, has been a social change fund-raiser for fifteen years, raising millions of dollars in the fields of women's human rights, hunger and poverty relief, HIV/AIDS, and movement-building.

25

My Life and the Gift Economy

Genevieve Vaughan

When I first met Gen Vaughan, I was fascinated by the depth of her think-
ing. I downloaded her book Women and the Gift Economy *(for free).*
In it I learned how generously nature offers us her gifts and how freely
mothers give, and how that openhanded paradigm is so different from how
our society—based instead upon a quid pro quo system of exchange—
operates. Gen introduced me to stories of indigenous matriarchal cultures
that functioned based on principles of abundance and generosity. I learned
that matriarchal cultures do not mean that women are on top, but rather
that both men and women are valued equally, in differing roles. My inquiry
into what our culture might learn from old-growth cultures deepened, as
has my exploration of women and money. I am deeply thankful for this
deep dive into Genevieve's personal story, so generously offered, and for the
wisdom she has nurtured through years of study and contemplation.

NINA SIMONS

I was born in 1939 to a wealthy family in Corpus Christi, Texas. We
lived next to the bay, and I could hear the waves at night and tune in to
all the moods of the water every day. Next door there was a big vacant

lot along the bluff that went down to the water, and in the spring it was full of wild verbenas and those delicate pink primroses that grow together in clumps all over south Texas. When I was eleven we moved closer to town to a bigger house with a huge garden that my mother loved. I spent a lot of time there, playing and getting to know the plants. Later I went away to boarding school and was only home on vacation, but throughout my life I always kept the sense of closeness to nature I had as a child.

I went to a girls' boarding school in Dallas—Hockaday—and then to Bryn Mawr College in Pennsylvania. I laugh saying that I had an education in feminism just by attending all-women schools. I remember some very late nights staying up discussing philosophy and everything else. But in fact it was the '50s, and I really just missed the feminist movement, and the civil rights and anti-war movements too. I graduated from college in 1961. Then in 1963 I married an Italian and moved to Italy.

People thought about things very differently in Italy. There was Marxism. There had been the wars. I learned to see my country from the outside, as the country of the Marshall Plan, but also as the country of the bombs on Hiroshima and Nagasaki and soon the country of the Vietnam War. I had always been concerned with the issues of poverty and wealth, and in Italy I learned about exploitation. That is, I learned that everybody's wealth comes from somewhere, usually someone else's poverty, or many people's poverty. My family's wealth came from oil and gas. At the time, it didn't seem like that was hurting anybody. (But back then nobody knew that cigarettes cause cancer, either, and we all smoked up a storm.)

My husband, who was quite a bit older than I, was a philosophy professor. He became part of a European current of thought that was considering the market—the exchange of goods—as a model for language—the exchange of words and ideas. Most of the intellectuals in Italy at that time had a Marxist perspective, and my husband's work was along those lines. He had been at Oxford and had studied the English philosophy of language. I had never thought much about what language was, or what meaning was, but through him I realized that this was the biggest question in twentieth-century philosophy. I started studying Marx's analysis of the market and commodities and trying to apply it to language as well.

During the '60s and early '70s I gave birth to our three daughters. This influenced my thinking a lot in that my children were learning language before they could use money or exchange things. To me that meant that language could not be derived from the market. If anything, it had to be the other way around.

Also, in college I had studied Mauss and Malinowsky, who wrote about indigenous gift economies, and I knew that indigenous peoples in the Americas did not have money or markets as such. Couldn't it be that the market derived from language and that language, if it had an economic origin, came from gift giving? Actually I was doing a lot of gift giving myself as a mother, bringing up my children. I did not like manipulation, and so I tried not to threaten or cajole or punish them. (It was the epoch of Dr. Spock.) That is, I tried not to make exchanges like, "If you do this, I will pay you back with that." When they were little it was mostly just gift giving and receiving and turn taking, and imitation. So I thought, All societies have to have mothering, or the children do not survive. And children learn language just during the time that mothers are giving to them unilaterally, before they understand what exchanging is or money is. So language must come from mothering itself.

At that time everybody was enthusiastic about Chomsky's idea of language as a genetically inherited capacity with a universal grammar.* I thought we should put women and mothering back into the mix by talking about a "universal grandma."

In the '70s, several important things happened in my life. I wrote two academic essays, which were published in important semiotics jour-

---

*Noam Chomsky is an American linguist, philosopher, and political activist who developed a theory of language according to which every intelligible sentence conforms not only to grammatical rules peculiar to its particular language, but also to a universal grammar underlying all languages and corresponding to an innate capacity of the brain.

nals in 1980 and 1981. In them I distinguished between communication and exchange. Communication, which I later realized could be derived from the Latin word *muni,* meaning "gifts" (so "giving gifts together"), was something prior to and more life enhancing than exchange. I didn't yet have the courage to use the word *gift* or to talk directly about mothering, but the idea was there. In 1978 my husband and I got a divorce, and soon after I joined a consciousness-raising group in Rome and became a feminist. On a trip back to the United States I bought Lewis Hyde's book *The Gift: Imagination and the Erotic Life of Property,* which confirmed for me what I had already been thinking and writing about the gift economy.

I began to realize that what we needed was an economy without trade, one that did not have a market at all. We need to go back and start over with mothering/gift giving as the model for the way we get the goods to the needs. Most people who talk about gift economies (they are almost all men) talk about debt and obligation, the duty to give back. However, a lot of mothering takes place without that. It's true that giving can also be done manipulatively, but then it becomes a kind of exchange. What is needed is an egalitarian gift economy.

In my consciousness-raising group I learned about patriarchy, and I realized that patriarchal hierarchies were what made gift giving oppressive. Exploitation was really people below having to give to people above, and manipulation was people above giving to people below—with strings attached.

In the group we talked a lot about women's free labor in the home. To me housework was and is a huge gift women are giving to society. However, I think the solution is not wages for housework but the creation of a free economy. "Free" is a mode of distribution. We are already doing a lot of it. We just need to create a mode of production to enable it. Nature gives everything free. She practices a gift economy. Native peoples acknowledge this so much more than we do. They co-muni-cate with Her, give gifts together with Her. They create circulations of gifts including Her in their co-muni-ty, and they give thanks. This is so different from Christianity, where we are always "paying" for our sins or feeling guilty—preparing ourselves to pay.

To me it seems that patriarchy and capitalism have grown up in denial of the gift-giving and maternal part of our humanity. This is what is wrong with our system. The gifts of the many are channeled to the few, and the abundance of the planet is destroyed, while any "excess" wealth that might have been used for nurturing is wasted in wars, which do not nurture anybody. The gift economy is easy and delightful in abundance, but it is difficult and even self-sacrificial in a context of scarcity. The patriarchal-capitalist system succeeds by creating scarcity and controlling the flow of gifts, never allowing enough abundance to accumulate for the gift economy to become generalized. Patriarchal hierarchies obstruct maternal egalitarianism.

In 1980 I started using the money I had inherited from my family for social change, contributing to projects based on women and what I called "women's values." My funding was itself a kind of gift giving, and I doubt if I would have dared to do it if I had not had the idea of the gift economy to back me up. Then in 1983 I came back to the United States to try to "make a difference." I had a radical idea, I had money, and I had a few good collaborators. I asked a cousin of mine who was involved in progressive politics to find out which groups I could give to, and she did. That is how I started a funding program that lasted about twenty years, until I had used up most of my money and also decided to give up my oil and gas properties because of the environmental devastation they were causing.

I tried talking about the gift economy when I first got back to the United States but nobody really understood. Because I considered gift giving as material communication, though, I kept doing it, hoping that the consciousness would rise somehow. Now, after thirty years, everybody is talking about the gift economy. The zeitgeist has altered. I don't know if my "material communication" had anything to do with that, but at least it didn't hurt.

In addition to contributing to many organizations for women, peace, and the environment, I started the Foundation for a Compassionate Society, a multicultural all-women activist foundation doing projects for social change in and around Austin, Texas, as well as nationally and internationally. The foundation was active in the '80s and '90s and finally closed in 2005. During that time I also wrote and edited several books on the gift economy, and many articles.

The foundation closed with a final conference on matriarchal studies, which we organized in collaboration with Dr. Heide Goettner-Abendroth, who initiated matriarchal studies in Germany some twenty years ago. When I went to her first international conference in Luxembourg in 2003, I knew the gift economy had found its context and immediately invited her to do a conference in the United States. Matriarchies are egalitarian societies that have maternal values. Many of them still exist. They are not mirror images of patriarchy. They are the natural "home" of gift economies. Patriarchal researchers in the past misunderstood them completely in terms of their own bias toward power-over.

Here are some of the ways the gift economy is being practiced at present in our own society, whether it is recognized as such or not. These and other similar initiatives make up a general flow that is turning in the direction of gift giving.

- Income-sharing intentional communities
- Wikipedia
- Free software
- General Public License (Copyleft)
- Blood banks and organ donations
- Community gardens
- Hitchhiking
- Ride sharing
- Yellow Bikes
- Couch surfing (a free in-home hospitality network for travelers)
- AA
- Burning Man
- Rainbow Gatherings

➤ Remittances of immigrants to their home countries
➤ Some alternative currencies—time banks
➤ Some volunteerism and nonprofit work
➤ Community solidarity work
➤ Social movements

I believe that solving social problems is giving gifts to the community, so I include the movements for peace and justice and the environment as part of the gift path. On the other hand, the commercialization and militarization of aid in emergency situations such as Katrina and the aftermath of the earthquake in Haiti demonstrate the harsh and paranoid mentality of patriarchal capitalism, its inefficiency and opportunism. In fact most of the "gift giving" that is done by governments and international bodies like the World Bank and IMF is just an instrument of economic colonialism.

As the gift economy has become more widely known and practiced, the basic connection between giving-receiving and mothering has unfortunately not been made. This keeps people from recognizing the kinds of values that are necessary for acting in a humane way. Patriarchal governments and systems act in ways that are contrary to the human heart. I believe that our construction of gender in the West puts little boys in a category opposite to that of their mothers and this implies to them that they should be not-nurturing. This (false) implication takes them away from their heritage as gift-giving, mothered children.

Instead I believe that we are all *Homo donans*—a species of gift givers—not just *Homo sapiens*—a species of knowers. We are an extremely maternal species because we nurture not only materially but also verbally, through language. Males and females, whether or not they are actually engaged in caring for children, nurture each other all the time in a generalized way, when they speak.

I have moved back to Italy and am spending my elder years writing and studying about the gift economy and language, trying to explain these connections in detail and to show how, by embracing this alternative positive self-fulfilling concept of our species, we can remake our human relations, forming a viable maternal co-muni-ty with each other and with Mother Earth.

 Genevieve Vaughan created an international all-women activist foundation (1987–2005) and the network International Feminists for a Gift Economy (2001–present). Her books are *For-Giving: A Feminist Criticism of Exchange* (1997); *Homo Donans*, a Web book (2006); and two anthologies: *Il Dono, the Gift: A Feminist Perspective* (2004) and *Women and the Gift Economy: A Radically Different Worldview Is Possible* (2008). These books, as well as a film on her life, her songs, her children's books, her many articles, and the complete video records of three recent conferences can be downloaded free from her website, www.gift-economy.com.

26

Circles of Mutual Mentorship

Nina Simons

When I was in my twenties, I had a very difficult time trying to find mentors. Each time I thought I'd identified a woman whose professional or life experience offered me a glimpse of things I wanted to develop in myself, she'd be unavailable, or she'd turn me away.

Once, for instance, I was hired to be a production assistant for a film crew. I was elated, partly because the producer was a woman, a rare thing in those days, and very accomplished in her field. Although I noted her fairly tough way of doing business, I was enthusiastic about how much I might be able to learn from her, working at her side. However, she kept creating distance between us, assigning me tasks that kept me far away. At the time I wondered whether she might have been somehow threatened by me, a young ambitious woman, rather than moved to help me develop my skills and my potential. I was sorely disappointed, though I knew I had done nothing directly to alienate her.

In the twenty-plus years since, I've wondered about the reasons for my inability to find mentors. I know I felt hurt by the experience of being seen as competition, instead of as an ally, and I promised myself that if I ever had the opportunity, I'd like to make it easier for young women to find women to connect with in relationships of mutual support and strengthening.

At the first women's retreat I hosted in 2002, called UnReasonable Women for the Earth, a new way to see mentorship arose. A friend and colleague, Kristin Rothballer, lobbed a seed idea into the dark soil of my heart when she introduced an idea she called Reciprocal Mentorship.

Kristin noted that our culturally inherited ideas about mentorship were flawed and outdated. They presupposed that in any mentoring relationship, the elder typically had more to offer than the younger participant. She knew from her own experience that this was not the case, and that young women had much insight and wisdom to offer older women. She suggested a new model for mentorship, one founded on believing that each person brought equal value and merit to the relationship, and to our capacity to enhance and encourage the emergence of each other's leadership.

My own way of discovering my "assignment," or sense of purpose, seems often to occur when an idea or phrase lands within me and won't let me go. I considered Kristin's idea for several years, noticing how often I felt awakened, inspired, or enlightened by words or ideas offered to me by a younger woman. I also noticed how each time I mentioned mentorship from a stage, there'd be a group of younger women awaiting me afterward, wondering how they could get involved, tap in, or connect with other women for mentorship. It became clear to me that something wanted to happen, and that I had some part to play in it, although I still did not know how.

In 2008, I encountered a group of four remarkable young women. Three were participants in the Cultivating Women's Leadership training I offer with my teaching partner, Toby Herzlich, and another I met when speaking at a conference. Their ages spanned from twenty-two to thirty-two, and they were immensely bright, lit-up, and capable women, each executive directors of organizations doing impactful, timely, and purposeful work in the world. Out of the blue, two of them e-mailed asking me for referrals for a coach.

I realized that I didn't know anyone exactly right to recommend to them, and inwardly I felt sad about my own lack of available time. I was deeply inspired by each of them, cared about them as people and leaders, and wished I could somehow fulfill their needs for growing their own capacities through connection.

I'd been learning through experiencing our trainings just how powerful it is to have women show up for each other in challenging, authentic, and mutual support. I'd seen how often, intuitively and effortlessly, we reflect each other's greatness and capacity in a way that reveals it to the woman who may most need to see herself differently. I'd learned how much ability we have to strengthen each other when we gather in circles for mutual reflection and hear, see, and reflect each other into flourishing.

Then it struck me: since I yearned to interact with these women, perhaps we could create a virtual circle together, for the purposes of mutual mentoring, honest and challenging (but loving) reflection, and support. I floated the idea to the four of them, and they enthusiastically agreed.

We've been meeting for over a year now. Sometimes we manage to get together by Skype once a month; sometimes it's only every three months. But invariably, I am stunned by the clarity, courage, and insight they each bring to the circle. Often, when we share our stories, there seems to be an invisible thread that connects the themes of our lives. We take turns facilitating the calls, and I learn so much from the creative and adventurous ways they each lead the circle.

One fantastic outcome has been that they've befriended each other and often turn to each other for feedback or assistance when the group's not available. Another is that I regularly get to practice mutuality, realizing I don't need to be "in control," to lead or be the smart one. Their presence reminds me to practice my own humility, and I am learning at least as much from each of them as I imagine they might be from me.

How do I learn and get strengthened by them? They are far more self-assured than I was at their ages. Since most of their parents raised them to know they could be anything, and life hasn't shown them differently, they have a stronger sense of belief in their own abilities and possibilities than I did at their age. They are each fiercely honest and hold me to a high standard. It feels like they're often more nimble at integrating creativity and intuition into their problem-solving than I am, as I seem to have more prior conditioning to unlearn. And yet, though the octaves of our issues sometimes differ, we resonate deeply with similar themes. I am inspired by their courage, their commitments, and their ways of holding their dignity unerringly through difficult situations.

How did we do it? Just as when I started a women's circle locally a few years ago, we made it up as we went along. We agreed to certain ground rules, like being honest, practicing active listening, and encouraging the expression of our own, and each other's, vulnerability. We spoke about what each of us desired from the circle, and we revisit our plans regularly to hold ourselves accountable and to see how we're doing. We discussed what kinds of forms we wished to integrate, including check-ins, formalizing feedback, meditating together, rituals, or playful, creative time. Sometimes we decide to end our calls with a proclamation of what we wish to grow/nurture in ourselves, so that we can revisit it next time and explore our progress. Generally, we take turns making notes about our calls on the chat portion of Skype, so that anyone who misses a meeting can see what happened.

As we are discovering the many benefits of connecting in circle, even virtually, I am amazed to realize how much more capacity we have together—to keep strengthening and growing each other—than we may have previously imagined. Whether it involves learning to fundraise, facing employment challenges, personal relationship hurdles, or navigating life-threatening illnesses, knowing we're at each other's backs has been a source of strength for all of us. Practicing and exploring this mutual mentoring circle reminds me how much better we are, invariably, together.

Nina Simons, the editor of this book with Anneke Campbell, is a social entrepreneur experienced in both the nonprofit and corporate worlds. In 1990, she cofounded Bioneers (www.bioneers.org) and is currently co-CEO. From 1989 to 1994 she worked for the entrepreneurial start-up company Seeds of Change, initially as its marketing director and subsequently as its president. From 1995 to 1997, Nina was director of strategic marketing at Odwalla, the fresh juice company. Nina's current work with Bioneers focuses largely on writing and teaching about women's leadership, nature, and restoring the feminine in all of us.

27

Learning a New Leadership

Jess Rimington

Jess Rimington is a young leader engaged in passionately and skillfully connecting individuals all over the world who hold a common vision: they care deeply about advancing sustainability. When she realized—in high school—that no network existed to help young people connect and learn from each other about healing our ecological relations, she decided to create one. When she attended our Cultivating Women's Leadership training she found that her idealism and vision were reaffirmed, and she found mentors whose honesty, vulnerability, sense of justice, and shared authority she respected. Her exuberance, strength, and clarity as an accomplished leader give me hope for our collective future.

NINA SIMONS

In 2004 I was eighteen years old and about to graduate from high school. I distinctly remember saying to my mom one night, "I just feel like something big is trying to come through me." I was about to defer my university admission for one year in an attempt to create a program that could connect schools in learning partnerships globally and empower students to take collaborative action for the good of their local communities.

Two years prior I had had the opportunity to travel to Soweto,

South Africa, for the Children's Earth Summit, held in conjunction with the World Summit on Sustainable Development. I went to represent a youth program for which I was a volunteer. Not only did this trip open my eyes to how big, complicated, and fragile our world is, it also exposed me to prejudice in an unexpected way. This was right before the United States went to war in Iraq, and a number of youths wanted to vote the Americans out of the summit. To respond, I had to articulate on the spot how crucial it was for people to move beyond stereotypes and see one another as human beings rather than as representing particular nations or creeds. It made me realize that to create a better future, we first need to learn how to relate to and work with one another.

It was this thought that inspired me to link my high school with a school in Ethiopia during my senior year. It was unfamiliar territory for many students who had not had the opportunity to develop global awareness or the chance to practice applied empathy. I learned that for a program like this to be successful, it had to provide more support, curriculum, and greater opportunities for connection.

So I contacted another education nonprofit and proposed that I work for them to create a sister-school program to further their mission. After they turned me down and I could not find another existing program to join, I was discouraged. At a dinner party my father said to me, "Why don't you start your own program?" I laughed at first. Then I realized he was serious.

I was the first in my family to actually be going to college, and deferring my education was no small matter. My high school counselor and others thought it was a terrible idea. I remember pacing around the street near my house, trying to make the decision. I was so nervous. What if I failed? How could I, at only eighteen years old, start something like this? All I had was a thousand or so dollars I'd saved and a bold idea.

Now it's five years later. I have graduated from a university, and One World Youth Project is an international nonprofit that has served sixty-seven schools in twenty-six countries and twelve U.S. states. We facilitate partnerships between schools and youth groups worldwide for the purpose of cultural exchange and community service toward eradicating poverty, encouraging environmental sustainability, providing for maternal health, and combating HIV/AIDS and malaria. Our belief is that recognizing their existence in a global community of shared challenges at a young age helps better equip youths to be the effective global citizens we all need to be in the twenty-first century.

My success has caused people to call me a young social entrepreneur and a leader, but if I were to describe myself, I would say I'm an "assembler." I greatly enjoy bringing the right people to the table and empowering them to work together toward something as massive as global systemic change. But when I went to college, I started to see this collaborative skill as something different from "leadership." It was not a quality that was taught in my university leadership textbooks or referenced in political science lectures.

Many of the female professors I had at Georgetown University prided themselves on their poker faces, strong masculine qualities, and "necessary" analytical detachment. I saw some of my female friends developing these qualities in themselves as they played dress-up in power suits and marched off to job interviews. I was uncomfortable with this model. I knew deep down that I did not want to become detached, to act as if showing vulnerability was a danger, nor did I want to lose my passionate connection to the work I wanted to do. I wanted to hold on to what I'll call the "assembler" qualities that came more naturally to me: honesty of emotion, an open heart, collaboration, and a sharing of power.

I had inklings that another way to be effective in a large arena was possible, but I was told that my ideas were idealistic and naive. There seemed a consensus that the kind of work to which I was choosing to dedicate my life was done only out of some kind of ego, that all success was motivated by this—consciously or unconsciously. I drove myself crazy trying to search my soul to figure out if this was true for me. The answer always came out a resounding "No."

I'm not a religious person, but I have always known that my work was in service to something greater than myself. But without "God" as an easy explanation, it seemed hard for others to understand that *this* something greater was a commitment to another world being possible, a just world in which human needs and challenges are shared and met. I took Gandhi's quote very literally: "Be the change you wish to see in the world."

So I struggled to find my larger community. Although my fellow teammates with One World Youth Project confirmed for each other daily that our work was beyond ego and beyond just a "job," I worried that this was perhaps a phase of youth—and that in ten years I would be left very much alone again in the vastness of my dream.

I call the spring through fall of 2008 my "awakening." I had the opportunity to attend a Cultivating Women's Leadership training, and afterward I joined a "mutual mentoring" circle of female non-profit leaders and also formed a circle of young women in Washington, D.C., who met weekly to discuss topics relevant to our lives. I went from feeling as though I was one unreasonable, unique person swimming against the tide to feeling as though I was part of a community of sane women trying to build acceptance for a new way of approaching leadership.

I had never been in a group of people where every person truly, deeply, authentically, and loudly wanted every other member to succeed—not out of self-interest or strategy, but because they believed in each other's vision and cared for each other through empathy based in love. I have never felt so safe in a group and so listened to. These are values I now try to bring into my own workplace as a team manager.

If someone had asked me two years ago to list the top five characteristics that describe myself, "woman" would not have been one of them. I did not understand the value of being a woman as a piece of identity beyond the biological distinction. Through the exploration of leadership in mutual mentoring with other women, I have gained a piece of my identity. My experience with women's mutual mentoring has shown me that I am not alone in dreaming on a large scale or in my community-building approach to leadership.

I have learned four important lessons.

The first is the concept of loving other women loving themselves. If you are a woman, you probably have experienced the competition and jealousy that we promote among even our female friends. Some of this is innate to human nature in general. However, I believe that a part of it is also learned and perpetuated through societal stereotypes. My experiences among women have proved to me that caring for each other's vision as though it is a part of ourselves is not only healthy and sound but also necessary to change the world.

The second is that leadership is not a finite resource. The idea that only a few can "rise to the top" as "true leaders" has been shoved down our throats since grade school. I still have to fight those years of conditioning. For instance, I remember when I gave up a speaking engagement to another staff member whom I considered a mentee, because I wanted to prove to her that she could succeed beyond her expectations. I was told both implicitly and explicitly that doing this was not smart. But we have to shake off these culturally imposed assumptions, because the challenges we face are too complicated and systemic to be tackled by the "lone leader."

The third lesson is that "being nice," in the traditional sense, isn't always nice. I think women in particular grow up with a drive to please and to comfort. Such accommodation can limit us. It helps neither ourselves nor society to flourish to our full potential. I am learning to operate from a place of heartfelt intention to speak truth with compassion and sometimes fierceness and to accommodate only when it's a deliberate choice.

Finally, "dreaming big" is not naive, rather it is necessary. Over the past few years I have been able to overcome my fear of vocalizing my big dreams for systemic, massive change. I will no longer apologize for these dreams or cushion them with comments like "I know it sounds idealistic, but . . ." I will no longer temper my vision, because I know that the world needs my voice, my big vision, and my bold ideas.

Jess Rimington (www.jessrimington.com; www.oneworldyouthproject.org) serves as director and founder of One World Youth Project, an educational nonprofit that facilitates high-quality partnerships between schools and youth groups worldwide for the purpose of cultural exchange and community service toward the achievement of the U.N. Millennium Development Goals. Rimington was named a Rising Talent by the Women's Forum for the Economy and Society and has received Earth Island Institute's Brower Youth Award and Do Something's BRICK Award for her activism. She is the principal author of the U.N. Millennium Development Goal Curriculum for Secondary School. Rimington has traveled the world to promote grassroots programs related to youth participation. She is a spoken-word artist, consultant, travel writer, and photographer. Rimington has a degree in foreign service and a certificate in international development from Georgetown University.

28

What Life Knows

New Ideas from Biology
That Could Change the World

Janine Benyus

As a naturalist, educator, and writer with a humble and wise presence, Janine Benyus is inspiring as she invites a new relationship to the natural world. Her work has helped to shift my worldview to see nature as teacher, to be revered and honored as our four-billion-year-old mentor. The endless and brilliant applications of biomimicry (a word she coined) for inspiring innovation in business, science, and industry may well hold the greatest promise of all to shift our eco-cidal course. Janine leads by evoking awe and wonder and fostering collaboration as she reminds us that nature is our context and our greatest ally in learning how to live on Earth.

NINA SIMONS

The earth is ringing . . . it's ringing . . . it's ringing off the hook, and I feel like we are in a dream, running through molasses to answer it.

Life on Earth is heading for an evolutionary knothole, a narrowing of choices brought on by the relative youth of our species. If we are to make it through that knothole, splinters and all, we must mature—

quickly—into a welcome species on this planet, a keystone species. Keystones like elephants, sea otters, beavers, and prairie dogs are creators of opportunity, living in ways that make it possible for other species to thrive. Like all elders on this planet, they are intimately attuned and beholden to the realities of their habitat, knowing that survival depends first and foremost on an accurate reading of context.

Fifty miles north of Phuket and hours before the Indian Ocean tsunami of 2004, elephants started trumpeting and wailing, and those tethered for work actually broke their chains. For these old-timers, the warning was clear, coming in the form of underground oscillations called Rayleigh waves, high-speed signatures of the earth's rupture. Elephants sensed these waves via sensors called Pacinian corpuscles on the bottoms of their feet, and each and every individual headed upland and inland. It is believed that we humans can also pick up Rayleigh waves through sensors in our knees, but thousands of people ignored the sensation and ran down to the retreating sea. Rescue crews were shocked to find very few nonhuman animal corpses in the aftermath, and they puzzled over reports of flamingoes, lizards, insects, and snakes that had also headed for the hills. We are a young species with a lot to learn. We see through a glass darkly, and we would be wise to borrow a clearer lens from organisms that have shaped and been shaped by their habitats for millions of years.

These days, I am tuned to the tuned-in.

Meet the Seven Sisters Oak, a 1,200-year-old Southern live oak on Lake Pontchartrain, for whom Katrina was just another storm in a millennium of bad storms. This oak survived, as did almost all the historic live oaks in New Orleans. Live oaks know something about thriving on a windblown coast. My question is this: How many of the architects rebuilding in New Orleans are asking live oaks to tutor them in wind tolerance?

After all, this is an organism that grows not tall, not skyscraper size, but round—sixty to eighty feet high and nearly as wide. Its trunk and branches are spiraled like the cables of a suspension bridge for strength and ease of flexing. When the wind howls, the trunk does what's called reformation; it bends and twists and dances, and its leaves actually curl into cylinders to let some of the wind go through. The rest goes up and over its rounded canopy, and, if you live in the lee of a live oak, it will help the wind go over your house as well.

But what you can't see is that a live oak is larger below than it is above—its roots span an outrageous 150 feet, like a fractal anchor in the soil. A live oak's roots are intertwined and even grafted with the roots of nearby trees. This Gulf Coast community is not a go-it-alone society. Having your roots connected to other trees is very useful when a big wind blows. In record gales, sacrificing some limbs is a good strategy too, not just for that particular tree, but for the whole neighborhood. Ecologists studying soils before and after hurricanes found that the periodic pulse of nutrients after a branch cleansing is essential to forest health. Even class 5 hurricanes can be a blessing, says the live oak, as long as you're designed for it.

Biomimicry means learning from the locals, and by definition, no one solution fits all. Biomimicry is not a list of solutions, but rather a durable way to find solutions. Consulting nature begins with acknowledging that other organisms have faced and solved the same functional challenges that we face. Their advice comes with 3.8 billion years of experience gained in context and centered on the continuation of life.

We humans are not the first to build, nor to shape materials. Diatoms are photosynthetic plankton that live in both fresh and salt water, fixing up to 25 percent of all carbon, and making cell walls out of silica (what we know as glass). These elaborate structures are made in seawater without emitting toxins, without high pressure, and of course without creating carcinogens. Yet, in the manufacture of *our* silicon chips and solar cells, we release numerous carcinogens into the waters of Silicon Valley. The high-tech industry, for all its software marvels, is still incredibly toxic on the hardware side. In labs at the University of California at Santa Barbara, scientists are learning to mimic the way the diatom forms silica, a mimicry that could and should revolutionize the way computer chips are made.

Another exciting example of biomimicry is helping erase the

poisons from otherwise sustainable wood products—plywood and particleboard. If we want to ease the demand for large, clear-bole trees, we need to find ways to join waste chips and small-dimension lumber into strong shapes. Unfortunately, many of the glues we use in wood composites contain a toxic passenger called urea formaldehyde. We use it because it's strong and waterproof, something most glues can't claim. But the blue mussel has humbly known how to glue itself to rocks without formaldehyde for millions of years. Its inscrutable bonding agent actually cures underwater.

For thirty-five years, scientists have been trying to mimic this feat, not by harvesting the critter and extracting a compound, but by taking a page out of its recipe book. Finally, at Oregon State University, a scientist figured out how to make a mussel-inspired glue inexpensively. Columbia Forest Products, North America's largest plywood manufacturer, is now using this Purebond resin in its cabinets, and I just ordered them for my kitchen. If every manufacturer began to use this, imagine what it could mean for air quality in all our new and retrofit buildings.

Here's another favorite example of biomimicry: biological chemist Geoffrey Coates rocked my world many years ago when he found a way to use CO_2 as a feedstock for biodegradable plastics. Not that using CO_2 is unusual in the natural world—mollusks use CO_2 to make seashells, and plants use CO_2 to make sugars, starches, and cellulose. Coates said, Why don't we use the carbon in CO_2 to make polymers (plastics) ourselves? We've got enough of it! In fact, we're the only species that would look at the excess CO_2 in our atmosphere and say, "Pump that poison underground." Mollusks would instead make more seashells, and plants would make more wood. Coates has devised a catalyst that mimics plants, and he's making tough yet biodegradable polycarbonates for packaging and other uses at his company called Novomer. Isn't this the kind of research we should be supporting? If what we research is what we get, then the materials we'll be buying in five, ten, or twenty years will be those we mimic today.

Life has a beautiful and economical way of shaping its high-tech materials. When organisms need more functionality, they don't use more stuff. They just add shape to matter, because, as Julian Vincent puts it, "shape is cheaper than material." In the humpback whale's case, a scalloped line of bumps on the front edge of the flipper allows the giant mammal to pirouette during bubble feeding with very little friction. A scientist named Frank Fish—no pun intended—said to himself, These tubercles may teach us how to reduce drag in all kinds of flow. He put bumps like these on an airplane wing and achieved a 32 percent reduction in drag. This is an industry where a meager 1 to 2 percent change is momentous! Tubercles also increased lift on the wings by 6 percent, inspiring Frank's company (WhalePower) to create highly efficient fans and wind turbines.

From planes to trains, nature's wisdom is helping us move with grace. The storied bullet train in Japan recently got a lesson from a water-diving bird called the kingfisher. The problem was that the bullet train was blunt in front, and as it sped through tunnels, it built up a pressure wave that burst as a sonic boom upon exit. In Japan, thousands of apartments are within rumbling distance, so an engineer at JR West was given the challenge of quieting the high-speed train.

As it happens, the engineer was a master birder. That very night he went to the equivalent of an Audubon Society meeting and began to think: What in nature goes from one density of medium to another? He thought about the kingfisher that dives from air into water to catch fish, and he thought about its spearlike beak. It's millions of years in the making, but the kingfisher's beak is small, and that's a big train. Would it scale? He tried it, and that's the train you ride today. The beak design not only cut down on noise but saved 15 percent in electricity and helped the train travel 10 percent faster!

While each of these bio-inspired products is a relief, full healing will not happen until we learn to mimic the brilliance of nature on a systems level. Ecologists have a beautiful way of depicting the full-web society of a coral reef or a forest or a prairie. Their food webs show how intricately the eater is related to all it eats. The picture is one of a full, three-dimensional weave, with no room for what we call waste. Our job is to learn to knit the same network into our economy, so materials such as metals, already removed from the earth's crust, can be regathered and upcycled into new products. To do that we need a take-back economy that is logistically flawless, with new methods of collecting precious materials that have been dumped into landfills and scattered in our waters.

For biologically based products like food and fiber and starch-based plastics, we need to create not just a take-back but also a give-back economy, which returns nutrients to the farmlands and forests they came from. Anything less, and we'll be mining soil fertility for our "stuff" just as we mined fossil plants and animals for our energy.

Speaking of soils, the reinvention of agriculture has begun, and it stems from a careful observation of wild communities. There are so many models—the buffalo-grass ecosystem as a model for holistic ranching, the three-story jungle as a model for agro-ecological farming in South America, and here in our wheat belt, the tallgrass prairie as a model for a perennial, polyculture farming.

These same ecosystems are teaching economists about resilience, cooperation, and true development rather than runaway growth. When you sample water coming out of a mature, healthy forest, you see very few fugitive nutrients, because every nutrient that has been drawn from soil to shoot is used over and over and over again. Creatively redesigned and repackaged, materials cycle from plants to fungus, fungus to bacteria, bacteria to insects, insects to birds, birds to mammals, and so on and so forth, spiraling through the network again and again.

That's how *our* economy has to flow. Industrial ecologists pair companies together so that one company's discards are hungrily gobbled up by the next company. Conjoined in a food web, companies realize that materials are precious and waste is unthinkable, and that only thoughtful design can shutter mines, make landfills irrelevant, and keep materials circulating forever.

At a systems level, life performs its greatest miracles. Air is purified, water is filtered, nutrients are cycled, soil is built, and each new generation creates a more lush, livable habitat. In the sheer act of staying alive, life creates conditions conducive to life. How can we, as a young species, learn to do the same?

At the Biomimicry Guild and the nonprofit Biomimicry Institute, we believe the answers to some of our most pressing sustainability questions are flying, slithering, and leafing out all around us. The problem is not a lack of knowledge about life's wonders. It's a lack of access to life's know-how by the very people who need it the most—the people who design and architect and engineer our world. Creating the flow structure that will deliver life's wisdom to human designers of all stripes is a job we have begun.

One of our absolutely favorite new projects is a website called AskNature.org. It's part digital library and part social networking site. Our goal is rather Googlesque. We want to organize the world's biological information by design and engineering function. So when you ask a question, like "How does nature remove salt from water?" you'll learn all about mangroves, kidneys, and the nasal glands of seabirds, for instance. You'll be introduced to the science and the scientists studying these adaptations. Our hope is that AskNature will be a place where biology and design cross-fertilize and where bio-inspired breakthroughs will be born.

We designed AskNature as a moderated wiki, then seeded it with ideas from a yearlong project that was an utter joy for us. A team of lucky natural historians at the Biomimicry Guild read through the biological literature with a list of knotty technical challenges before us—questions like, "How can we store energy without toxins?" Worthy challenges? Meet life's evolved answers. We finally had to stop at 2,100 entries, the very best of which you'll find on our site.

Because life thrives via diverse and locally tuned ideas, we found incredible abundance: not just one way to do water-based chemistry, but 146 ways. Do we need 146 ways to do water-based chemistry? You bet, because that's how life does it. We do it with toxic solvents. Do we need 49 ways, new ways, to generate energy? You bet we do. Do we need 23 new ways to absorb water and 44 new ways to store it? Absolutely. Do we need 58 new ways to manage extreme temperatures? Unfortunately, yes. And do we need 42 new ways to cooperate? Oh yeah.

To provide a continual flow of information, we partnered with E. O. Wilson's Encyclopedia of Life project. This $50 million project will create a Web page for every species on Earth. Scientists worldwide will contribute everything they know about a species, from its first hand-drawn identification to the latest proteonomics info, all on one page. Thanks to the project's high profile and incredible usefulness, most scientists of the world will flock to upload their data. When they do, they will find an entry field that asks: What can we learn from this organism (functional adaptations for biomimicry)? Those tasty tidbits of wisdom will flow forever into AskNature.

Our community in turn will creatively match important biological ideas to worthy societal challenges. Having all of life's strategies organized by function is new for biology, and an important enabler of innovation. And, because AskNature publishes science in a design context, it may be considered "prior art" in patent battles, helping block the patenting or enclosure of nature's ideas. To be clear, I am all for the patenting of an application—such as a tape that mimics how a gecko walks—but I believe that no one should be able to own the scientific *knowledge* of how a gecko walks. That is a wisdom commons that belongs to all who live on this wondrous planet.

For similar reasons, we're also committed to making AskNature a free, public-domain resource. Imagine any innovator, anywhere in the world, at the moment of creation, being able to ask, "How would nature solve this?" We believe that nature's time-tested counsel, appearing upstream in the design process, can help change the world.

We also believe that respect—which is the true legacy of biomimicry—can transform how we treat other organisms. Respect is a far more powerful emotion than pity or guilt—common feelings that lead to conservation giving. We believe that respect leads to gratitude, which in turn flames an ardent desire to protect the genius that surrounds us. That's why we insist that a formal "Thank you" should be a part of any biomimicry process. First, quieting human cleverness, then listening, then emulating, and finally, giving thanks for our inspiration.

At the Biomimicry Institute, we've started a program in which companies and inventors can return a percentage of their profits to conserve the habitat of the organism that inspired their breakthrough. We think it's the least we can do (and it's good manners too) to honor the original patent holders by preserving the habitat that nurtured them into being.

We biomimics have the world's best job. It's not often that you witness, much less get to help midwife, a whole new discipline. As biomimicry emerges, just in the nick of time, we are doing our best to help reverse the "gold rush" mentality of prior revolutions. This time, we vow to see nature in a whole new way, as mentor rather than workhorse, university rather than warehouse, temple rather than trash heap.

When we as a species truly listen to the elephants' counsel, we free them from their chains forever. Perhaps only then can we do as the indigenous people who survived the tsunami of 2004 did—follow them to safety. For our lost culture, regarding nature as elder will ultimately be a gift to ourselves and to the planet, an essential part of our growing up. If we're lucky, becoming nature's apprentices will not only end our loneliness; it will bring us home at last.

Janine Benyus (www.biomimicryguild.com) is a biologist, innovation consultant, and author of six books, including *Biomimicry: Innovation Inspired by Nature*. Her company, the Biomimicry Guild, helps clients such as HOK Architects, Interface, Herman-Miller, Kohler, and Seventh Generation create sustainable products and processes. Janine also cofounded the nonprofit Biomimicry Institute, a biomimicry design portal on the Web, and the Innovation for Conservation program to conserve the habitat of the mentor organisms. Her latest book project is *Nature's 100 Best*, a look at what ingenious (and often endangered) species can teach us about becoming true natives.

PART FIVE

*Restoring the Feminine
in Our Strategies,
Institutions, and Culture*

29

V to the Tenth

Eve Ensler

Thank heaven for Eve Ensler, who has the audacity, vision, capacity, and courage to shift public awareness on a mass scale—to create vehicles for women to publicly celebrate their bodies, sexuality, and vaginas, while naming and ending the global pandemic of violence against women. Eve's fiercely dedicated work with V-Day, The Vagina Monologues, *the Congo, teenage girls, and her continuing quest for healing is altering the ways women see themselves and each other, and bringing to public awareness the gender-based violence that has so permeated our collective culture. Not only is she boldly transforming culture through art, but her strategy of creating vehicles for expression, and open-sourcing them so that they are available to women's groups and colleges globally, also embodies a decentralized, generous, and feminine approach.*

NINA SIMONS

It's hard to believe that almost fifteen years ago, I said the word "vagina" on a small stage in a little theater called Here in New York City. When I first read those monologues, my most pressing concern was being able to get the words out of my terrified mouth. I certainly could not have conceived what would follow, in terms of both the development of V-Day* and the life of *The Vagina Monologues* itself. I had no intention, to be honest, of even writing a play. I was already a way, way, way downtown playwright. I assumed a play about vaginas would permanently secure that status.

If I have learned anything in these past fifteen years, it is how to hold two opposite thoughts at the same time. The most radical play I'd ever written turned out to be the play that was accepted and invited into the mainstream. Saying the word I was not supposed to say is the thing that gave me a voice in the world. Revealing the very personal stories of women and their private parts gave birth to a public, global movement to end violence against women and girls.

In terms of existing in the world of opposites, I see now that living between the play *The Vagina Monologues* and the V-Day movement, between the ambiguous energy of theater and the less nuanced world of activism, has both stretched and inspired me. The art has made the activism more creative and bold. The activism has made the art more sharply focused, more grounded, more dangerous.

The trick in both has been to avoid ideology and fundamentalism in one direction, and fragmentation and irresponsibility in the other. The trick has been to create certain universal givens—the play, the intention of the movement—and then to trust individuals and groups to bring their own vision, culture, and creativity to the experience. The trick has been to create something that is both concrete and fluid, something that can spread quickly and yet has integrity, something that is owned and changed by many but has certain ingredients and laws that allow this adaptability. The trick has been to live in the contradictions while maintaining principles, beliefs, and purpose.

I believe this friction has been, at the core, what has energized and spread V-Day throughout the world so quickly. The excitement and danger of just saying the word, performing the play in tiny villages, in conservative cities with unlikely performers (ministers, doctors, telephone

---

*The author is the founder and artistic director of V-Day (www.vday.org), a global movement to end violence against women and girls.

workers, members of parliament) and in unusual venues (churches, synagogues, women's living rooms, stadiums, and factories) has propelled the play to be performed in forty-five languages and 130 countries, raising nearly $70 million for women and girls.

There are so many victories: women speaking the word where it had never been uttered; women standing up against local and national governments, religious forces, parents, husbands, friends, and university administrators and presidents, and against the voice inside themselves that judges and censures. College students across the world are making V-Day a radical annual event. Recently someone who toured colleges told me there are only two things on every college campus, a Starbuck's and a V-Day.

Women are reclaiming their bodies, telling the stories of their own violations, desires, victories, shame, and adventures. Women are finding their power, their voice, and their leadership abilities by becoming accidental activists. Women are finding each other. Women are standing up for women in other parts of the world. Women are releasing memories that have numbed their bodies and depleted their energy. Women are standing on the stage, on edge, in reds and pinks with New York accents, Southern accents, African accents, Indian accents, British accents, speaking, screaming, whispering, laughing, and, of course, moaning.

There are so many tales and images I can share. I was in Manila when I saw a group of thirty former "comfort women"* between the ages of seventy and ninety chanting *"Pooke"* in Tagalog with their fists raised.

I was in Iceland when the president of Iceland publicly declared himself the first vagina warrior president.

I was in Narok, Kenya, when hundreds of girls danced in the African sun as the first V-Day safe house was opening so their clitorises would not be cut.

I was most recently in a Catholic girls' school in Cap Haitian, Haiti, which was overflowing with more than five hundred people, mainly men, who were so engrossed with the show that they were literally screaming back at it.

---

*"Comfort women" is the translation of a Japanese term for prostitutes (usually unwilling) in World War II military brothels in Japan and its territories.

I was in Islamabad, Pakistan, when the first production of *The Vagina Monologues* happened in a clandestine back room, where the women were dressed in red saris and *salwar kameez* (pajama-like outfits) as they performed for our sisters from Afghanistan. When they were reading the Afghan monologue, there was both so much weeping and so much laughing that women's chadors fell off—an amazing moment.

I was in Juarez, Mexico, when seven thousand people came from every direction to stand up to stop the murders and the disappearance of the women in factories there.

I was in New York when Mary Alice, one of the great actresses, nearly took down the Apollo Theater with her moans at the first V-Day, celebrating African American, Asian, and Latina women.

I was in Bosnia when the monologue "My Vagina Was My Village" (a monologue about a raped woman during the Bosnian war) was performed by girls who had been in the war and whose family members had been raped.

I was in South Dakota when the first production for the Indian-country campaign happened and Indian men bravely and emotionally broke the silence. They handed out red feathers instead of tickets.

I was in Washington for the first performance by deaf women, and I learned how to sign "vagina."

So much has happened. So much has changed. We can point to places where violence has been reduced or has been stopped altogether, where the consciousness has most clearly shifted. We've had huge victories. We have broken through many barriers. We have changed the landscape of the dialogue.

We have reclaimed our stories and our voice, but we have not yet unraveled or deconstructed the inherent cultural underpinnings and causes of violence. We have not yet penetrated the mind-set that allows every single culture to permit violence, expect violence, wait for violence, and instigate violence. We have not stopped teaching boys to deny being afraid or doubtful or needy or sorrowful or vulnerable or open or tender or compassionate. We have not become or elected leaders who refuse violence as a possible intervention, who make ending violence the center of everything, rather than amassing more weapons and proving how macho and unbending they can be.

We have not made violence against women abnormal, shocking, unacceptable. The world is still profoundly unsafe for women. We have not come to see this as an ecological issue. Violence toward women is equivalent to the poisoning of the skies, the destruction of the ozone layer, the polluting of the seas. The disempowerment of women is equal to global warming. The long-term crippling effect of violence against women is that women have stopped being full selves, fully alive, fully creative, imaginative, productive, sexual, in the same way that the earth is being lessened and species are being killed off, fish are dying, forests are slain through violence, through disrespect, through dishonoring, through stupidity, through greed.

We have not yet become or elected leaders who are brave enough to make ending violence against women the central issue of their campaign. Essentially, we have not cracked the tectonic plate at the center of the human psyche that is still more terrified to love than to kill.

If we are going to end violence against women, the whole story has to change. Ending violence is more than a lifestyle shift. It's the culture that has to change, the beliefs, the underlying story of the culture. Ending violence against women is actually about being willing to struggle to be a different kind of human being. It means redefining power. The only point of having power, it seems to me, is to give it away, and inspire other people to have it.

Last year, during V-Day's spotlight on women in conflict zones, I traveled to Haiti and the Democratic Republic of Congo. In the DRC, I heard the worst stories of atrocities I've ever heard in my life. Yet even here, there was the transformative power of telling the story, and a power in the listening.

There was a little girl, this beautiful nine-year-old girl. She and her mother were taken in one direction in the middle of the night, her father in another. She was held and she was gang-raped for two weeks. When she was returned, she had a fistula, a hole inside her, so she couldn't hold her pee or poop. Many, many women in the hospital I was in had fistulas, 250 of them in this community of raped women, and more were arriving every day. But she was this incredible spirit, and at one point I just took her and put her on my lap, and as she sat on my lap, she peed, because she had no ability to hold it. I think that was probably one of the most powerful moments of my entire life, because I felt that she had come into me and I was with her. I realized in that moment that nobody had held her since she'd been raped, because everyone was so afraid that she would pee on them.

I think that had I not gone through what I have been through, I would have been afraid in that moment, but instead I felt blessed. I knew once again that, paradoxically, being a survivor of sexual abuse and violence myself has opened doors. It's a wound that tore open something in me that's never really been reconstructed. It's been incredibly painful and at the same time, an incredible gift.

We have to be willing to go into the wounds, and open those wounds, whatever they are—even if they're self-inflicted wounds from being a perpetrator. Having worked in a prison for eight years with women who committed violent crimes, I now think that dealing with what you've done to other people is actually harder than dealing with what's been done to you. All of us are perpetrators in one way or another, given that we live in a racist, sexist, and unequal world.

Eve Ensler (www.vday.org), an award-winning playwright, performer, and activist, is the author of *The Vagina Monologues* (which has been translated into forty-eight languages and performed in over 130 countries). Eve's other plays include *Necessary Target; Conviction; Lemonade; The Depot; Floating Rhoda and the Glue Man; Extraordinary Measures; The Good Body; The Treatment;* and, most recently, *OPC.* Ensler is the founder/artistic director of V-Day, a global movement to end violence against women and girls, which has raised over $70 million in eleven years. She is also the author of *Insecure at Last: Losing It in a Security Obsessed World* and her newest work, *I Am an Emotional Creature: The Secret Lives of Girls Around the World* (February 2010).

30

Plastic and Public Policy

Getting the Estrogen Out of One
and Into the Other

Charlotte Brody

From her early years as a feminist nurse and community organizer, Charlotte Brody has become a primary player in the national effort to stop chemicals from poisoning our bodies, land, air, foods, and waterways. Charlotte's story reveals how the biases and imbalances inherent in our culture have affected our policies, science, media, and corporations. Working with the BlueGreen Alliance to shift chemical policy in the United States, she brings a fierce commitment and strategic perspective to protecting the health of life on Earth. Her vision is systemic, lucid, and wise, and she reminds us what science and governance could be if they were reformed toward truly serving the common good.

NINA SIMONS

On the bookshelf in my office, I have a very early edition of *Our Bodies, Our Selves*. The list price on its cover is thirty cents. I've carried this book from home to home for almost forty years, because *Our Bodies, Our Selves* changed my life. The book and the women who collaborated

236

in its writing sketched what gradually became a vision for me of how I might work for social change and earn a living at the same time. I went to nursing school because of *Our Bodies, Our Selves*. I worked with coal-mining families and cotton textile workers and as an executive director of a Planned Parenthood affiliate in North Carolina because of *Our Bodies, Our Selves*. And starting with *Our Bodies, Our Selves,* I learned an enormous amount about women's hormonal cycles and the role of estrogen and progesterone.

Since I left Planned Parenthood in 1994, my work has focused on toxic chemicals. When I learned that a toxic component in #7 plastic, bisphenol A, abbreviated BPA, was first synthesized to be a pharmaceutical version of estrogen, my two worlds collided. BPA was put back on the research shelf after drug companies decided that diethylstilbestrol (DES) was a better option. After millions of women had been prescribed DES to prevent miscarriage (which it did not prevent), we learned that DES led to cervical cancer and other reproductive system problems in the children of the women who had taken it when pregnant.

As DES was being taken off the market, the chemical industry was finding new uses for the synthetic estrogen BPA: the lining of beverage and food cans and clear polycarbonate plastic. Today BPA has even more uses, from the paper our fish comes wrapped in to the debit card receipt copy that we get when we pay for it. Is it safe for us all to be exposed to this synthetic estrogen? Steve Hentges, Ph.D., senior director, BPA Group, American Chemistry Council, in his May 14, 2008, testimony to the U.S. Senate Committee on Commerce, Science, and Transportation, says there's nothing to worry about. "After more than five decades, no reliable evidence has shown that bisphenol A in consumer products to have caused [*sic*] any human health problem."

Steve Hentges has become an important person in my life. He is the man the chemical industry sends around the country to tell public officials that they shouldn't take action to limit exposures to bisphenol A. Steve Hentges is a nice-looking guy with a doctorate who, when the nightly news runs a story about bisphenol A, assures us that we don't need to concern ourselves with the findings of the study of Chinese workers exposed to BPA who report four times more erectile dysfunction and seven times more difficulty ejaculating than a control group. Dr. Hentges explains that the Chinese workers are being exposed to higher levels than we're getting from those big plastic bottles in water coolers and the linings of various cans. Well, he's right about that.

But there's also a study showing that the higher a pregnant woman's BPA levels are during her first sixteen weeks of pregnancy, the more likely it is that her child will show atypical gender behaviors at age two. At the levels of exposure that we're all getting, girls have more masculinized behaviors and boys are more feminized.

That study doesn't prove anything, according to Steve Hentges. It just shows a correlation or a connection, not a cause. True enough. And when Steve Hentges dismisses correlations, he does it well. He does it with millions of dollars of campaign contributions and the lobbying power of the U.S. petrochemical industry, all singing behind him and chanting amen.

Yet somehow Steve Hentges and the choir aren't convincing everybody. As much as women may want men and boys to express their feminine side and women and girls to be as tough as they want to be, we don't want those behaviors to come from chemicals that leach into our food from the plastics that contain that food. So Hentges et al. couldn't stop the Connecticut legislature from banning bisphenol A from infant formula and baby food cans and jars and all reusable food and beverage containers. He didn't stop Wal-Mart and Sears and Toys "R" Us from phasing out baby bottles containing bisphenol A or REI from taking Nalgene water bottles that contained bisphenol A off their shelves. Hentges hasn't stopped other counties, states, companies (and most recently the Food and Drug Administration) from listening to young mothers, nurses, and environmental justice and health activists, and he hasn't stopped these concerned individuals from taking action to limit our exposure to bisphenol A.

Given the power of corporations and the difference in budgets, it's fair to ask, why is Steve Hentges not winning every legislative and corporate policy boxing round he enters? He might say it all comes down to hysteria. And I might agree. But I don't mean a neurotic disorder. I mean the Greek root of the word that defines hysteria as suffering in the womb. The power of we womb-sufferers in the voting booth and the marketplace is beginning to transform how we make policy decisions in the United States.

The electoral gender gap is one of the indicators of that growing power. Women had been voting for president for more than fifty years before 1980, the year the gender gap started making a difference in presidential elections.

In 1980, men voted for Reagan over Carter 54–37 percent, and women were about equally split, 46–45 percent. In the Obama/McCain election, the gender gap was a stunning 13 percent. And while women have been running households since the hunter-gatherer divide, corporate marketing campaigns that recognize that women are the primary decision-makers for most purchases in this country are a new phenomenon.

Whether these two signs of a new kind of power are empty flirtations with societal transformation or the real thing depends on whether women's way of thinking actually begins to change the way big societal moral decisions are made. The Steve Hentges of the world may continue to win the war, even if they lose a few battles. Or they may not. I don't know who will win. But I do know what's at stake. And I started learning this from Carol Gilligan.

When I started reading Carol Gilligan's 1982 book, *In a Different Voice,* I was interested in what she had to say about how women were making the decision about whether or not to have an abortion. I'd been moved by the kindness, concern, and hard work of the counseling staff in the Planned Parenthood clinic where I worked. I wanted to have more to say when I responded to the antichoice groups' claims that women didn't have enough information, enough intellect, enough autonomy, or enough moral capacity to make their own decisions about an unintended pregnancy.

So the next time I was in a city that had a bookstore that sold feminist literature, I made sure to bring Gilligan home. I expected to be moved by her research on how other women decide when and if to have an abortion. I didn't expect to have Gilligan challenge all of my very own insecurities about intellect and decision-making.

Carol Gilligan describes the difference in moral decision-making between women and men as the difference between judgments based on relationships or based on rules. Gilligan was the first person to make me seriously ask, what if men and women aren't just different? What if male ways of thinking have got it wrong? What if Sigmund Freud was exhibiting more sexism than genius when he proclaimed that "women show less sense of justice than men, that they are less ready to submit to the great exigencies of life, that they are more often influenced in their judgments by feelings of affection or hostility"?

What if the feelings of affection and hostility actually provide us womb-sufferers with a greater sense of justice?

Carol Gilligan describes Kohlberg and Kramer's Moral Justification Scale. I had never heard of Kohlberg and Kramer when I read her book, but I recognized the scale as my own internalized critique of my womb-dominated brain. On level three of the scale, morality is seen in inter-personal terms—helping others. Beginning at stage four, rules become more important than relationships. At the sixth and highest Kohlberg and Kramer stage, relationships become subordinate to universal prin-ciples of logic and reason and rules.

I was stuck on level three; I was terrible at subordinating relation-ships to principles. My heroes were the Robin Hoods who became thieves to feed the hungry and became forgers to get Jews out of Nazi Germany. I kept seeing how the rules didn't fit every situation. I kept noticing how the rules seemed to be written to benefit a certain set of people. In nursing school, I kept paying attention to how much we didn't know, how many times medicine had been wrong. I kept being drawn to the people who practiced medicine as art as well as science. In the world of politics, I couldn't stop being skeptical about political theory. Jefferson, Marx, Chairman Mao, and Milton Friedman had interesting, big, round ideas. But to me it felt like they were pushing their theories into little square holes, sweeping away all the pieces that didn't fit.

Reading Gilligan let me hear the still, small voice that asked whether or not these guys needed to pay more attention to what didn't fit into their theories. I started to notice that if adherence to rules is all that matters, what we can't capture in a rule doesn't exist. After I read *In a Different Voice,* I began to understand how often male-pattern rule-based thinking, supported by money and political might, was blinding all of us to the more relationship-based, complicated truth. Problems were unsolvable because we weren't looking at the whole problem. Capital punishment? Parental consent for birth control and abortion? Neat rule-based systems for issues too complicated to be addressed by simple rules.

In a Different Voice helped me understand that we need to build campaigns and social change organizations in which the facts matter but so do relationships. Gilligan encouraged me to stick up for the human story rather than always deferring to the intellectual argument. When I make the commonsense case for what's wrong with having lead in some red lipsticks when other red lipsticks don't contain lead, Gilligan helps me stand up to the Steve Hentges–type risk-assessment argument that argues that small amounts of lead are safe.

When Hentges argues that "no reliable evidence has shown that bisphenol A in consumer products to have caused [*sic*] any human health problem," he is stating that the rules say you have to have proof of human harm before you can limit a chemical company's product. If proof of cause is the rule that matters, then Steve Hentges wins. But if commonsense relationships of accumulated evidence and the innovative ability to do something safer have merit, then we have more states and companies and even the federal government limiting dangerous chemicals, and we get more regulation and less exposure to dangerous chemicals in the products we use every day. And we get healthcare reform that factors in the suffering of the family of a child with cancer. We get military policies that don't exclude the collateral damage of bombed-out villages. All those extraneous findings that mess up our submission to Freud's great exigencies of life get taken into account.

American women are experiencing real womb suffering. And there is real reason to believe that chemicals are playing a role in these growing health problems: Uterine fibroids are the number one cause of hysterectomy in reproductive-aged women, accounting for more than 200,000 of these surgeries annually in the United States alone. Uterine fibroids are a significant cause of pelvic pain, heavy menstrual bleeding, abnormal uterine bleeding, infertility, and complications in pregnancy.

At least 12 percent of women reported difficulty in conceiving and maintaining pregnancy in 2002, an increase of 40 percent from 1982. The rate has almost doubled in younger women aged eighteen to twenty-five. About 30 percent more babies are being born prematurely. And the low birth weight that accompanies prematurity can have deleterious lifelong health effects.

As the evidence mounts that these and other health problems are connected to chemical exposures, the political opportunity is growing to create a new federal chemicals policy that captures the complexity of how chemicals can harm health, and to move chemical manufacturers toward safer alternatives. In my daily work I get to be part of growing this national effort and to witness the widening and deepening of a campaign that now includes both the Planned Parenthood Federation of America and the North American Hazardous Materials Management Association. Safer Chemicals, Healthy Families includes traditional environmental groups like the Environmental Defense Fund and the National Resources Defense Council but also Moms Rising, Women's Voices for the Earth, and the Breast Cancer Fund. The power of real estrogen is coming together to challenge the producers of chemicals that are synthetic estrogens and chemicals that have other harmful properties.

My former Commonweal colleague, Rachel Naomi Remen, likes to quote Dame Edith Sitwell's description of William Blake: "He was cracked. But it was through the crack that the light came." The wound that women share can be opened to let in the pooled light that changes the way our society makes decisions. If the history of the twenty-first century includes the story of how we developed an approach to public policy that was less rules-based in favor of one that was oriented to put relationships at a premium—a policy that consequently gave us new tools to solve long-standing problems—the estrogen-mimicking bisphenol A will have its own chapter.

 Charlotte Brody is a registered nurse and the director of chemicals and green chemistry for the BlueGreen Alliance, a national, strategic partnership between labor unions and environmental organizations dedicated to expanding the number and quality of jobs in the green economy. Formerly national field director for Safer Chemicals, Healthy Families, the director of programs for Green for All, and the executive director of Commonweal, Brody was also a founder and executive director of Health Care Without Harm; the organizing director for the Center for Health, Environment, and Justice; the executive director of a Planned Parenthood affiliate in North Carolina; and the coordinator of the Carolina Brown Lung Association.

31

The Return of
the Ghost Dancers

Edward Tick, Ph.D.

*Unlike those who employ conventional approaches to help heal veterans, Ed
Tick understands that post-traumatic stress disorder is really a wounding
of the soul. Working with veterans as whole people, with deep respect for
the healing process and an appreciation of the deleterious spiritual impacts
of warfare, Ed leads from his heart. As the numbers of people who've
been damaged by warfare continue to rise globally—both literally and as
a result of surviving the combat of life in prisons and many inner-city and
other impoverished communities—Ed's healing modalities have tremendous potential application. Through his care, listening, and compassionate
reframing, veterans are transforming into spiritual warriors to help wean
our culture's addiction to war.*

NINA SIMONS

In the history of the United States and its Native Americans, the
Ghost Dance was a messianic movement that arose at the end of the
nineteenth century, when many of the indigenous people had been
defeated, had been moved to reservations, and could no longer bear
arms against the genocide by the Euro-American culture. Across the

continent thousands of traditional people began dancing, praying, and chanting the Ghost Dance in a movement that would, they believed, bring back the spirits of the dead—the dead warriors, the dead wives and children, the dead buffalo, the dead Earth. They danced and prayed to see the spirits, because they knew that the spirits are there and with us all the time.

A recent headline in *USA Today* read: "Veteran Stress Cases Up Sharply; Mental Illness Is Now No. 2 Injury." It is good that the Veterans Administration is finally admitting the degree and extent of invisible wounding from our present wars. It is good that the invisible wounds of war are getting publicity and the public is being educated to their reality. But there are two mistakes in this headline. One is that post-traumatic stress disorder (PTSD) is neither an individual pathology nor a mental illness. The second mistake is claiming that the psychological, spiritual, and moral dimensions of the war wound are the "number two injury." They are number one.

War has been epidemic since the beginning of recorded history. Scholars declare that we have had over 14,600 wars in the last five thousand years of recorded history—and these are only the wars with definitive outcomes. When we go to war now, we use such advanced technology with such brutal firepower, moving at such rapid speed, that it is impossible to participate in combat in the modern era and come out sane.

The ghosts of war populate our world. All over the country, all over the world, people perceive these ghosts. Our veterans who have nightmares of the dead are not just seeing an individual pathology; they are seeing the ghosts. In Vietnam today, in Korea, in African nations, and among Native Americans on this continent they have longed called Turtle Island, people perceive the ghosts through their dreams, their visions, and their flashbacks.

Commonly, PTSD nightmares are pathologized as individual problems rooted in personal psychology. However, when we take the spiritual approach, when we understand how war affects us, how it damages our soul, we can see that these nightmares are visits from the spirits, the spirits of the dead, the spirits of the land, trying to talk to us, trying to return to us, asking us for help.

What is this invisible wound of war we now call post-traumatic stress disorder? It is classified as a stress and anxiety disorder. It is not merely that. That is a civilian category. The person suffering PTSD may be loaded with stress and anxiety, but these are not the words that adequately describe the emotions we experience during war. PTSD is not an individual pathology or illness, nor is it a medical condition to be healed by the battery of medications in which we drench our veterans and survivors.

First, PTSD is a soul wound. A soul wound means that all the functions ever attributed to the soul are distorted, damaged, lost, and confused by the horrible wounding of war. The way we think, the way we feel, the way we act, the way we love, the way we participate in employment, whether or not we can participate in society, our moral sensibility, and our aesthetics are all profoundly distorted and disturbed by the experience of war. PTSD is a cry of the soul trapped in the underworld. It is a frozen war-consciousness that makes the whole world look like a war zone. The self shrinks, barely staying alive and struggling to tolerate daily life, while the world looks like it is exploding around us. If we need to use the acronym PTSD, let's call it post-terror soul distress.

PTSD is also a social disorder. Our entire tribe is disordered when we are at war. The PTSD symptoms that individuals suffer are also our epidemic social ills—suicide; homicide; skyrocketing crime, divorce, child abuse, and domestic violence; drug and alcohol abuse—all the things we are suffering the most as epidemic conditions in our society are the symptoms of post-terror social disorder. When a country is at war, nothing is normal for any of us. We all feel the pain; we all have the disturbance.

If we must fit the condition into psychological categories, PTSD is better understood as an identity disorder. That is, the experience of war is a death and rebirth. It is an initiation. Since the beginning of time, traditional cultures have used the journey into warriorhood not to create people who will destroy and kill, but to create people who understand and appreciate the preciousness and fragility of life and who are here to protect it. That is what a spiritual warrior is and does. Our First Nations people teach us that their warriors are peacemakers and peace bringers, not destroyers.

When we send people off to war, they are changed forever. "Who am I now?" is a question every survivor has to answer. The death of innocence has occurred, and the death of the old self has occurred. We have to help our survivors find their new self and create a new identity that includes the wounding and includes the war experience. As well, we have to help them find a way to bring all of it back to everyone in the tribe.

What is the usual contemporary response? We give our survivors massive amounts of medication, separate them, send them off to hospitals, or let them go off and hide in the woods by themselves. Or we practice therapeutic strategies that teach them not to talk about the wound, not to talk about their experiences, and to avoid anything that might cause stress. But the truth is—war hurts, and it should. We don't ask the veterans their stories, and they don't tell them to us. That is wrong, and we have to stop it.

This old strategy that isolates and medicates our veterans effectively cuts their tongues out. We need to restore their voices in our communities, in our larger society, and around the world. Aeschylus, the Greek playwright, himself a veteran of the Battle of Marathon where his brother was killed, said, "Truth is the first casualty of war." Only when we restore the stories, when we restore the voices of our veterans and survivors, can we restore truth. When we understand that PTSD is a spiritual wound and a social disorder, the recipe for healing is clear. That recipe is what the traditional people have been teaching us forever. The recipe for healing PTSD is spirituality and community.

When we understand that PTSD is an identity disorder, we can work with our survivors to achieve an identity transformation that *includes* their wounds. We cannot and should not try to be pain free after war. Instead we need to be in a new, constructive, openhearted, and compassionate relationship to our own and each other's pain and the world's pain. In the Civil War, PTSD was called "soldier's heart." My nonprofit organization dedicated to healing the aftereffects of war takes its name from that.

PTSD is an incomplete initiation. Our veterans and survivors are stuck in the underworld. We need to go down there, meet them in hell where they are stuck, and walk out with them. When we do this, our hearts will be broken also, but we will discover depths of love, commitment, and devotion that only people who have served in hell together know. We can complete the initiations and bring them back from hell. Many veterans, as they heal, say, in effect, "I'm no longer a Vietnam veteran, I'm no longer a Somalia or Grenada or Panama or Gulf War veteran. I'm a warrior whose service was in Vietnam or Panama or El Salvador. I've joined the world class of spiritual warriors, and my service was unfortunate, but I can carry it because I've returned and I have a new identity with new meaning."

We need to reformulate our relationship to veterans. Vets, soldiers, and warriors put their lives on the line for the rest of us; whether we think the cause is legitimate is beside the point. The wounding to war survivors transcends politics. Most people go into the service to preserve and protect the people, country, and values they love—and they are willing to sacrifice their lives for them. All too often, however, when they are in the middle of combat or overseas deployment or a long service contract and they cannot exit or return, what they discover is that they are not serving such high values; they discover that the service is illegitimate. We need to say to all of our survivors: You protected us, now it's our turn to protect you. You went out on the front lines for us, now come back into the tribal circle, into the community circle, and let us protect you. You served in our name, now we will serve you.

I have just returned from leading my ninth journey of reconciliation and healing to Vietnam. I cannot express how beautiful it is to run a reconciliation group with veterans from America, Canada, Australia, North and South Vietnam, and the Viet Cong—all of them loving and embracing one another as brothers and sisters who have survived the same hell.

I want to end with a quick story about one modern ghost dancer, a man named Bob who was an infantry grunt in Vietnam. He participated in the destruction of villages. He had severe PTSD. Divorced twice and with recurrent nightmares, he was on the verge of his third divorce. He had over two hundred college credits but could not finish a degree, and he could not keep a job.

We went back to Vietnam together twice. There he saw the ghosts, not only in his nightmares, but as we were driving through the rice paddies. He saw the people he had killed, the people we had bombed, and the children and our veterans and his comrades who had died. He saw them all walking toward him as ghosts.

Bob saw the ghosts and knew they were real. So we honored his dead. We, the first Westerners to visit this remote region since the war, returned to where he had served in the jungles north of Ho Chi Minh City. We returned to where his comrades fell, and we prayed. We honored the Vietnamese dead. We practiced reconciliation with these former enemies and entered a universal brotherhood. We did rituals for the souls of the Vietnamese lives that he took. We practiced restoration projects. We built a school in the Mekong Delta. He adopted some Vietnamese children and now sponsors them in school.

In particular, there was one fourteen-year-old boy, the first Viet Cong soldier Bob had killed. For decades, Bob had seen this boy in his nightmares, and then walking toward him again in Vietnam. Finally, we climbed to a Buddhist pagoda on Nui Ba Den, Black Lady Mountain, and did a memorial service for that boy. During that ceremony, Bob saw the boy's soul come to him on top of the sacred mountain. The boy's soul came to him beaming, smiling, with arms out, embracing him and saying, "Thank you. I've returned. From now on I am your spiritual ally and guide and friend. We will walk and serve together for the rest of our lives."

From the moment of that vision on, Bob began sleeping like a baby. This was eight years ago. He has not had a combat nightmare since then. He is reconciled with his wife and now has a great marriage. He continues to support Vietnamese children and veterans. He is active in his community in veterans' affairs. He has become a modern ghost dancer.

Edward Tick, Ph.D., has been working with survivors of war, violence, and trauma for over thirty years. He is founder and director of Soldier's Heart: A Veterans' Safe Return Initiative (www.soldiersheart.net) and guides educational, healing, and reconciliation projects nationally and internationally. Tick is author of *Sacred Mountain: Encounters with the Vietnam Beast; The Practice of Dream Healing: Bringing Ancient Greek Mysteries into Modern Medicine; The Golden Tortoise: Viet Nam Journeys; War and the Soul: Healing Our Nation's Veterans from Post-traumatic Stress Disorder;* and *Wild Beasts and Wandering Souls: Shamanism and Post-traumatic Stress Disorder.*

32

Transforming Economics

Donna Morton

Donna Morton employs humor and strategic insight to awaken people to ideas that can accelerate change through economic leverage. She teaches us to question our assumptions about money and explore seemingly unlikely strategies to alter its distribution and use. In her research of effective and innovative policies across the globe, and her creative envisioning of cutting-edge projects to bring energy independence to indigenous communities by combining arts, finance, and traditional lifeways, she demonstrates what it means to be an economic artist. I am inspired by her commitments to justice, creativity, and whatever works, as well as her nimble and expansive mind.

NINA SIMONS

After spending years in the environmental movement, I realized two things: that I cared hugely about people and jobs, and that one of the consistent barriers to moving forward on all these interconnected issues was an inability to figure out how we were going to pay for the changes we want to see. That seemed to me a missing piece of our story. Economics is pivotal to addressing the biggest issues of this generation: abating climate change and addressing global poverty. My work in reinventing economics has shown me that if we can lead from softer and more ancient ways of knowing, we can build big-picture solutions that integrate people, planet, and profits.

The Centre for Integral Economics and our new project called First Power seeks to fill in those gaps and build solutions across organizations, sectors, genders, and cultures. But I have to start by noting that economics, as much as it pretends to be a hard science, is not. It is a collection of stories, which makes it more of an art. The most powerful part of that recognition for me means that we are empowered to edit. Narratives have authors, and seeing authorship in economics invites a discussion of who wrote the stories and who ought to be writing the stories now. We are empowered to hit CONTROL-ALT-DELETE on the pieces that fail us. If we see the authors and note who is missing, we open space for new voices. Women originated economics, and today we need to play a role in its reinvention too.

In my story of economics, there is not anything inherently evil about money or markets. It's all energy; any economic activity can be neutral, negative, or even positive. There's something exciting about entrepreneurs racing with a hot new idea into a marketplace. However, damaging ideas prevail in conventional economics, ideas that drive the wrong kinds of growth, reward dangerous practices, and leave out key feedback loops that used to control economic activity in smaller and more local contexts.

We need to tell more complex stories about growth in balance with living systems. We need to demand that growth align with the values of communities and with life itself. We need to be aware of the larger context of economics and the stories left out of corporate and government ledgers. Dollars and jobs can lift or lower the quality of the future, and citizens need to insert themselves and ask the larger questions. To me the questions are: What does that marketplace look like? How does it treat people? How does it despoil communities and trash environmental ecosystems? How does it play within the rules of a game that all of us have a hand in building?

I have been called an economist; in reality I am more of an economic artist. I believe economics can be made to express the highest aspirations of human beings. Economics can—like poetry, the poetry of a Mary Oliver, an Alice Walker, or a Lee Maracle, for instance—express a higher purpose. I think we, as citizens, have a right to demand beauty even from economics and its structures. Toronto, spearheaded by artists and others, just passed an "ugly tax that rewards beauty"; it's a tax on billboards, and its revenues are redirected into the arts. Economics that now blames, shames, and separates can instead express love, install trust, demand honor, and lift the soul.

I love teaching and have done community-based workshops that teach economics as a values-based discipline. I often use poetry to illustrate the nobility of humanity and deeply held values, and then we look at how those values can be translated into economic tools and institutions. It makes economics both real and soft, inviting curiosity instead of intimidation. Historically, and in the ways we hear about economics daily, we are made to feel afraid of economics, we are made to feel disqualified. Economic empowerment can start in a single day. I have seen it; I have witnessed an elderly woman cry and break through to a new sense of power, and a single mom cut through layers of lies to a sense of how her values, brought inside economics, could help others. I believe that economic literacy is one of the most fundamentally important next steps in rewriting our collective history.

Our economic infrastructure in Canada, much as in the United States, was built by robber barons. It was built to suit the interests of the few, paid for by the many; citizens had no role in building the rules we live with more than a hundred years later. Bringing people inside economics is critically important. We need the largest "we" in human history to turn this mess around and to craft a next economy that heals. The "we" I am talking about includes hairdressers and cab drivers and restaurateurs and activists and artists and antiglobalization street youths and aboriginal communities and people who have been incarcerated and people who have been in the sex trade. We all have a right and a responsibility for crafting this next economy. No one is going to hand it to us. We're the ones who must separate economic activity from harm. We're the ones who will build new rules that are tied to new values.

The good news is that "we"—progressive citizens from every walk of life—have been doing this work all over the globe. For years now a lot of my work has included shopping the globe for the best economic practices that exist. The most powerful policy stories come from the richest places, and the most whole and creative policy stories often come from some of the world's poorest places. My favorite examples include taxes in Europe, budget and currency innovations from South America, and financial innovations like microcredit in Southeast Asia. Always I am inspired by aboriginal models from all around the world.

We've spent a lot of time looking at the participatory budget movement in Brazil, which I find very inspiring. In these communities, the citizens who didn't like the way a local government was making decisions about budget allocations came together, with the encouragement of the Porto Alegre government, and they decided that the decisions about both taxation and budgetary expenditures would be made by the community as a whole. Inviting people to touch economics—inviting dreams, values, and aspirations to show up in the structure of the economy—now that's economic and social innovation!

Other great examples come from Scandinavia and other E.U. countries. I spent ten years full-time looking at an innovation known as tax shifting or ecological tax reform. The best models for tax shifting are Denmark, Norway, Germany, the U.K., and Spain, whose governments have literally started to use tax policy to integrate the environment and the economy. They've started to wring out waste and tax inefficiency. They've even encouraged jobs by untaxing labor. Basic economics, even conventional economics, teaches that when you tax something, you get less of it. It is the building block of every first-year economics class, but in our culture and on our continent, we tax things we want more of—we tax jobs, we tax income, and we tax investment. At the same time we don't tax the things that are harmful—we don't tax pollution, we don't tax sprawl, we don't tax the wasteful use of natural resources.

At the core of tax shifting is a transition from taxing "good" things to taxing "bad" things. Of course, the devil's in the details, and tax shifting at any level of government is very difficult. I would argue that it's even more difficult in the United States, because there's a knee-jerk reaction about taxes. But it's time to take back even the tax debate from reactionary politics. Progressives have abandoned the tax field, and the open space has been exploited for generations. I have done only a few talks in the United States, and still I believe that, especially right now with climate change actually showing up on the public agenda, we have the opportunity to start a more intelligent dialogue about taxes.

We are a communications organization as much as a policy center, so we started playing with language to get people talking about taxes. We tested a whole bunch of things, and, oddly, we landed on the notion that talking about taxes was sexy. Maybe taxes are the sexiest, least-utilized agenda for progressives to get what they want. It's sexy to make polluters pay. It's sexy to hit gas-guzzling activities in the wallet and sexy to revitalize downtowns and pull profits out of building more suburbs. What if lots of the capital we need to reinvent the world is available by addressing harm directly?

I believe that social housing could get a huge boost from taxing single-level parking lots and boarded-up buildings. Lurking behind parking lots and empty buildings are land speculators. Speculators pay little or even no taxes; they don't make things, they hire as few people as possible, and they are waiting for land values to go up based on the activities of others all around them. For land speculators, every bit of productivity around them, every thriving business, every park, every bit of infrastructure that the taxpayers pay for benefits them, and when they sell off that land, they get money for nothing. It's a massive form of robbing the commons, and we and our elected officials look the other way.

For me that land could become a fabulous place to start building affordable housing. We just need to tax it back into best use and offer carrots to developments that serve people and places.

There's ways and means. You could try an experiment at the level of your local government. The biggest opportunities to test ideas like tax shifting are at the local and regional levels. Local government economics is where the bike rubber is hitting the road: where we are looking to take back control of our communities, where we want to pass bans on toxins and address climate change, and where we can prove that a diverse set of voices crafting economic policy is superior to the work of a few experts. So I want to encourage us all to embrace our inner tax wonk.

As an economic artist, I can bring all parts of me to reinventing economics, including my experience being raised by a single mother in a rough neighborhood, my studies in liberal and fine arts, my gifts of storytelling from my aboriginal blood, and my participation in civil disobedience. We need to claim our whole selves in order to build whole economies. We need to build hybrid structures and draw on the alchemy of difference. There are new solutions being crafted in the spaces between activists, artists, and entrepreneurs. There is a fire in people who are deeply committed to change, people who want to see the world different than it is today. Creativity is essential to reinventing economics and seeing our own assets; all of them are important. Our mortgages, credit cards, and retirement plans are assets that can be harnessed to reinvent the world.

We can build very different financial institutions and community-controlled funds that can catalyze change. I live in a place where we have a $13 billion financial institution that's run by people who want to change the world. Vancity Credit Union is run by women. Both the CEO and the chair of the board are visionary women. The origin of Vancity was a path to build credit for poor people—many of them women who could not get loans without husbands or fathers co-signing. Through pooling assets, standing together, and holding fast to their values, they have built something huge. Look at most of the creative nonprofits or values-based businesses in British Columbia, and Vancity assets show up.

We need to take actions against predatory lenders and move toward financial institutions we can trust and relate to. We can stop giving our money to banks and credit card companies and investments and retirement plans that act against the planet and against communities. We must fund at least part of the work at hand ourselves. What if we have the creativity, the plans, the technologies, the skills, and even the money to reinvent our places and abate climate change?

Many people in the philanthropic community and many foundations have had their money invested in the very sources of harm their programs attempt to address. Philanthropy will not fix the world, nor will government programs do it for us. We need more hands on deck, and my faith is in organized citizens, visionary communities, values-based businesses, and hybrid projects that align us and our money with what we care about. As my friend Carol Newell, cofounder of Renewal Partners and the Endswell Foundation in Vancouver, B.C., likes to say, "Get off your assets." Her company invests in cutting-edge businesses. The foundation spent down its assets but jump-started sustainability work in B.C. significantly. Even small assets pooled together can catalyze the economy that we all want.

The First Nation Finance Authority (FNFA)—entirely owned by First Nations across Canada and founded by Deanna Hamilton—pools assets of First Nations to provide infrastructure investments. Recently they expanded their work to include energy and clean technology. Through First Power and several First Nations, we are working with the FNFA on a series of projects that will harness the savings on converting diesel-generated power to renewables.

What if Native Americans and First Nations led the change to renewables? We are working on a project that will, over the span of a few years, move remote communities from their 100 percent reliance on fossil fuels to having all their electrical needs met by green power. Leaders like Carol Anne Hilton of the Hesquiaht First Nation see energy and food security, jobs, and economic development as related projects that nest and rely on each other. She is the economic development officer for her nation and is excited by the prospect of Native communities owning their power, their food, their economies, and their futures through collective finance tools. She is one of many women who have held context over time and who are now bringing a new depth of vision and crafting new stories.

Together with several leading First Nations, renewable energy leaders, and artists, we are designing a project in which wind turbines will look like totem poles and artists will culturally modify solar panels, so that elders and youths, carvers, and spiritual leaders will all be united in building green jobs. Oral traditions can be put at the center of this training so that the use of video, storytelling, and hands-on teaching methods can replace textbooks and classrooms.

What if North American cultures that had complex economies and lived sustainably for thousands of years are central to reinventing the world and economics? There are many stories of economics done differently that can inspire and guide us. Most essentially, we need the voices and stories of those who have been left out; we need a wider web of visions that hold that environmental issues, social justice issues, and economic reinvention issues are interconnected.

We need new and ancient forms of intelligence now more than ever. We need the Ph.D.s, and we need to gather from the margins—from Native reservations, cooperative housing started by single mothers, and permaculture teachers—to know what they know. New voices will remind us that inside all of us is an ancient, cellular knowledge of what matters. Dr. Helen Caldicott taught me at fifteen that the love a woman feels for her baby is a force that can save us, and I still believe that almost thirty years later. Love can be harnessed, it can be distilled into politics, it can build housing for the homeless, and it can be used as a homeopathic to heal economics.

I have heard the voices and the stories, and I believe that love-rendered economics is possible; I have felt it well up inside me like a song.

 Donna Morton is an Ashoka Fellow and cofounder of First Power, a project that supports First Nations in owning renewable and clean technologies through culturally based training and finance (www.first powercanada.ca). As well, she is a cofounder of the Centre for Integral Economics, an enterprising NGO advancing sustainability through tools like tax shifting and community finance (www.integraleconomics.org). Both organizations are based in Victoria, British Columbia, Canada. Morton is a frequent speaker and commentator and is featured as one of thirty global leaders who use economics to deliver communiqués about the environment in the international TV series *Architects of Change* (www.actfortheplanet.org).

33

Green Worker Cooperatives

Omar Freilla

If we seek to distribute power and authority more equitably, to reinvent business for the common good, what might such a healthy and sustainable business look like? Cooperatives are worker-owned and decentralize their governance while performing services that support the people and constituencies they are meant to serve. Omar Freilla sought to identify a solution with cascading benefits to his community: to create jobs, improve people's self-esteem while building equity, and recycle discarded materials to create value and divert stuff from the waste stream. His work achieves all of this by employing his relational intelligence, nimble mind, and deep caring for his community to design a business that measures its successes through benefits to people, planet, and profit. His humility, sincerity, and real caring inspire me to stand in support of his integrated vision and leadership.

NINA SIMONS

When the light switch goes on, where does the power come from? When we go to the bathroom, where does the water go after we flush it down the toilet? All the things that we don't want—the waste—where does it go?

I come from one of those neighborhoods where a lot of this stuff goes. The South Bronx is my home. I was raised there, and I live there still. Growing up, I learned pride from my mother, but I learned early on from my surroundings that my community and I were Second Class.

As a kid I had access to two playgrounds across the street from my apartment. One was an isolated island with little equipment sandwiched between a highway below and rumbling trains above. The other was a vacant lot full of rubble and trash where a building had once stood. The dilapidated playground and the vacant lots, the abandoned buildings with windows painted to fool highway commuters into thinking they were occupied, the broken sidewalks, and the police brutality, these things screamed out at me: They Don't Care About Us. And every time my mother and I visited the wealthy and overwhelmingly white business districts in Manhattan, I would notice something I wasn't used to seeing in my neighborhood: trees!

I didn't know anything about dirty industries back then, or why asthma was so common among the kids at school, but I understood neglect.

We live in a wasteful society, and a wasteful society needs a dumping ground. So in the South Bronx we're living with a lot of trash, as are many other communities around the country, like Richmond, California, and Bayview Hunters Point in San Francisco. These low-income communities and communities of color function as steam-release valves that make it possible for the lights to be turned on, for people to drive their cars, for the water to be flushed down the drain.

When you look out the window of a housing project in my community, you might see a red-and-white smokestack, which is the New York Organic Fertilizer Company. This is a company that processes sewage sludge. My neighborhood handles about half of New York City's sewage sludge—the sewage sludge from half of 9 million people. In the summertime there's a horrible odor that spreads all over the place. It makes you want to run away, but people can't afford to leave.

New York produces about 50,000 tons of trash every single day. Of that amount, approximately 13,500 tons is construction and demolition debris. About half of all of New York City's trash is processed in just two neighborhoods, the South Bronx being one of them.

The additional pollution due to truck traffic to and from all these plants is major and the consequences immense. Environmental issues have always been a public health issue. One of the highest rates of asthma in the country occurs in the South Bronx, with the rates for asthma hospitalization six times the national average. If you go into a classroom and ask kids how many of them have asthma, at least 30 percent of the hands in the classroom will go up. If you don't have asthma, try breathing through a straw and you'll understand what having an asthma attack actually feels like.

The reason why our communities wind up suffering from this state of affairs is that disposal follows the path of least resistance. It's simple but true. Garbage is like water; it goes where there is the least resistance. This is how a power plant or a garbage transfer station gets sited. If the place is cheap and the geography works, then someone is going to build something on it.

How can a community say no? If someone tells you that they're going to build a power plant in your neighborhood, what would you do? Would you be calling a lawyer? Is someone in your family a lawyer, or do you know someone on the city council? We live in such a segregated society, by race and class, that those resources aren't spread across the board evenly. And race and class in this country have always been intertwined. Since the very beginning, slavery was an economic system. Race and class have always been linked, and it's impossible to say it's one or the other.

We can understand economics as an ecosystem in and of itself. It's human made. It's what drives or guides how we eat, how we sleep, and how we get food on our table. So when we talk about what it takes to move toward a green economy, if we are truly going to be able to transition to a pollution-less world and move to zero waste, we must realize that some communities bear a disproportionate amount of our waste and that our economic system requires it to be that way. We're talking about an economic system that is destroying communities and destroying people's health.

This is why communities like mine are fighting, and why it is that we talk about environmental racism and environmental classism, and why it is we fight for environmental justice. We're fighting for our lives.

Even with modest resources, we have begun to fight. When we get enough people in a room, and enough skilled organizing, we can stop something from happening, especially if we become aware of a project ahead of time. It just takes people power. There are more and more communities in this fight, but even as we have successes, one of the things that has been increasingly frustrating—and it's the reason we started Green Worker Cooperatives—is this issue of jobs.

Someone waves a carrot in front of a community and says, We want to build this power plant, or this warehouse distribution center or even an oil refinery, and in so doing, we're going to bring jobs to the community. In our area, unemployment rates are as high as 24 percent. The Community Service Society in New York did a study a few years ago that concluded that almost half of the black men in New York City were out of work. For Latino men the statistic was just slightly less, about 42 percent. We all know about the loss of manufacturing, the traditional source of blue-collar jobs. This situation makes people desperate, and people desperate for work will say, Okay, fine.

Those of us in places like the South Bronx need jobs, but we don't want jobs that kill us in the process. We want jobs that give us health insurance, not to protect us from the job itself but to protect us from walking outside and getting hit by a car. Besides, when we hear companies say they have a job for us in a power plant, we understand that not many people actually work in the power plant, and most of those that do are engineers. And as far as I know, the public schools in my community are in no shape to turn out any engineers, at least not yet.

So I was organizing with a local community group, Sustainable South Bronx,* and working with the New York City Environmental

---

*Sustainable South Bronx (SSBx) is a community organization dedicated to environmental justice solutions through innovative, economically sustainable projects that are informed by community needs. In 2001, SSBx was created to address policy and planning issues like land use, energy, transportation, water, waste, education, and, most recently, design and manufacturing.

Justice Alliance, and I was getting tired of constantly being the nay-sayer, of constantly working to stop this plant from coming in, of stopping the city from doing this or that. And one day it popped into my mind: As long as we've got a vacant piece of property, let's create something to fill that piece of land that will bring healthy jobs, whether it's a park or a green manufacturing plant. Let's create green-collar jobs. Let's create plenty of green-collar jobs that don't kill people in the process. We love our communities. We love clean air. We'd one day like to see some green trees. We need to create this kind of work and make it be homegrown.

Much as we tried to attract green businesses, there weren't any CEOs with a green conscience coming to the South Bronx and trying to give workers a piece of the action. I was always thinking about what would be a better way. So I started the Green Worker Cooperatives as a separate organization with the support of the folks at Sustainable South Bronx. I had no knowledge of business. As a matter of fact, I didn't know that much about worker-owned cooperatives either. But I knew enough to know that they were a much better alternative to the "winner take all" capitalist approach that has sacrificed communities like mine, and they are truer to the idea of democracy than anything we have going now.

We're learning as we go. We decided to follow the precautionary principle and opt for zero waste. In the spring of 2008 we launched our first cooperative, ReBuilders Source, a worker-owned business engaged in reuse. In a sense, you can think of it as a worker-owned Home Depot for used stuff. We salvage building materials. Anyone who has ever renovated a kitchen knows that there is an incredible amount of waste and expense. You've got to pay to throw all that stuff out. The benefits are that not only are we reducing this waste, we're creating jobs, we're minimizing the pollution, and we're preserving any number of natural resources because we're not cutting down the trees and strip-mining the mountains to get those materials in the first place.

My mom gets to feel proud that I'm doing good things, even though she thinks I spend too much time going to meetings and picking up garbage.

This idea of the worker cooperative is a positive antidote to the current corporate models. It is made up of workers owning their own workplace whereby they are empowered to decide their own fate—in other words, true democracy. There are many benefits to a worker cooperative. It retains wealth in a community. You don't have someone who makes a thousand times what the lowest-paid workers make and who winds up living maybe ten states away or even in another country. Worker cooperatives do not leave town, and thus they avoid layoffs. They enable accountability, because it's not enough to say, "We don't want a smokestack in the neighborhood." True accountability means that if there's going to be a smokestack, the smokestack needs to be pointed into the boardroom. Because it's in the boardroom where those decisions happen.

There are plenty of worker co-ops in the United States. Rainbow Grocery and the Arizmendi Bakery are in the Bay Area. In other parts of the country, Burley makes bicycles, and there's the Northland Poster Collective. Cooperative Home Care Associates is in my neck of the woods and consists of over a thousand workers, all of whom are home healthcare aides who have raised the standard for work in their field.

Because of the success of ReBuilders Source, we've just revamped our co-op development strategy. Now we have groups of people coming to us with their ideas for green and worker-owned cooperatives, and we work with them to develop a business plan and secure the financing they need to make it real. We've got another six co-ops in development. They range from green catering services to a local and healthy foods diner, a furniture refurbishing outfit, a manufacturer of solar thermal panels, and a worker- and youth-owned green community center.

So this movement for worker cooperatives is growing. We've developed our approach to meet the need for work in our community, work that respects our human dignity and allows us the space to fully grow as human beings, work that builds up our community instead of sacrificing it. We believe deep down in our hearts that another world is possible, and we are going to be the ones who will make it happen.

Omar Freilla is passionate about creating a green and democratic economy in the South Bronx, where he grew up and where he now lives. He is the founder of Green Worker Cooperatives (www.greenworker.coop), an organization dedicated to incubating environmentally friendly worker-owned businesses in the South Bronx. He has a master's degree in environmental science from Miami University and is a graduate of Morehouse College, where he also founded the organization Black Men for the Eradication of Sexism. Freilla is a recipient of the Jane Jacobs Medal for New Ideas and Activism.

34

Reconnecting Children and Nature

Cheryl Charles, Ph.D.

Retooling education and how we raise our children is clearly essential to a sustainable future. If one of our worst systems errors has been in believing we are apart from, rather *than* a part of, *nature, what could be more essential than reestablishing kids' connection to the natural world? Educator and author Cheryl Charles reflects on her effective work to bring nature back into childhood and education and notes how her own ongoing relationship with nature informs and enhances her life.*

NINA SIMONS

Ecology is a term my grandfather, Perl Charles, taught me. Granddad was a lifelong conservationist—and always a teacher and storyteller. As we went horseback riding together, he told me to look around. He liked to have us follow the same trail through all the seasons and notice the changes. He also loved to take us to a place where we could get a big view—often from a mountaintop in the desert Southwest where we could see horizon in every direction. He said, "Places like this teach perspective." With his strong and gentle guidance, integrity, humor, and heart, he taught me. He showed me that all parts of any environment, living and nonliving, exist in relationship to one another, and that every part matters and is connected.

I have carried this wisdom with me throughout my life. These two themes of being out in nature and connecting all the parts in community have guided and motivated my work and my leadership. I have spent most of my adult career focused on the importance of children's healthy development, the health of communities, and the health of the environment—and how these are all connected.

I began my career as a teacher in an inner-city high school in Phoenix. At that time, textbooks might have references to wildlife or endangered species, but there was no mention of the world of habitat, there was no sense of the web of relationships among living things. I realized early on that ecoliteracy involved all subject and skill areas and actually involved a way of life, and I wanted to see that reflected in the development of curriculum. Within a few years, I became the national founding director of what remain the two most widely used environment education programs in North America, designed to integrate ecological concepts into the educational system at the K–12 level. The names of these programs are Project Learning Tree and Project WILD. When I left these programs, we had reached about 17 percent of teachers in the United States, and it delights me that these two programs continue to thrive and serve as outstanding resources for educators and others today.

But as we were developing this curriculum, a profound change in the actual nature of childhood crept up on us. Most children and youth today have limited direct experience with the outdoors, a trend that has only escalated in the past ten years. If they are outdoors, the experience is more likely to be in organized sports and on playground equipment, often on asphalt playgrounds. Shuttled from school to church to soccer to dance class to day camp, most of our children are—with all good intentions on the part of parents, teachers, and caregivers—being given a virtual, vicarious, electronic, passive, and cocooned experience of childhood. Or they are left on their own for hours and hours at a time, hooked into what I call the electronic umbilicus of today's kids' contemporary lifestyles. This umbilicus comprises the computer, the cell phone, the television, and video games. I am not at all antitechnology, and there are always exceptions, but on the whole, the defining experiences of today's youth and children take place indoors, at home, in school, or in a car.

Teachers and others can make life better for children, and for ourselves, by opening the door to the first classroom—the natural world—from backyards to neighborhoods to schoolyards and public places. Instead of children being indoors, stuck in place, they should be outside, where ecoliteracy lessons can penetrate deeper into body, mind, heart, and spirit. It's about emphasis, re-righting the balance. They need direct experience, and schools need to change to allow for that.

This is certainly happening in some places. Robin Moore and Herb Wong's environmental schoolyard in Berkeley, California, built in the 1970s, is an early example; now there are many such powerful learning gardens and schoolyard habitat projects all over the country. Nature-based preschools are beginning to increase as well. Awareness is building. My colleague Richard Louv's book *Last Child in the Woods* has made a huge contribution and made my work in the Children and Nature Network easier: to build a worldwide movement to reconnect children with nature.

The research is also catching up to common sense. There is now a substantial body of work indicating that the simple act of going outdoors reduces people's stress, anxiety, and depression. With people of all ages, the results are dramatic. People's overall health, peacefulness, and general well-being are enhanced to the degree that we spend some time outdoors on a regular basis.

There are immediate physical payoffs for getting children outside, but there are more far-reaching benefits as well. If we are in the outdoors often enough to watch and experience the seasonal changes, we learn about "place." We learn about the natural cycles and changes within an ecological setting. In so doing, we are more inclined to have a complex and informed understanding of that natural system—and potentially other natural systems. We will be far more likely to care about the health of living systems over time, more likely to make informed decisions, and more likely to effect responsible actions.

In Illinois, I was asked to speak to seven hundred fourth and fifth graders who were assembled in an old auditorium. About twenty minutes in, I took a chance: I asked if anyone would like to come up to the stage, and a number of children did so. One was a fifth grader who took the microphone from me with confidence. She said, "Nature is important in my life because I feel better when I'm outdoors. And when we get to play outdoors we learn about the natural world, and this means we will do better taking care of nature when we're grown up." She had just nailed the two most important points that I needed to make in my speech, so I thanked her. Afterward, she came up to me and said: "What is ADHD? That is what they tell me I have."

There's no doubt that the symptoms of attention deficit disorder are mitigated by outdoor experience. People tell me stories all the time about how a school program that encouraged their children to play outside or plant a garden made a huge difference in dealing with the children's ADD or ADHD. I get many phone calls and letters from parents and grandparents telling me that their children were failing in school, and after learning plant restoration, mucking about in wetlands, or just playing and running around outside, they found a sense of calm and an ability to focus, which in turn made it possible for them to do well in school.

I walk my talk every day. In the midst of a hectic schedule, my beloved husband of thirty-six years has become housebound with Parkinson's. It's been challenging to accommodate to this phase of our lives together, and it's become a part of my personal self-care to take long walks by myself. For an hour or more every day, I go outside and I check on my bird neighbors. We live in an older urban community that is a good model of how, with some care and planning, one can enjoy nature in the city. There's a small lake, surrounded by bike paths and lots of native vegetation; it's home to a number of migratory species. I carry my camera and binoculars, spotting in one week a gorgeous male cardinal, a family of kestrels, and a great blue heron and getting pictures of each. I get to recall my early days with my grandfather, and I am gradually restored in a feeling of balance.

Cheryl Charles, Ph.D., an innovator, entrepreneur, educator, author, and organizational executive, is president and CEO of the Children and Nature Network (www.childrenandnature.org), cofounded with a collaborative group of leaders including Richard Louv, author of *Last Child in the Woods: Saving Our Children from Nature-Deficit Disorder*. Charles was the founding national director of the two most widely used environment education programs in North America, Project Learning Tree and Project WILD. Her most recent book is *Coming Home: Community, Creativity and Consciousness*.

35

Chica Luna Productions

Women Creating Social Change by Using Popular Media

Sofia Quintero

In today's media world, we are bombarded constantly with stories that perpetuate negative stereotypes, describe women as victims, and are secondary to a hero's journey. Sofia Quintero realized early on that to transform our culture, media must change. Her work as an author and activist challenges negative assumptions and stereotypes. Through her work at Chica Luna, she cultivates tomorrow's media makers to tell stories from diverse women's perspectives, while writing novels in which young women can recognize themselves. These novels integrate learning and complexity and they cultivate a moral compass. Sofia is a woman of great heart and mind whose systemic and wholehearted response to the pervasive lack of vision for young women inspires me.

NINA SIMONS

We in the hip-hop community have a saying: "Keep it real." But I always ask, "What if what's real needs to change?" There is no value in keeping it real if what's real is oppressive. That certainly has been the case

271

with the way women—especially women of color—have been depicted in entertainment media.

I firmly believe that it's going to be women who will keep it real because they're going to bring hip-hop subculture back to its roots in resistance. Before it became a global commodity, hip-hop was a strident vehicle for personal change and social transformation. As it has grown from subculture to commerce, more often than not it has become a purveyor of oppressive ideologies by entertainers of color against their own people.

Now I may be one of very few women utilizing hip-hop in the realm of commercial fiction, but I am not the only woman who is using storytelling in popular culture to promote social change.* However, there needs to be a lot more of us, and we can stand to be more diverse. This is one reason why I cofounded a nonprofit organization called Chica Luna Productions. The mission of Chica Luna is to identify, develop, and support women of color who strive to create socially conscious entertainment.

Why entertainment? Because entertainment is as political as anything we might see on CNN or the Fox News network. You think *Crash* is a political film? So is *Hustle and Flow*. We readily call *Thelma & Louise* a political film, but we should also recognize *Miss Congeniality, Maid in Manhattan, Chasing Papi*—all these are also political films. All movies, whether you see them on cable, at the art house, or at the multiplex, are political films. Therefore it is imperative that we build a cadre of socially conscious filmmakers, especially among women who will make commercially viable films that tell our stories, whether they are critiques of the way things are or offer visions of the way things should be.

One of Chica Luna's signature programs toward this goal is a project called the F-Word—and yes, the *F* does stand for feminism, because we encourage women to embrace feminism and make it their own rather

---

*Quintero is the author of a critically acclaimed series of novels, written under the pen name Black Artemis.

than disavow it based on how it has been defined or misrepresented by others. The F-Word is a one-year filmmaking institute for women of color ages sixteen and older, and not only do they learn the craft of filmmaking—including all the technical aspects that are usually male dominated—they also undergo political education, community-building, and self-healing. Political education includes media literacy, because we rarely learn how to read a film for its social, political, cultural, and economic messages.

Why is community-building a significant part of our curriculum? Because if women are going to build a movement, they must learn to collaborate across their differences and produce each other's films. This industry *will* pit them against each other for the scarce resources to make their films. Not only because they're women, but because they're *activist* women. And, finally, the F-Word involves self-healing to dismantle the internalized oppression that women of color have suffered from all the negative messages they have received about themselves. When we fail to do the *self* work to dismantle that internalized oppression, despite our good intentions, we often replicate the very same messages that we want to counter.

There's another thing we say in the hip-hop community: "Don't talk about it—*be* about it." The films produced by women in Chica Luna's F-Word program cover a variety of topics, carry different sensibilities, and definitely have different tones. There are films about gentrification. There are films about first love. There have been dramas and comedies. What they all have in common is that they are universal stories told by women of color.

Often when we see popular media created by a woman, automatically we assume, "Oh, that's just for chicks." That is, when the experiences of women are central, we dismiss any possibility that the story contains universal truths that can potentially resonate with anyone and everyone. The same thing happens to people of color, queer folks, and other communities or minorities that have been disenfranchised. When these communities create popular media, what may be "popular" about their stories comes under scrutiny, or at the very least is doubted. The simple act of people from those communities telling their own stories rather than having their lived experiences depicted by those *outside* their community suddenly renders those stories "too specific." They are not considered universal, and this notion is precisely what Chica Luna exists to challenge.

Those of us who cofounded Chica Luna hope that one day it will be the Sundance Institute for women of color who want to create commercially viable but socially conscious narrative films. We want women of color to create films like *Girlfight,* not *Chasing Papi.* But the challenge facing all activist filmmakers is the belief that pervades the entertainment industry, which is, if you want to send a message, use Western Union. As if every studio picture or television show or commercial radio station is somehow devoid of political, social, cultural, and economic assumptions and statements and conclusions. All media—especially entertainment media—is selling us something. If it's not a product, it's a belief; if it's not a belief, it's a value; if it's not a value, it's a lifestyle. This is why it's imperative that we start to seize popular culture as another strategy for making change.

This is also why I cocreated Sister Outsider Entertainment. My creative partner and I took the name of our company from a groundbreaking collection of essays and speeches by lesbian warrior-woman and poet-activist Audre Lorde, who once said that poetry is not a luxury. At Sister Outsider, we seek to promote quality urban entertainment, not only in film but also on stage and in publishing and other media. Our intention: to build Sister Outsider as a socially conscious multimedia production company that is profitable enough to reinvest in the social justice infrastructure—supporting nonprofit organizations like Chica Luna nationwide on a variety of issues both within and outside of media—keeping the movement going and growing.

I look at cultural activism as something that can occur on three levels. One is on the individual level. For me personally, that is not only the fiction I write as Black Artemis, but also the unapologetically feminist novels that I write under my real name. Then there's the collaborative level, when I team with like-minded people, and we do anything from facilitating media literacy workshops to creating an organization like Chica Luna. And then there's the entrepreneurial level—establishing Sister Outsider Entertainment—because we must seize the means of production and create our own work, and not be reliant on the same system we're trying to change to get our messages out.

What drives this work? What compels me, and others like me, to attempt to commercialize consciousness? Prior to experiencing my own creative recovery, I would be at a nonprofit organization or government agency engaged in policy analysis and advocacy as my paid work during the day. Then in the evening I worked with the grassroots organizations and other community activists on anything from fighting police brutality to defending multicultural education in public schools. These experiences gave me the stories that I wanted to tell. But I wanted to tell these stories particularly to those who are not already engaged in social justice movements. Writing novels and even doing stand-up comedy was a way to marry political activism with my creative impulses. I didn't stop being an activist, I just switched to another strategy.

But why popular culture? Why entertainment? Why don't I become a documentary filmmaker, or a literary novelist? Because the truth is that what my people, who are not engaged in social justice movements and who are the most negatively affected by that disengagement, are consuming is popular films, novels, songs, and videos.

If I want my nephew to read a book by bell hooks, I introduce him to her with a book like *Picture Me Rollin'*. I made a decision to create commercial popular media because there is no art-house theater in the 'hood. Young people and adults in the 'hood don't subscribe to the Independent Film Channel, if they even know it exists . . . if they even have cable. There is no bookstore in the 'hood—not even the major chains, so forget about the progressive independent store. There is, however, a street vendor in front of the subway station selling books with titles like *Every Thug Needs a Lady*. And there are several movies at the multiplex that are little more than Cinderella in blackface, while the feminist critique of those films has been relegated to a radio commentary on a public station that the young people in my community bypass on their way to a station like La Mega or Hot Power Something-or-Other.

I am particularly concerned about young women who, through this entertainment, are being sold a false sense of empowerment by the films they watch, the books they read, and the rest of the popular culture they consume. Despite all the girl-power icons and language, the average young woman today does not explore, define, or pursue empowerment on her own terms. Rather, she capitulates to the male gaze and convinces herself that she's empowered because she chose to capitulate rather than to resist. And why does she not resist? Because she is afraid.

And she should be afraid. Everywhere she looks, popular culture tells her that she's damned if she does, damned if she doesn't. If she doesn't wear those low-riders and tube tops, men will not break off a piece of their power and lend it to her. However, if she does don the low-riders and the tube top, and then becomes a target of both wanted and unwanted male attention, she asked for it. So she'd better make like Buffy or Dark Angel and know how to kick butt in those leather pants and stiletto heels. Of course she's afraid. She has only two choices. Either she can choose to be invisible or she can choose to be targeted.

That's not empowerment.

Nor does she see genuinely empowered and fearless women as individuals or working in collective in the films she sees and the books she reads. Young women are reading this genre known as chick lit, and depending on who you're speaking to, chick lit can either be a compliment or it can be a diss. Well, I decided to write a chick lit novel, but *Divas Don't Yield* is not *The Devil Wears Prada* or *The Nanny Diaries*. This is not a novel about a woman vying for the corner office while navigating the boss from hell. This is not about a woman searching for the perfect pair of Manolo Blahniks, or any of the typical chick lit tropes.

In my novel, the characters are a group of unapologetic activists who drive from New York City to San Francisco to attend a women's conference, each packing a little more baggage than she thought. These are young women who are grappling with issues of race, class, sexual orientation, and faith. As much as they like to dance and chew the fat and tell jokes, they also have serious discussions about issues that affect them and their communities, much like the women I know that you usually don't see in popular fiction.

So I do this work because I came to understand that we cannot seriously begin to heal our culture if we refuse to critically engage and deconstruct and offer compellingly progressive alternatives to the media we consume under the veneer of entertainment. We, as activists, need to translate our issues into accessible narratives that broaden our conversations beyond the elite groupings we have formed, even though we didn't intend to form them. If we want to expand our ranks and recruit more people to our causes, we have to meet people where they are and take them to someplace better. And popular culture—films, novels, songs, plays, and other forms of entertainment—is a very powerful way to do that.

Sofía Quintero (a.k.a. "Black Artemis") is a Bronx-born writer, activist, educator, producer and comedienne of Puerto Rican–Dominican ancestry. A self-proclaimed "Ivy League homegirl" who earned an MPA from Columbia's prestigious School of International Affairs, she is a longtime cultural activist and social entrepreneur who creates socially conscious entertainment through her novels and videos. Sofía is the cofounder of Chica Luna Productions and Sister Outsider Entertainment. This year, she published her critically acclaimed young adult novel *Efrain's Secret* and will launch the Web series Homegirl TV.

36

Turtle Heart
Toward an Ocean Revolution

Wallace J. Nichols, Ph.D.

For me, few things are more heartbreaking than the global pollution, warming, and overfishing that are altering Earth's oceans and affecting all that live here. Wallace J. Nichols is turning the tide by advocating creatively for sea turtles. By engaging with people of different nations and cultures, he mounts successful campaigns to halt the poaching of sea turtles, while enlisting local recruits to become their protectors. As a trained scientist, he knows the data, but his work is informed by and infused with his love, empathic understanding, and tactical creativity, employing the wholeness of his human capacity to lead change.

NINA SIMONS

As a child, I fell in love with the ocean, like lots of kids do. We used to spend summers on the Chesapeake Bay, where we'd catch snapping turtles. We would get them into our arms, these big turtles, and paint numbers on their shells. Then we'd throw them back in the water. They would swim around and we'd eventually catch them again. Sometimes they'd have numbers on their shells.

When I became an adult, I discovered that I could make a living

278

doing basically the same thing. Now I'm chasing turtles around in the ocean, marking them, releasing them, maybe recapturing them, thinking about them, and then calculating their population size with complicated mathematic models.

Seventy-one percent of our planet is ocean. Eighty percent of the biodiversity is in the ocean. Ninety percent of our planet's habitat is oceanic. Yet we refuse to accept that we are an ocean planet. As such, our relationship with the ocean is damaged. We're abusing the ocean.

What is it going to be? Will it be a "brave new ocean" scenario? Are we going into a situation where we'll rely exclusively on technology, a "lockdown" state with millions of tiny computers constantly monitoring us and enforcing every activity? Or will we be able to make the societal, psychological, and spiritual changes needed to protect our ocean?

Basically, what we need is to understand and respect our Mother Ocean. She is our mother, our grandmother, our great-grandmother, and so on.

I'm a scientist through and through. But I'm a *highly* biased scientist. First, I have an inordinate fondness for sea turtles. That's kind of a fancy way of saying I'm a turtle freak. I love them so much that I dream about turtles. I think about what they're doing. I think about where they're going.

Second, I love my girls, my kids. I love *your* kids. I love *all* kids. I wake up in the morning thinking about the ocean, the sea turtles, and the kids, about my own Grayce and Julia.

And, third, I love the fishermen and their families that I get to work with. All over the world there are amazing people making their living in, on, and under the ocean.

As a marine biologist, a scientist, I serve all of them. I work for our ocean, our ocean planet. That's my job. Therefore, I'd like to give you a little review of the bad news and then tell you why there's much cause for hope.

We face a global ocean crisis. Two big, landmark ocean reports have come out this decade: a federal government report and one by the Pew Oceans Commission. These exhaustive reports say essentially the same thing: we've put too much into the ocean, we've taken too much out of the ocean, and we're destroying the edge of the ocean—the land and the water at the edge of the ocean.

We've put too much in the ocean.

Our massive consumerism, our daily consumption of things and the packaging of these things, is drowning us. When all this stuff ends up in the ocean, it floats far and long. Animals like the albatross that have evolved on the planet without plastic are eating the plastic stuff, and unknowingly they are feeding it to their young.

Sea turtles eat everything they can get their mouths on. They have been doing that for over 100 million years. Their intake comprises jellyfish, algae, and other soft-bodied animals found out in the ocean. When we add plastic to the ocean, they eat it, but they cannot survive on plastic. I could show you a hatchling green turtle from Australia that didn't survive its first meal, of plastic. Smaller animals, such as pelagic crabs, also feed on the plastic bits. The squid, the tuna, the sea turtles, the bigger animals eat those crabs, and, of course, we eat many of the bigger animals. So this plastic comes right back to us. (No more single-use, disposable plastic items, please! Let's make it a national policy.)

We're also putting too much heat into the ocean. Global warming is essentially ocean warming.

We're putting too much sound into the ocean everywhere.

Agricultural runoff ends up in the ocean. All of our pesticides on our farms, on our lawns—they all end up in the ocean.

We're taking too much out of the ocean.

For centuries we've been taking animals like sea turtles out of the ocean in numbers that just cannot be sustained. While we're taking the last of the bluefin tuna, the price keeps going up—more than $170,000 was reportedly a recent record for one fish sold in Japan. That brand of economics is driving the ocean extinction crisis. Whales and even dolphins continue to be hunted because subsidized and government-backed demand continues.

We've eaten many of these animals into oblivion. Rule number one for fishing is, don't take more than the ocean can stand to lose.

Moreover, as much as 90 percent of what is caught in a shrimp trawl can be non-shrimp, including animals like sea turtles, shark, fish, crabs— virtually any species living on the sea floor. Around the world, fisheries are collapsing. Coastal people are looking for alternatives. I was recently in the Kei Islands, Indonesia. A young man told me all about the new jellyfish fishery, which is booming. We are fishing down the food chain because that's mostly what is left in the ocean now, in many places.

We're destroying the edge of the ocean.

By 2025, nearly 75 million Americans are expected to live along the coast. Some love the coast so much they'll pay $6 million for a house just so they can walk out their door onto the beach or listen to the sound of the ocean while sleeping. This is what's happening on a global scale. The trend is for big cities to exist along the world's coastlines. People are buying second, even third homes along the coasts, pushing the population out along the coasts everywhere.

Mangroves, so important to the vitality and health of the ocean, to the protection of coastal areas, to the reproduction of our seas, are being developed to produce more shrimp, the number-one seafood in the United States. Most of the shrimp we consume comes from destructive shrimp farms around the world.

We need to leave *some* of the coast alone, period. We need to let it stay there for the animals. We need to preserve the remaining coastal wilderness.

So, what do we need to do for the ocean? What's our call to action? We need to start an *ocean revolution.* We must realign our relationship with the ocean. And to be sure, there's hope for the ocean. There's a lot of hope.

We continue to increase our ocean knowledge. We used to understand the ocean as impenetrable, mysterious, and boundless. Now we know it to be fragile, still quite mysterious, but finite. We know that dilution is not the solution to pollution and that the ocean is not an endless bounty. Technology is helping us learn about the ocean in new and transformative ways, although I'm not saying that technology alone will save the day.

For example, in the '50s sea turtles were tracked using weather balloons. Simple flipper tags have been used for decades. But in 1996, when I was still a graduate student in marine ecology, we satellite-tracked a loggerhead turtle named Adelita. She was named after a local fisherman's daughter, herself the namesake of the heroine of the Mexican Revolution. Since that time, naming turtles after fishermen's families has become a tradition.

Back then, debate was rife among scientists about the loggerheads of western North America. Specifically, where did they come from? Genetic evidence suggested the possibility of epic ocean-spanning migrations. But the vastness of the Pacific Ocean made that hypothesis unthinkable, even revolutionary, at the time.

One August afternoon, we put the turtle, with a transmitter attached to her shell, into the ocean off Baja California, Mexico. Each day, the small box on Adelita's back relayed her location to us via satellite. We studied the data, then uploaded it to the Internet. Tiny dots aligned on a map, surrounded by nothing but blue. Soon, other people took note. Scientists and turtle lovers and millions of kids tracked her on the Internet, connecting their hearts to this turtle as she made it all the way across the Pacific Ocean.

At night, I couldn't sleep. I'd lie awake thinking about Adelita, praying for her safety, wondering what was beneath her and above her. Was she hungry? How did it feel to be going home after so many years? I became obsessed with checking my e-mail for her latest position.

Alone, but not *alone,* Adelita stroked on through the deepest, wildest, most humanless expanse of our planet. We tracked her due west out of Baja making a steady twenty miles per day, a healthy walking gait for you or me. By January 1, she was just north of Hawaii. From there, she tracked west and ever so slightly north. Sure enough, she was headed straight for Japan. Three hundred and sixty-eight days after we lowered her into the Pacific, Adelita's signal finally went dark—her last location put her near Sendai, a port in northern Japan. Her exact fate remains unknown.

In the years since, much has changed, scientifically, environmentally, and, most significantly, socially. In January of 1999, I helped

found Grupo Tortuguero—the "turtle-people group"—a grassroots network of individuals, community leaders, organizations, and institutions
from Baja and around the world dedicated to sea turtle conservation.
We are encouraging people and their communities to conserve sea turtles by strengthening relationships within the growing environmental
community, developing innovative programs and participatory research
projects, and sharing knowledge and information as widely as humanly
possible.

Now in its second decade, the Grupo Tortuguero works to restore
sea turtles to their ecological role on Baja's reefs, sea-grass beds, bays,
and estuaries. In places like Bahia Magdalena, Cabo Pulmo and Laguna
San Ignacio, and the Loreto Marine Park, these diverse habitats provide
refuge for the endangered turtles.

When the Grupo Tortuguero gathered for its first annual meeting
in 1999, forty-five fishermen, scientists, and conservationists showed up.
Each member pledged to save at least one sea turtle during the following
year. Within a decade, the Grupo Tortuguero grew tenfold and filled
half of Loreto's municipal auditorium. The meeting is now equal parts
conference, fiesta, and family reunion. Successful conservation efforts
require good science, but music, beer, and tacos don't hurt. Countless
thousands of sea turtles have been rescued, protected, and rehabilitated
by members, mostly fishermen and their families.

Grupo Tortuguero's former coordinator, Rodrigo Rangel, grew up
on Isla Magdalena in Baja California, one of a long line of fishermen.
Sea turtle meat was common fare in his home. "At first, my family
called me an *ecologista* and tempted me with sea turtle soup," he said
of the time he first told his family of his new profession. "Now they
respect my work, and they help me to protect sea turtles. The sea turtle
revolution is happening . . . one person at a time," he explains.

The explosion of information related to tracking and studying these
animals gives us tremendous help in protecting them. Using telemetry,
we were able to learn where they go, but we want to know more. So,
working with Dr. Jeff Seminoff and *National Geographic,* we put small
cameras on their backs, which opened a whole new chapter in our

understanding of the ocean. We used to think green turtles in Baja ate just algae and seagrass, but now we know they also eat sea pens. Sea pens are invertebrates. This is very exciting stuff for a sea turtle "freak."

We learned that the deep ocean is much more diverse than we once thought. On the sea floor in the Gulf of Alaska, 2,700 meters down, there is a diverse underwater forest. We're able to study the sea floor, and we also have the technology to study the surface of the ocean remotely, from the comfort of our labs. Buoys all around the planet inform us about temperature and ocean currents. We're now studying the ocean from space and can monitor what's going on with chlorophyll, algae blooms, and temperature off the coast of Baja California. Using space-based technology, we can see what fishing boats and ships are doing.

This impressive technology can be used to save our Mother Ocean. Or it can be used to further destroy our Mother Ocean. That's what the phrase "ocean revolution" refers to: amassing the collective knowledge, building the global network of scientists and activists, and sharing creatively and widely in the service of life. Ocean revolutionaries learn from diverse points of view, build strong relationships, and communicate with spirit, innovation, creativity, and love.

Thousands of individuals around the planet are leading this revolution. Some you've heard of, most you haven't.

Leaders like Dr. Sylvia Earle are calling on the world to protect the ocean's most diverse and productive places. She calls them "hope spots," and their protection is vital to our future.

But there are also people like Francisco Fisher, who was a sea turtle hunter and now calls himself a sea turtle protector. Francisco was in prison for poaching sea turtles. Members of Grupo Tortuguero visited him there. When he got out after six months, he offered to help our efforts. He said we were among the few people who cared enough to visit him in prison. Following his release, Francisco participated as the principal spokesperson in a national communications and outreach effort that reached millions of Mexicans on live TV and radio, as well as many of the national newspapers. He bravely told his personal story and described the impunity and corruption that endangers sea turtles.

He quit the turtle-hunting business and began working in the fish-packing plant, scrubbing lobster tails.

Julio Solis is the director of Magdalena Baykeeper, fighting for his bay, the coast, and its sea turtles. Previously, Julio was a fisherman and a "pirate," taking whatever he could for himself and his immediate needs, not thinking much about the future. I hired him to help with boat logistics and turtle catching. But he taught me what he knew and he'd always say, "You know, this is just a job for me. I don't care." Little by little he got more interested, then he began to take on more project responsibilities. He began to manage, analyze, and present data at meetings. Eventually, he became the director of his own NGO. He gave a talk at the 2008 International Sea Turtle Society Symposium, a gathering of a thousand scientists from seventy countries, and people cheered and cried. Now Julio mentors the next generation of ocean revolutionaries.

People can do remarkable things to heal the ocean. This is where I continually find hope, in the face of waves of bad news. We need to live like the ocean matters, because it does; like we love the ocean, because we do. We need to surf and scuba dive and swim; we need to familiarize our kids with the ocean; and we need to teach them about sea turtles.

We need to celebrate, and howl, and make the ocean revolution a real thing.

Wallace J. Nichols, Ph.D. (www.wallacejnichols.org), is a scientist, ocean activist, author, and dad. He's the codirector/founder of Ocean Revolution and a research associate at the California Academy of Sciences. He works with many nonprofit organizations, youth, fishermen, and researchers around the world to build an ocean revolution.

37

Global Women Rising

Atema Eclai, Melinda Kramer, and Kavita Ramdas

Perhaps the uprising of women around the world is the earth's own immune system kicking in. There's no doubt that women's ascent is occurring in every part of the globe, and that this emergence is among the most hopeful trends today. Coming from very different nations, backgrounds, and perspectives, Atema Eclai, Melinda Kramer, and Kavita Ramdas convey their insight about this trend and what it signifies. Atema Eclai speaks of her traditional village upbringing in Africa, and of how her mother's courage informed her vision and capacity to strengthen and uplift women toward leadership. Melinda Kramer works with diverse women globally through the Women's Earth Alliance on issues of ecology, health, and sustainability, and she notes the commonalities she's observed in their approaches and commitments. Kavita Ramdas's perspectives have been informed by the brilliant efforts of international activist grantees of the Global Fund for Women, as they have innovated what personal and community healing looks like from each of their own hearts and communities. Informed by their personal and professional experience, these three contributors explore how women are altering the leadership landscape to create enduring change at every level—large and small. Their styles, grace, and eloquence combine to illuminate a pathway toward greater hope, health, sufficiency, and peace.

NINA SIMONS

Atema Eclai: Women have always been leaders. And women will always be leaders. But the shape of their leadership is different. Most of the women whom I walk with or have seen in the world practice a leadership that is very collaborative, and that claims sisterhood. If one of us suffers, everybody suffers. When one of us succeeds, every one of us succeeds. Therefore, when women approach leadership, it's not just about themselves, but it's about women, young people, men, and everybody else.

We know that there has been a lot of suffering among women all over the world, but the women I know do not approach world problems as victims, they approach them as something they can change and as people who can succeed.

The HIV group in South Africa is a case in point. There was a huge taboo around even mentioning this disease. These women decided that they were going to make the world look at HIV/AIDS as a disease that has come to them, and they refuse to die without speaking about it. Many women have reclaimed themselves by declaring that they are not going to be defined by HIV/AIDS, but rather they will be defined by who they are in spite of it and by what they can do in fighting it.

So there are pockets of hope. In 1987, I started working in the northern part of Kenya, where I come from. My job as a district commissioner for this particular community was to set up schools. As I was at work setting up schools, I found out that girls would go missing. On one occasion I learned that twelve girls had died after the practice of genital mutilation. At that time, you couldn't even talk about that. You couldn't go to the ministry of education and complain. You couldn't go to the health services and talk to doctors about it.

But the women in that area decided to organize and decided for the first time to say: "No, our children are not going to be cut. We are going to use different methods to teach the key things in our initiation system, without the cutting of body parts." This grassroots movement is now coming to fruition through external groups courtesy of international groups that give donations to the women doing this work, because locally the governments won't sponsor the effort.

In southern Sudan, a group of women who were tired of their husbands going to war decided that they were going to use the traditional ways of knowledge to make their husbands stop fighting. The men would go to war, come back in December, make their wives pregnant, and then leave again. The women were frustrated, and they decided that they were not going to continue to produce children for this war. They came up with a very creative solution that was based both on their tradition and on modern technology.

The older women, who are highly respected, even by the men, decided to tell the warriors that their ancestors would no longer allow the women's wombs to produce children if they came home only for a little while. And indeed, it so happened that the women did not get pregnant when their husbands came home. In the meantime, the women started using family planning pills, which they knew their husbands would not approve of. The men would, however, accept the traditional method, whereby the women said: "Our ancestors do not want more bloodshed, therefore, we are not going to get pregnant again."

That is how women in traditional societies maneuver when it comes to issues of leadership. I have seen this over and over again: they let crises motivate them for leadership. As the program director for the Unitarian Universalist Service Committee, and before that as well, I worked with partners in many countries, running workshops in conflict management. In Nairobi, for instance, instead of fighting the government for their right to trade, the people were fighting each other. These divisions prevented them from being able to see themselves as traders who all wanted the same thing. I am a facilitator in a training-for-transformation program called DELTA—Development, Education, Leadership Training in Action. We ask questions like: Why are these conflicts happening? What do the people want? What can they do about it? By answering these questions together, people discover they can be change agents; they can be part of the solution.

Out of frustration, out of crisis, women bring up hope. Out of war, they reclaim their land in peace, and this particular leadership shines because women support each other collaboratively. The most beautiful example of this happened in Liberia where I had been hired—by the World Council of Churches during the summers of 1999 to 2001—to give leadership seminars so that the women of this war-torn area could start to see themselves as leaders.

Kavita Ramdas: Liberia had been torn apart by civil war for decades. Women feared their sons would be abducted to be child soldiers and their daughters would be raped. They feared that their children would never finish school. They feared for their lives. They banded together through their churches and found that both Christian and Muslim women were tired of the men making war. This small group of women determined to bring an end to the war. They consciously used their own traditions to make a point. Liberian women usually wear bright, colorful clothes and jewelry. But for the protests they all dressed only in white, which was a color that expressed their desire for peace.

They stood at the side of the road on which Charles Taylor's motorcade passed every day on the way to the Presidential Palace. They stood for many days and many weeks—women who had been raped, beaten, women who had seen their families torn apart. At first they were twenty women, then fifty, then hundreds, and eventually thousands of women, Muslim and Christian, wearing white, singing, dancing, holding signs saying PEACE.

Their movement coincided with growing pressure from the United Nations, and eventually opposing forces were pressured into holding negotiations in nearby Ghana. But the talks dragged on for weeks even as troops and militias battled for control on the streets of Monrovia.

At the Global Fund for Women, we were in contact with women on the ground in Liberia. These Liberian women wanted to bring their protest to Accra, the capital of Ghana, where the peace talks were taking place, to surround the venue of the peace talks. We provided some funds for the women's transportation and other needs. Linking hands, they formed a human chain around the offices and barricaded the officials who were negotiating inside.

In a now-famous clip from CNN, you can see the women simply sitting on the floor with their arms linked and refusing to move. The police were called in to physically remove the women from the premises. The women stood up and began to unwind the white headdresses that covered their hair. In a few moments, the police retreated.

Atema Eclai: There is a tradition in West Africa whereby when an older woman takes off her clothes deliberately in front of a man, it is believed that the man will be cursed and that his whole family will be affected. These women who were unwinding their headdresses showed that they were serious, that they were not going to leave until a peace agreement had been signed.

This strategy worked. After the peace accord was signed, the women of Liberia mobilized in support of Ellen Johnson Sirleaf, who became the first elected female head of state in an African country.

Those trainings we gave sowed seeds among the people. The seeds then blossomed, and the women started to recognize themselves as change agents. Of course, it takes many elements accumulating for change to occur; it takes timing and it takes support, but once women recognize themselves as leaders, the possibility is for the most amazing change to happen.

Melinda Kramer: Across cultures, women have met at the well, where they collect water and bring it back to their community. Traditionally, the well is also a gathering place for women to strategize, plan, support each other, and source from; I like to think about the Women's Earth Alliance, which I founded, as being a well.

The organization was inspired by a visioning session where we invited thirty women from twenty-six countries to come together and identify the key challenges and barriers in terms of their agency, access, and ability to lead. It was an opportunity to collectively design a long-term initiative that would support women's leadership for generations to come. Today we are hundreds of women strong. We are advocates, mothers, entrepreneurs, educators, health workers, lawyers, journalists, and community leaders from around the world who are uniting to ensure the long-term health of our communities and our earth.

Women's Earth Alliance (WEA) is an alliance based on reciprocity, respect, deep listening, peer-to-peer learning, and dynamic exchange. The result is collective action. WEA is a global organization that empowers women working on the front lines of environmental causes through the coordination of training, technology, and advocacy support.

An example of how we work is our Sacred Earth Advocacy Network, which brings together women with specific professional skills and grass-roots women who are working on local environmental or social justice campaigns. The program is based on the principle that interpersonal connection is the necessary foundation for meaningful societal change. During the first stage of this program, attorneys, policy professionals, and other advocates participate in journeys of experiential education, which introduce delegates to environmental injustices affecting indigenous lands and to indigenous women who are environmental-justice leaders.

For example, recently in the southwest United States, a group of female public-interest attorneys visited with Native American women leaders who are dealing with significant environmental assaults from mining, water pollution, and toxic waste disposal. Our delegation engaged in personal dialogue with these leaders and visited sacred sites that were suffering from environmental degradation.

In the second stage of the program, which is happening now, these delegates join our Advocacy Network, where they offer their professional skills to the Native American women in the form of focused technical advocacy assistance. This might mean interpreting or distilling an environmental impact statement; enforcing environmental laws through administrative advocacy and litigation; advancing an environmentally just and human-rights-oriented federal and international policy agenda; or widely distributing information about environmental justice.

When I look closely at the campaigns of these women leaders who are succeeding, I realize that some of these strategies, although they look innovative, may be what women have been doing from the beginning of time. But now they're adapting and adjusting to the scale and scope of today's challenges.

Throughout time and across cultures, women have been stewarding the earth's natural resources as mothers, as protectors, as nurturers, and as caregivers. Women have fought fiercely to ensure that we have clean air, clean water, healthy food, and healthy forests. The new challenges—climate change, water privatization, water shortage, and toxic waste—affect women disproportionately. In developing countries, women are walking miles and miles to access water and firewood, and their bodies are literally receptacles for the toxins in our air and water and food.

As a result, women are adapting, stepping forward, and voicing what needs to change from a personal, emotional, rights-based approach. Women have spent decades inserting our rights in environmental policies at the United Nations and in our own governments. On the grassroots level, we work to interpret and articulate what is happening to the environment through our own experiences, because there is no way we can separate our own wounds from those being inflicted on the earth.

So that is how we lead. Through firsthand experiences women have brought a human element to the environmental movement, which melts away the argument that "people come before trees and the environment can wait." Nature is not something "out there" to protect. Women's holistic approach to environmental advocacy invites us to see our interconnectedness, to recognize how our own health, safety, and well-being are inextricably tied to the earth itself.

One campaign at a time, women are helping disband the constrictive notion of environmentalism as an "ism" and instead are merging the environment with other key issues and movements. I'll never forget the time I was sitting in a press conference in rural Missouri where a group of women had come together to fight the largest lead smelter in the country. One of the women, who was also a mother, stood up in front of the EPA and the press and said, "I'm not an environmentalist. I am a mother. I have a heart, I have a conscience, I have an investment in my children's future, and I have a community to support."

Many of the women I work with are successful because they don't wait for the experts to come and fix the problem. Mothers, grandmothers, and young women are picking up video cameras, combing through environmental impact statements, learning the science of harmful chemicals, and writing letters to their government officials. They are learning what they need to learn to become the most effective spokespeople for an issue.

Finally, women are modeling collaborative leadership in really exciting ways. I believe that part of this innovation has to do with the very real limitations that hold women back. We face significant social, political, and economic barriers that we must navigate on a daily basis, and so we aren't trying to go it alone. As a result, women's circles, collectives, cooperatives, and self-help groups cover the globe. Women are pooling their resources, building trust and real connection. These circles are nothing new. Women have been gathering in these ways for millennia. But now we recognize that the age-old strategies employed by women are highly effective and are changing the face of the environmental movement itself.

Kavita Ramdas: There's no shortage of exciting and inspiring ways in which women are taking leadership. I hear a lot of discussion about how if you educate women, then wonderful things will happen. I would like to turn that on its head a little bit and suggest that women actually have a lot of work to do educating the rest of the world.

There is an assumption that you have to have a degree and a fancy title behind your name to let people know that you are a possessor of knowledge, when, in fact, people in communities all across this world have incredibly deep resources and reserves of knowledge. We may call it indigenous knowledge, we may call it community knowledge, but that knowledge has a potential that is yet to be unlocked and shared with our world. When 51 percent of the world's population is systematically denied a voice, and systematically denied the opportunity to share what they actually do know, you end up depriving everybody.

One example is in Afghanistan. The period under the Taliban in the late '90s was a time of gender apartheid and incredible oppression and subjugation for women, but what people often forget is that the process of subjugating women also hurt boys and men. Sixty-five percent of elementary school teachers in Afghanistan were women. When they were forbidden to teach, it was not girl children alone who suffered; boys also suffered. Boys no longer had teachers in their schools, and many ended up in religious schools or madrassas that were being run by the Taliban.

This notion that somehow women are some kind of special interest group is just a fallacy. We can't allow ourselves to be having a conversation that somehow suggests, Oh, yeah, we'll take care of the people who care about trees, we'll take care of the people who care about whales, we'll take care of women. That's like saying, We'll take care of only one half of our body.

One of the things that we've seen is that there's no dearth of leadership at local levels. People throw their hands up in the air and say, Oh, in the twenty-first century, there's no statesmanship, there is no real leadership. Where is the shining hero on his white horse? But we have plenty of heroes, and we have extraordinary leaders out in the world, just waiting for their voices to be heard, and that's what people like Jensine Larsen with World Pulse, and Atema with the Unitarian Universalist Service Committee, and Melinda with the Women's Earth Alliance are doing.

That's what we know at the Global Fund for Women. Women leaders are rising up all over, even in the bleakest of places. We have an extensive network of advisors who are activists, academics, and policymakers, with the pulse of what's happening in their region and of the women's groups doing critically important work to advance women's human rights. We fund their organizing and advocacy at national and local levels. We've given grants in 167 countries: 650 grants last year, totaling $8.65 million.

So, for example, we made the decision to fund Women Waging Peace in Liberia because our advisors from Africa were informing us about the wars in Africa and the unique challenges that women faced there: mass population displacement, spillover of conflict into neighboring countries, and the sponsoring of rebel groups by neighboring governments. One of our advisors gave us a heads-up about the urgency of the situation in Liberia, and we were able to provide critical funding to make a successful intervention happen.

We know women are the best stewards of the limited resources they have and get, so we just give them the most that we can within our own limited means. Women can use these operating support grants for travel, to attend conferences and gatherings, and to pay for the basics.

So many times I am asked, "Ah, you run the Global Fund for Women, but what about men? Isn't there a Global Fund for Men?" And I say, Yes, actually, there are many global funds for men; they're called international financial institutions, and you can see what they've done.

But we should be encouraged, because the desire to include women is catching on even in mainstream circles. From the World Bank to large foundations, you can hear people say with pride, "We are investing in women. It's the best thing you can do; it's so important. You must educate them." However, we still need to translate that rhetoric into real action and into real change. What do I mean by that?

The Global Fund for Women is a grant-making foundation. We are also a public charity. We raise all the money that we give away each year. It might be astounding to you to hear that despite all this rhetoric about women, in 2007, of the $90-plus billion that went to support private philanthropy in the United States, less than 6.8 percent went to organizations serving women and girls, much less to organizations actually led by and run by women and girls. I would say that it is immoral to talk about bailouts for the richest people in this country, and then expect that the people who are among the world's poorest—women and children—should be able to get by with a mere 6.7 percent of the private philanthropic resources of the richest nation in the world.

I want to say another thing in relation to civic and political leadership. We should be very clear that with increased presence and participation in the political process comes a huge diversity. If we are 51 percent of the world's population, why would you expect us to be any less diverse than the other 49 percent? For instance, we don't expect any one male candidate to represent all men's views, so why is it we expect Hillary Clinton or Sarah Palin to do so for women? We represent a rainbow of diversity, secular women and deeply believing women, left-leaning women and conservative women. We all have a right to be heard. And it's our collective and diverse and collaborative leadership that will make the difference in our bringing change to this planet that we all love in our own particular way.

Atema Eclai, director of Human Rights and Social Justice programs at the Unitarian Universalist Service Committee (www.uusc.org), has worked around the world on issues of gender and security, conflict resolution and negotiation, microcredit, health, ending genital mutilation, and quality education. She has been a facilitator of many international meetings. Eclai was also a chief facilitating team member for Inclusive Security: Women Waging Peace, an initiative of the Women and Public Policy Program at the Kennedy School of Government.

Melinda Kramer is the founder and codirector of Women's Earth Alliance (WEA; www.womensearth alliance.org), an international organization that coordinates training, technology, and advocacy support for women-led environmental initiatives. From rural Kenya to northern India to Native American reservations, WEA has designed collaborative initiatives influencing issues of water, food, health, climate change, and women's empowerment. Before founding WEA, Kramer pursued issues of environmental justice, sustainable local economies, and indigenous rights with various organizations around the world. She lived in East Africa working with CARE Kenya on sustainable health and agricultural projects and later worked throughout the North Pacific Rim, nurturing the emergence of grassroots environmental movements in China, the Russian Far East, and Alaska with the environmental organization Pacific Environment. At the Natural Capital Institute, she was the communications manager and a key contributor to the Web-based communication tool WiserEarth.org. Kramer is a trained facilitator and speaks Kiswahili, Spanish, and some Mandarin.

Kavita N. Ramdas provides leadership and direction for the largest nonprofit foundation in the world that funds women's human rights: the Global Fund for Women (www.globalfundfor women.org). During her tenure, Global Fund assets have grown from $6 million to $21 million, and the number of countries supported has tripled. Annually, the Global Fund provides 650 grants totaling $8.5 million to women's groups in 171 countries. Ramdas serves on the Global Development Program of the Bill & Melinda Gates Foundation and the board of trustees at Princeton University. She speaks six languages.